ACTIVITIES
AND
PROJECTS
FROM
THE
NATIONAL
BUILDING
MUSEUM

Why Design?

ANNA SLAFER and **KEVIN CAHILL**

Contributing Author:
S. GOODLUCK TEMBUNKIART

Designer: Kevin Cahill
Primary Illustrator: S. Goodluck Tembunkiart

The book was supported in part by a grant from the National Endowment for the Arts, a federal agency; The Andy Warhol Foundation for the Visual Arts; The Friends of Robert W. Duemling; and The George Gund Foundation.

CHICAGO
REVIEW
PRESS

Library of Congress Cataloging-in-Publication Data

Slafer, Anna 1958-
    Why Design?: Activities and Projects from the National Building Museum/Anna Slafer and Kevin Cahill. —1st ed.
        p.   cm.
    Includes bibliographical references.
    Summary: An overview of design with activities intended to increase awareness of and participation in the designed world.
    ISBN 1-55652-249-5
    1. Design—Juvenile literature. 2. Design, Industrial—Juvenile literature. [1. Design. 2. Design, Industrial.] I. Cahill, Kevin, 1959-   . II. National Building Museum (U.S.) III. Title.
NK1510.S59 1995
745.4—dc20   95-12376
                                                                              CIP

Primary typefaces: Stone Serif, Franklin Gothic Condensed, and Lithos Written and designed on Power Macintosh 6100, 7100 and Powerbook 520c computers using Adobe Pagemaker 5.0 and Photoshop 2.5 software.

Photographs: Kevin Cahill, Tom Devol, Anna Slafer, Eileen Adams Additional photo credits: pages 11–12, USGS; 9, USDA; 96 (top) and 97 (top), Eric DeLony; 97 (center), Jet Lowe; 98–100 and 102–103, FEMA; 109, HABS/HAER; 106 (left), 157 (top), 190. 192, and 193, Eileen Langholtz

Page 10: Portion of map of Fairfax County, Virginia, in 1760, printed by the Office of Comprehensive Planning, Fairfax County, Virginia. Reprinted by permission of Beth Mitchell.

Pages 17 and 104: Adapted by permission of Ken Baynes.

Pages 20–23: Adapted from *Problem Solving in the Man-Made Environment*, Cranbrook Environmental Education Project, 1975. Used by permission.

Pages 44–46: Adapted from *Getting to Yes*, 2nd ed., by Roger Fisher, William Ury, and Bruce Paton. ©1981, 1991 by Roger Fisher and William Ury. Reprinted by permission of Houghton Mifflin Co. All rights reserved.

Pages 63–64: Adapted from *Personplace*, in *Education through Design: Middle School Curriculum Teacher Workbook*. North Carolina State University, 1994. Used by permission.

Page 72: Descriptions taken from *The 4Mat System: Teaching to Learning Styles with Right/Left Mode Techniques*, by Bernice McCarthy. ©1980, 1987 by Excel, Inc. Those desiring a copy of the complete work for further reading may acquire it from the publisher, Excel Inc., 23385 Old Barrington Road, Barrington, Il 60010, 708-382-7272. Used by permission.

Pages 101–103: Text and map—"350 Feet Above Flood Ruins, A River Town Plots Rebirth," by Isabel Wilkerson, Oct. 31, 1993. ©1993 by The New York Times Company. Reprinted by permission.

Bizarro ©1995 Dan Piraro. Reprinted by permission of Universal Press Syndicate. All rights reserved.

Published by Chicago Review Press, Incorporated
814 North Franklin Street
Chicago, Illinois 60610

ISBN 1-55652-249-5
Printed on recycled paper in the United States of America

1 2 3 4 5 6 7 8 9 10

THIS BOOK IS DEDICATED

TO OUR PARENTS AND TO THE FUTURE DESIGNERS WHO WILL INHERIT WHAT THE REST OF US HAVE DESIGNED

STOP

If you're satisfied with the way things are, read no further.

Contents

Part 1 Design awareness

Part 2 Designing

Preface

ABOUT THE MUSEUM

In 1980 Congress established the National Building Museum (NBM) in Washington, D.C. The mission of this private nonprofit institution is to examine and interpret the many aspects of building in America so that people, by learning about the past and present, can make informed and enlightened choices in determining the built environment of the future. Museum programs and permanent and temporary exhibition explore the act, process, art, and business of building, and interpret the world of construction, engineering, architectural design, environmental and urban planning, building crafts and materials, and historic preservation.

This book was inspired by work done in the museum's DesignWise program. The program's goal was to provide junior and senior high-school students with hands-on experiences that would increase their awareness of the designed world, their ability to design, and the skills they need to become active participants in shaping their communities. In a series of summer institutes and a year-long program in Washington, D.C.-area classrooms, students worked with professional designers and educators to explore how design affects their lives and to solve a variety of design problems. Working individually and in design teams, students learned to ask the questions designers ask and to formulate solutions to increasingly complex design problems.

Susan Henshaw Jones, President and Director
Anna Slafer, Curator of Education
Ann Caspari, School Programs Coordinator
Amanda DiPaul, Adult Programs Coordinator
Jacqueline Eyl, Volunteer and Visitor Services Coordinator
Marcia Gregory, Assistant Programs Coordinator
Michael Hill, CityVision Coordinator
Eileen Langholtz, Youth and Family Programs Coordinator

ABOUT THE AUTHORS

Anna Slafer has been the curator of the National Building Museum's education department since its creation in 1985. In this role, she established the DesignWise program, cocurated the museum's first permanent exhibition, *Washington: Symbol and City*, and coauthored its award-winning teacher's guide. She has a bachelor of arts degree in ecosystems from UCLA and a master's degree in museum education from The George Washington University. She has developed hands-on programs for the Smithsonian Institution, the Los Angeles Children's Museum, the National Park Service, and other institutions.

Kevin Cahill is associate professor of visual communication and communication criticism at California State University, Chico. He also teaches visual thinking and publication design at University of Santa Cruz Extension. He has a master of fine arts degree in design from Cranbrook Academy of Art. While he was a partner in Communication Design, Inc., the three-person graphic design firm in Richmond, Virginia, he received many design awards, including American Center for Design 100 Awards and the AIGA Certificate of Excellence.

S. Goodluck Tembunkiart, contributing author and illustrator, is an architect and associate vice president with RTKL Associates in Washington, D.C. He received his bachelor of architecture degree from Cornell University and honed his teaching experience in the Architect-in-Schools program and as a guest critic at the Cornell/Washington program. He is a project architect/manager for large, multiuse spaces, including the U.S. Capitol Visitor Center.

Acknowledgments

The publication of this book would not have been possible without the unwavering support of Robert W. Duemling, president and director of the National Building Museum from 1987 to 1994. During his tenure, Mr. Duemling provided the essential support and resources needed for the museum to break new educational ground. Under his leadership several programs of national and international renown were established, including the DesignWise program. Mr. Duemling championed educational publications as a way of making the museum's programs available to a wider audience. He encouraged the staff to develop a strong philosophical underpinning for all programs and to articulate this philosophy to the public.

In designing this book we tried to practice what we preach by seeking critical feedback at each step of the journey. Several people went above and beyond the call of duty in assisting us. Eileen Adams gets the gold medal for transatlantic phone critique. Her enthusiasm, unflagging belief in the importance of this work, and insightful comments always kept us going. She also contributed much of the framework for the self-evaluation component in chapter four. Cheryl Best (a kindred spirit and a pleasure to work with on DesignWise at Central Park) provided a program director's very practical concerns and criticism—all with a New York sense of humor. She pushed us to never settle until the book became "as good as the DesignWise program." Meredith Davis, who played a critical role in shaping the DesignWise program at the National Building Museum, provided an extremely thorough, rigorous, and insightful critique. The questions and points she raised helped us clarify the pedagogical objectives and keep us on track. Alan Sandler has been a constant source of support to the museum over the years and a mentor to Anna. He was always there to remind us that the work we were doing was unique—and important. Goodluck Tembunkiart (whose name could not be more appropriate) cowrote the curriculum for DesignWise at Central Park, which was the precursor to this book. He is absolutely "the best," as is his wife, Julia Craighill, for putting up with the odd hours and pitching in with valuable advice.

Heartfelt thanks for technical assistance to the David Blockstein–Debra Prybyla team, who were a font of biodiversity resources; CSU Chico students Stephen Blake, Andrea Dehart, Molly Hamilton, Stacia Lay, Stephen Long, and Phil Quinn, who tackled "pet poop in the park" with boundless enthusiasm; Larry W. Canter, who graciously overnight-mailed his draft of *Environmental Impact Assessment*; Paul DeLong, mediator extraordinaire, who trained the staff in conflict resolution and clarified the related activities; Sharon Gillerman, whose expertise in education and ecosystems helped clarify several activities; Carol Maus, who is a great editor and friend, was always there when needed; Nancy McCoy, who set the standard for museum education curriculum and provided invaluable feedback; techno-wizard Phil Quinn, who was also always there when we needed him and kept everything running smoothly; Loren and Dennis Slafer, who moonlighted as long-distance computer consultants for their sister; Alexis Slafer, who defined landscape architecture and applied her analytical skill to the content; George Steele, a superb environmental educator, who generated great activities at a moment's notice; Dr. Robert Tinkler, who was always willing to check a history fact—even at 1 A.M.; Marc Wolfson, Public Affairs Officer at FEMA, who provided photos; James P. Zook, Director, Office of Comprehensive Planning, Fairfax County, Virginia, who provided planning information; Amy Teschner, CRP Editorial Director, for being clear-eyed, enthusiastic, supportive, and patient; editors Ann Grogg, Sheila Whelan, and Carol Maus, who sorted out style issues and monitored our grammar and syntax; and the education staff at the museum—who assisted in a million ways. They are the best staff a supervisor could ask for.

Special thanks must also go to Ellen Meyer, who brought the initial idea and funding for the DesignWise program to NBM's first director, Bates Lowry, who had the vision to see immediately the project's importance. Ellen's commitment and ceaseless optimism inspired the staff during that first year. She introduced us to the groundbreaking work of British design educator Ken Baynes. He and colleagues Eileen Adams and Krysia Brohochka are master educators who have the rare ability to translate research and "academese" into words, ideas, and games that everyone can understand and enjoy. Their workshop at the National Building Museum to kick off the program has remained an inspiration and model to us. Thanks also to the "big three" built environment educators, Rolaine Copeland, Ginny Graves, and Anne Taylor, who have been supportive advisors over the years; Rob Fischman, Todd Goodglick, Maggie Grieve, Betsy Lyons, Carol Rosenberg, and Gene Slafer, for advice and moral support; Nancy Hafkin and the group—thanks for keeping Anna going; and all the DesignWise and CityVision students—you were our inspiration.

Over the years, many museum staff members helped make the DesignWise program and book possible: Director Susan Henshaw Jones provided support needed for the book's completion. Cathy Kunkel was always there to help—smiling even while scrubbing paint off the floor. Joyce Elliot was willing to edit at a moment's notice. Lucy Lowenthal, Mary Cay Campbell, Beth Bolen, Mary Hewes, and Nancy Mannes were dedicated fund-raisers. Susan Wilkerson and Hank Griffith located historical images. Trustee Cynthia Field was a tireless advocate for the entire project. Gregory K. Dreicer, the wordsmith, provided expertise in the history of technology. Edward McWilliams was always there to handle a crisis. Interns Nancy Hove, Allison Gottsegen, and Rosette Millora enthusiastically researched and assisted in numerous ways. And deepest gratitude goes to Melissa McLoud and A. J. Pietrantone, who provided curatorial and administrative expertise and served as anchors and advisors from beginning to end.

MANY THANKS TO THE FOLLOWING DESIGN EDUCATION SPECIALISTS, DESIGN PROFESSIONALS, AND EDUCATORS WHO REVIEWED THE BOOK DRAFT:

Eileen Adams, Design Education Specialist, South Bank University, Great Britain; Dan Bairley, Architect, VA; Paul Baker, Site Coach, State Systemic Initiative Team, Delaware Department of Public Instruction, DE; Evan Bartlett, architecture/drafting teacher, Lane Technical High School, IL; Bob Benoit, Curriculum Coordinator, Butte County Schools, CA; Cheryl Best, Director of Education and Recreation, Central Park Conservancy, NY; Patricia Bruce, Director of Media Center, Forestville High School, MD; Elaine Bullock, fourth grade teacher, Watkins Elementary School, Washington, DC; Meredith Davis, Coordinator, Graphic Design Department, North Carolina State University, NC; Dorothy Dunn, Director of Education, Cooper-Hewitt National Museum of Design, NY; Victor Dzidzienyo, Chairman, Howard University School of Architecture and Planning, Washington, DC; Cynthia Field, Director, Office of Architectural History and Historic Preservation, Smithsonian Institution; Ruth Fishman, art teacher, Richard Montgomery High School, MD; Patricia Goodnight, science teacher, Bell Multicultural High School, MD; Robert Graeff, Director, Center for Product and Environmental Design, Virginia Polytechnic Institute and State University, VA; Donna Grogan, fourth grade teacher, Thomas Elementary School, MD; Rubye Grover, kindergarten teacher, Davis Elementary School, MD; Meggett Lavin, Curator of Education and Research, Drayton Hall, SC; John Newboe, architecture/drafting teacher, Schurz High School, IL; Gerald Proctor, President, Bally Design, Inc., PA; Harry G. Robinson III, Dean, Howard University School of Architecture and Planning; Anita Sanchez, Sr. Environmental Educator, Five Rivers Center Environmental Education Center, NY; Alan Sandler, Director of Education Programs, American Architectural Foundation, Washington, DC; Dr. Nana Seshibe, social studies teacher, Bell Multicultural High School, MD; Julia Miller Shepard, Assistant Dean of Education for Architecture, Denver Museum of Art, CO; Alexis Slafer, Director, Landscape Architecture Program, UCLA Extension, CA; Joshua Taylor Jr., Social Studies Specialist, Arlington Public Schools, VA.

PARTICIPANTS IN DESIGNWISE PROGRAMS

Over the years, an extremely committed group of administrators, architects, educators, graphic designers, landscape architects, and product designers helped create and realize the program's vision. Heartfelt gratitude goes to the following:

NATIONAL BUILDING MUSEUM DESIGN FACULTY AND ADVISORY COMMITTEE

Daniel Bairley, Kevin Cahill, Meredith Davis, Robert Graeff, Gerald Proctor, and S. Goodluck Tembunkiart.

EDUCATORS

Dunbar High School, Washington, DC: Cynthia Jones Donovan, Valerie White; Georgetown Day High School, Washington, DC: Deborah Haynes, Amanda Jonas, Amy Merrill; H-B Woodlawn Secondary School, VA: Nancy Kinneman, Bobbi Schildt; McLean High School, VA: Jean Grefe, Maureen Herspring, Patricia McKinstry; Winston Churchill High School, MD: William Cormeny, Michael Jon Foo, George Morse, Kent Walker; Woodrow Wilson High School, Washington, DC: Mary Reiger.

DESIGNWISE AT CENTRAL PARK

Staff: Cheryl Best, Renee Friedman, Kathy Grupper. Faculty: Kevin Cahill, Daniel Chelsea, Andrea Gross, Amelia Kennedy, David Merkel, Leslie Neblett, Sabine Stezenbach.

CITYVISION AT THE CHICAGO ARCHITECTURE FOUNDATION

Staff: John Engman, Phyllis Kozolowski, Bonita Mall. Faculty: Evan Bartlett, John Newboe.

Introduction

Have you ever . . .

Rearranged the furniture in your room? Tried to open a window that had been sealed because of climate control? Created a sign for a lost pet? Opened the wrong side of a milk carton? Built a tree house, a sand castle, or a house of blocks? Stood in front of your closet trying to assemble just the right outfit? Faced stairs when you needed a ramp? Felt great when something was so easy to assemble that you didn't need the instructions? Complained to a product manufacturer? Found your way easily through a building you'd never been in before? Tried to open a door by pushing when you should have pulled? Rejoiced to find that the bus stop you needed was just up the street? Misunderstood a road sign symbol? Saved a bag because it looked too beautiful to throw away?

If you answered yes to any of these questions, this book's for you. It will make you aware of why the world looks and functions the way it does and convince you that designing is as natural as walking or talking.

This book will also make you aware that design is the result of a series of choices. As a consumer, you play a critical role in the design process. Every purchase you make influences what is manufactured. Reeboks or Nikes? Pen or pencil? Paper or plastic bag? These decisions mean more than just pen or pencil; they determine the number of trees cut, the quantity of gas used to transport the lumber, and the amount of pollution produced by the processing plant. Your choices also affect animals and people: Where will the owls live if the trees are gone? Who will make or lose money—or a job? Design has an impact on you and you can have an impact on design. *That's* why we wrote this book.

How to use this book

TWO PARTS MAKE A WHOLE

The book is divided into two parts that work independently, yet enrich each other. The first part, Design awareness, contains activities for exploring the designed world around you—the products of design. Although most activities can be done by an individual, design is often a team effort, and a few require at least one friend or a group of people. This is noted in an activity's introduction, as is whether you need to photocopy the included worksheets. You'll find other helpful facts in the **Educators' index**, beginning on page 194, like whether an activity takes place indoors or outdoors, and the necessary time commitment.

The second part, Designing, provides a step-by-step method for solving real design problems—the process of design. Maybe you'd like to change something you don't like in your home, worksite, neighborhood, or city. Where would you begin? What steps would you take? What questions would you ask? This section provides techniques to help you answer these questions. It also contains a chapter on basic design skills, like drawing and model making, that can help you do the activities in the book and benefit you long after you've put it away.

TAKING THE <u>WHY DESIGN?</u> CHALLENGE

There are many ways to use this book. If you'd like to become a professional designer someday, it will give you insight into how designers think and work. If you're an educator, you'll find ideas for incorporating the real world into programs you teach. The **Especially (but not only) for educators** section in the Resources part of the book provides practical tips for using the activities in a variety of settings—from classrooms and museums to nature centers and camps. Perhaps you're a parent who is looking for fun things to do with your kids, or your child talks of becoming an architect, graphic designer, or product designer. If so, you will find activities that will help them explore their interest.Or maybe you've always been fascinated by design but for some reason decided not to pursue it as a career. This book will help you indulge your latent interest. Or perhaps you have a design problem in your community and you're not sure how to go about solving it. Or maybe you just want to throw a party and are looking for entertaining and interesting activities. If so, there are plenty to choose from.

YOUR ROLE

Design is basically a process of asking good questions, so you'll find this book filled with them—often listed in red. The questions are meant to put you in a questioning or critical frame of mind—the best state of mind in which to tackle not only the challenges on these pages, but those that life throws you everyday. And like those questions, ours help to point you in a direction, but don't give you the answers. Some answers will be obvious; some will require deeper thinking and research.

Things you'll need

THE SIMPLE BASICS

This book is about doing. To get going you'll need some very basic tools and materials, most of which you probably already have. And most of what you need to purchase will be inexpensive. The key is to be inventive with what you have around the house. You can get additional materials at art supply and hardware stores. You don't need everything listed below—each activity includes a list of necessary materials under the heading, **MATERIALS**. The following information, however, will be useful when making your selections or purchases.

PENS AND PENCILS

Your basic tools: A set of *colored felt pens* (varying in thickness) or *colored pencils* will help you think in color. Keep *black markers*, ranging from very sharp to blunt (they put down a lot of ink very fast), and an assortment of very sharp *pencils* always within reach. Pencils come in varieties ranging from hard to soft and dark to light; a selection will give you more options in your drawing. Although any *eraser* will work, a *kneaded eraser* works best on paper.

PAPER

Designers use a lot of paper. The kind they often start out with is *tracing paper* (also called "vellum"). Tracing paper is great for helping ideas take shape because its see-through quality enables you to layer images on top of your base image. The most efficient form is a roll, 12 to 18 inches wide, comfortable enough to slide under your arm and take with you. By the end of the book you may easily go through a couple of rolls. *Graph paper* is useful for creating measured images. *Regular white bond paper* is the stuff that feeds photocopiers. You can use *recycled paper* and you can recycle the paper you use. *Butcher roll* or *press ends* are rolls of very wide paper. Ask your meatcutter or newspaper printer for what are called "end rolls." They're usually free. *Poster board* or any other stiff paper is used for making models and mounting presentations. *Cardboard*—the thin, brown kind (the thickness you find in toilet paper rolls) and corrugated (in large sheets or cut from boxes)—is good for making large models. *Foam core* (white, paper-encased foam) is available in a number of thicknesses. Although expensive, it is very sturdy and useful for the more advanced presentation models.

ADHESIVES

Be careful here. The things people use to stick things together are often toxic. Read labels and ask for safe alternatives. *Glue* is the basic white stuff you've been using all your life. It takes a while to dry, but you won't find yourself permanently attached to your model. Glue also comes in stick form for use with paper. *Rubber cement* also works on paper (be sure to get a rubber cement "pick-up" for easy removal), as do *spray adhesive*s. You can buy an *electric waxer* (something like a tiny iron) that you use with special sheets of wax. When warm, these let you easily attach and remove pieces of paper. If you like to make models, a *glue gun* is a good, fairly inexpensive investment, but like the waxer, it requires electricity. *Tape*, both transparent tape and masking tape, will help bind the ideas together; duct tape will help them stand up. Drafting tape is a nice white tape that holds paper down without ruining either the paper or the surface. *Pins*—straight or t-shaped—are the nails for your models.

CUTTING TOOLS

You're going to need *scissors* and an *X-acto knife*, which is like a pen with a blade at its end (be sure to get extra blades), or a mat knife, which is larger and easier to hold and use for thick material. A *metal rule* (18 to 24 inches) aids in cutting straight lines. *Band-aids*, because you never know. . .

CAMERA

Cameras freeze a moment so you can clearly see what's going on and document it easily— which makes drawing easier. When you need an image immediately, use a *Polaroid* camera. Or if there's no rush, use a *35mm* camera and same-day processing. A *video camera* can be especially helpful in capturing and portraying movement.

COMPUTER

Computers are good tools for research and writing, and great drawing and design programs are available for them. The computer's advantages are information storage, speed, consistency, accuracy, and an ability to network with other people (often instantly).

The all-important journal

One of the most important tools you'll need is a journal. Many designers use a journal to help record and stimulate new ideas. Although it is similar to a diary—it's a bound book of blank pages in which you write things—the similarity stops there. Unlike a diary, a journal is not a private record of your thoughts and feelings. It's open for the world to see. It's for recording what you did, what you think about it, and what you're going to do, so that you can free up your mindspace to work on other ideas. It's created from words and images—your own and others'. It's for documenting the record of your journey to a design solution.

MAKE YOUR JOURNAL . . .

portable. You'll want to feel comfortable taking it with you wherever you go. It should look like it's been there.
durable. It should survive a backpacking trip and the nine months working toward the next backpacking trip.
responsive. It should work well with your favorite pencils and pens. You should like the way ink looks on the paper.
accepting. You should be able to tape things to it, glue things to it, and file things in it.
creative. It should be in no particular order, but be filled with order. It should make sense backward.
yours. But you should share it.

If you purchase a journal, you should feel an immediate attraction to it. If nothing attracts you, try making your own. You'll find this a good introduction to designing. Choose paper that you'll enjoy writing and drawing on—it can be recycled or wrapping paper—anything you want. A good size for inserting photocopies is 8½ x 11 inches. Choose a sturdy material for a cover and bind it all together (sew it, staple it, wire it, or connect it in some interesting way) so that it will meet your needs. If you get stuck, check with a photocopy store for ideas.

START YOUR JOURNAL

Open to the first blank page. The first step is always the hardest. To make it easier, get one of your fingers really dirty with something like ink. Make a "print" somewhere on the page. Now the book is yours.

Design is so obvious, it is almost invisible. Like the air we breathe, it surrounds us and is critical to our survival. It is one of the most powerful tools at our disposal.

Design
awareness

PART ONE

The activities in the next three chapters invite you to explore what design is, why we design, what affects design, and what design affects.

Design is . . .

How can one word mean so many things?

The activities in this chapter serve as an introduction to what design is all about. Each one takes a look at a different aspect of design—as a process, as a product, as something that brings meaning and pleasure to our lives, and as something that has impact on us and our environment.

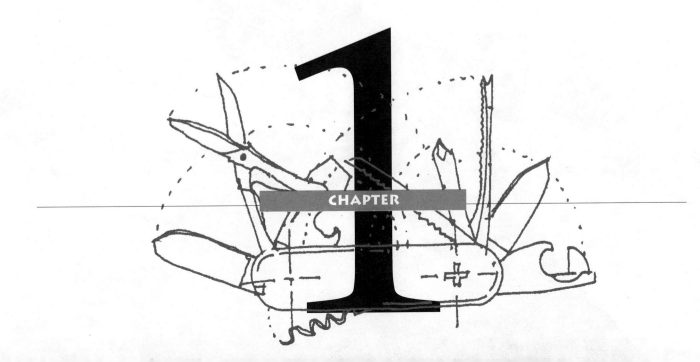

CHAPTER

The designing animal

Design is intrinsically human.

MATERIALS
- Journal
- Pen/pencil

We are unique among the animals on the planet in our ability to change the environment as much as we adapt to it. Change is our middle name. And when you're in the middle of change, it's often hard to see where you came from and where you're going to. Maps and aerial photographs (images of land taken from an airplane) are wonderful visual tools for letting us do just that. They enable us to stop and see the big picture and the detail—the forest (or what's left of it) *and* the trees. In this activity you'll examine aerial photos and maps from different time periods to see just how much human animals change their environment.

CHECK THE CHANGE

Every generation leaves its mark on the land. Look at the images on pages 10–13. They represent the past, present, and future of Vienna, Virginia, an area 15 miles west of Washington, D.C. These images were created at different times and show change over more than 200 years—from 1760 to the present and beyond. As you look, keep in mind that they are each at a slightly different scale—but that shouldn't prevent you from seeing the big picture and the detail. The images are

- 1760 map
- 1963 aerial photograph
- 1994 aerial photograph
- 1992 master plan (20 year projection reviewed every four years).

WHAT DO YOU SEE?
First, carefully examine each image. Try to figure out what the different shapes and shading represent. Record your observations about each image on a separate page in your journal. Be as specific as possible. Look for natural features, like open space and vegetation (the darkest areas on the aerial photos are vegetation; the lighter gray areas are fields), and built features, like roads, buildings, and schools.

WHAT ELSE DO YOU SEE?
What was the land used for in the past? How is it used now? What will it be used for? What occupies the most space? the least? How are the roads connected? What is located near the largest roads? near the smaller roads? Why? What, if any, evidence do you see of planning?

COMPARE THE CHANGE
Do you see things in one image that are not in the others? Look for changes in the size and number of features. What has changed the most? What has changed the least? What things have remained the same? When did the most dramatic changes take place? Why? How have the roads changed? Why? Who owned the land in 1760? Who owns it now? How can you tell?

BUT WHAT DOES IT ALL MEAN?
Although you may never have been to the town of Vienna, the changes you see are clues to the choices some people made about its development. If you were from another country and had no information about this area except what you saw in the images, what general conclusions could you draw from the changes? What might these changes tell us about Americans' attitudes about the natural environment? about land ownership? about mobility? about energy consumption? and about recreation?

NOW EXAMINE YOUR OWN FOREST AND TREES
What's changing in your community? Check out some old maps. They are easy to find in libraries or local government planning agencies. See the listing under "Maps" in the bibliography of this book for information on how to get aerial photographs from the U.S. Geological Survey. To look at the future, get a master plan from your town or county planning office. How is your town planning for the future? Who is making the changes you see? How are you involved?

What would it have been like to have been like to have lived in Vienna, Virginia, during each time period? Which do you think you'd have liked best? Why?

How might other cultures use their land differently?

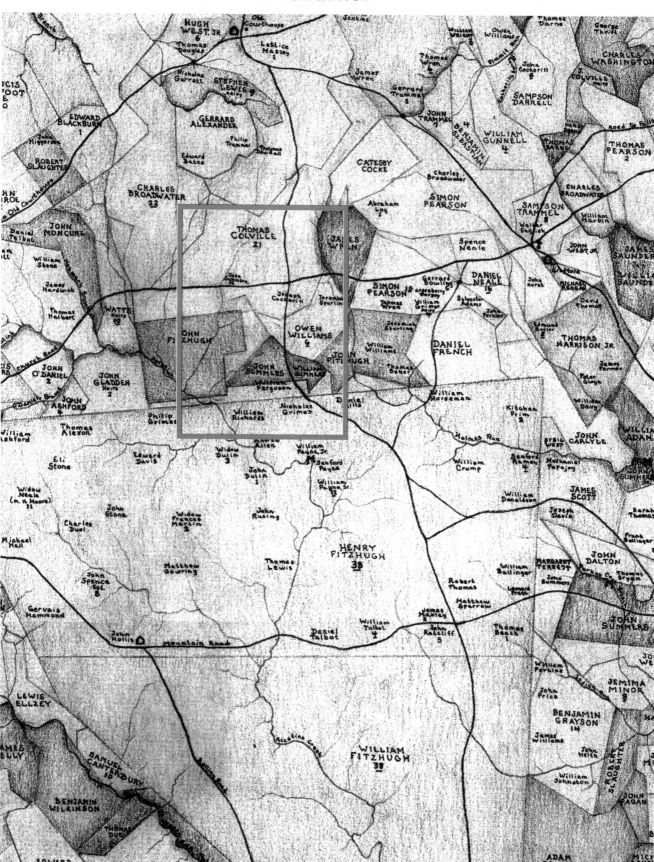

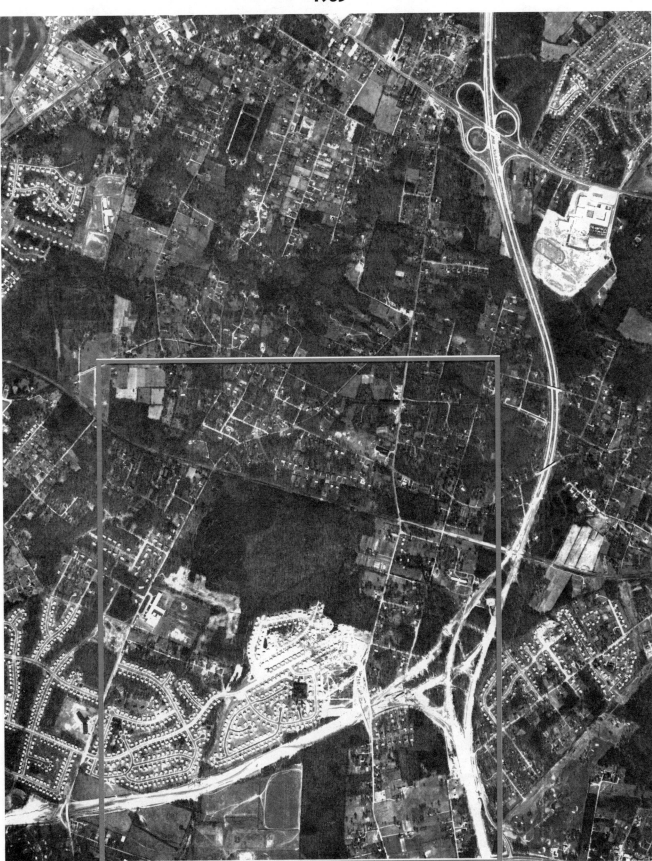

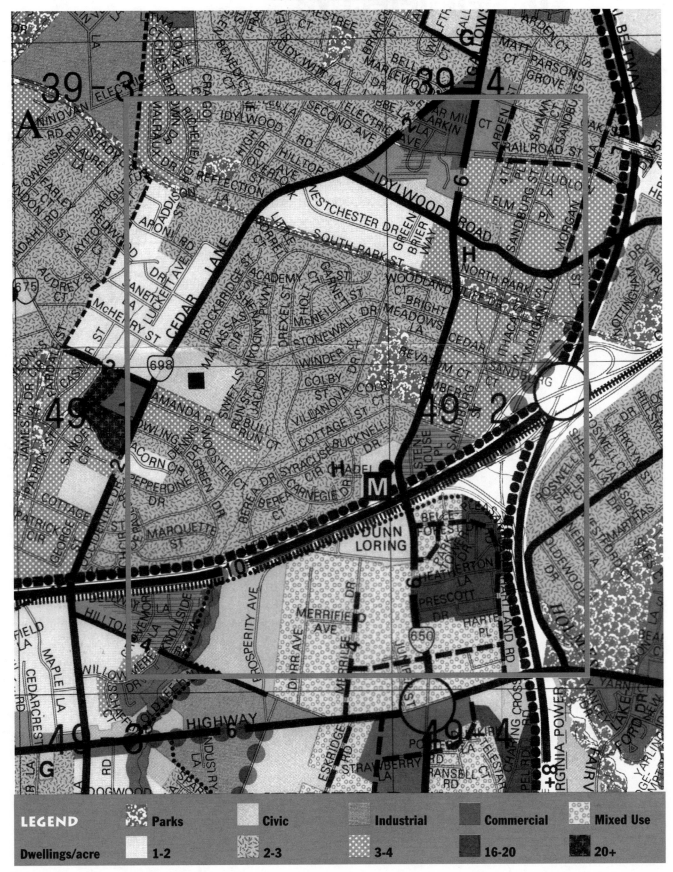

LEGEND

Parks · Civic · Industrial · Commercial · Mixed Use

Dwellings/acre · 1-2 · 2-3 · 3-4 · 16-20 · 20+

Design detective

Design is graphics, places, products, and systems created to satisfy a need.

MATERIALS
- Journal
- Pen/pencil
- Photocopy of worksheet if doing multiple objects (optional)
- Selected design (see list)

Can you imagine a world where almost everything has been created to meet your needs and desires? Hard to imagine? Well, guess what? You're living in one. Alarm clocks, newspapers, toothbrushes, cars, chairs, and the bus system—these are all design solutions created to meet our needs. And in many cases, they are meeting needs we didn't even know we had until an advertiser "suddenly" made us aware of them.

Whatever the design solution may be, you can be sure that a lot of time, thought, and resources were put into its creation. Designers make a lot of choices—and there is no one right choice. Rightness depends on how well the solution meets the need. In this activity you'll get to know this designed world better. You will look carefully at a specific design solution to discover the situation, desire, or need that sparked its creation, examine how it solves the problem, and judge if it's successful.

ANALYZE DESIGNS
Pick a design solution from one of the four categories listed on this page—graphic communications, places, products, or systems (things working together to accomplish a task), or choose your own. The solution can be familiar or unfamiliar, crazy or practical.

Use the questions on the worksheet titled "Design detective" to analyze the design. To do this you'll need to use the design yourself or watch other people use it. If you are watching other people, follow up with an interview using the questions on the worksheet as a guide. Be sure to include a sketch of the whole design and/or a diagram of its parts in your journal (see the example on the next page). You can use words to help describe how it works (an "annotated diagram").

TRY IT AGAIN
When you're finished, pick another design that solves the same problem and compare them. Which of the two would you prefer to own or use?

DESIGN SOLUTIONS TO CONSIDER:	GRAPHIC COMMUNICATIONS	PLACES	PRODUCTS	SYSTEMS
	magazine	stairwell	dog collar	city transportation
	advertisement	zoo	fork	city/town plan
	bumper sticker	shopping mall	key	house
	billboard	elevator	television	park
	CD cover	school	hammer	gas station
	map	park	watch	evacuation plan
	book cover	movie theater	door handle	telephone directory
	signage	kitchen	remote control	sewage disposal

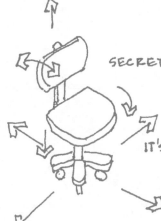

SECRETARIAL CHAIR

IT'S HIGHLY ADJUSTABLE
IT SLIDES, SWIVELS...
ITS HEIGHT CANBE
ADJUSTED.

PEOPLE PROBABLY USED
A MORE TYPICAL CHAIR
IN THE PAST... SOME
PEOPLE STILL USE THIS
KIND OF CHAIR WHEN
THEY TYPE AT HOME.
THESE WERE WOOD,
HEAVY AND NON-ADJUSTABLE

FIRM BACK SUPPORT

CUSHIONED SEAT
FABRIC COVERED
FOAM.

AVAILABLE IN MANY
COLORS.

NEW MATERIALS ARE
LIGHTER BUT POSSIBLY
NOT AS RECYCLABLE.
EFFORTS ARE BEING
MADE TO MAKE MATERIALS
MORE ENVIRONMENTALLY
FRIENDLY.

IT IS DESIGNED MOSTLY FOR ADULTS WHO
WORK ALL DAY AND ARE SURROUNDED
WITH WORK STUFF.

SOME FUNCTIONS ARE EASY
TO UNDERSTAND - SUCH AS
ROLLING AND SWIVELING.

ITEMS THAT ARE LOCKED INTO
POSITIONS ARE A LITTLE
MORE DIFFICULT TO MANIPULATE.

OFTEN THESE ARE MADE IN DIFFERENT COLORS
AND DESIGNED TO FIT THE BODY ERGONOMICALLY.
SEATS ARE SOFT BUT FIRM FOR LONG WORK HOURS.

THEY ARE SAFE AS LONG AS THEY
ARE USED IN FLAT AREAS.

IT IS DESIGNED TO BE AFFORDABLE
BUT SOME CHAIRS ARE BETTER
MADE, (CRAFTED, MORE DURABLE)
THAN OTHERS. THESE TEND TO
COST MORE BUT THERE IS A
POINT OF DIMINISHING RETURNS.

IT IS A PRETTY SUCCESSFUL DESIGN CONSIDERING
ITS POPULAR USE IN THE WORKPLACE.

WE RATE THIS AS PRETTY CLOSE TO A (1)

Worksheet

*Sketch your design solution in your journal—show the parts,
what they're made of, and how they work.*

What is the design solution you chose?

What problem does it solve?

How was this problem solved in the past?

For whom is it designed? (Note age, size, gender, physical ability, and cultural background.)

Do other people use it too? If so, who?

Is it affordable for the intended user?

Is it being used in ways other than originally intended? If so, how?

Is the design easy to use? Why or why not? (Note how color, material, shape, and texture affect use.)

Is the design attractive? Why or why not? (Note how color, material, shape, and texture affect attractiveness.)

Is the design safe to use? Why or why not? (Note how color, material, shape, and texture affect safety.)

Does the design work really well? Why or why not? (Note how color, material, shape, and texture affect function.)

How might you improve the design?

What is the impact of this design on other people, animals, and the environment?

Is this design successful? Rate it on a scale of 1 (very) to 4 (not at all).

What if?

Design is moving from the existing to the preferred.

MATERIALS
- Colored markers/ pencils
- Journal
- Pen/pencil

"If they can put a man on the moon, why can't they . . . ?" You fill in the blank. We get really frustrated when design seems to be able to solve huge problems, like sending someone into space, but not the simple ones that annoy us every day. Like the neighbor's dog who is always barking, or the gum stuck to the bottom of your shoe, or your disappearing keys. The goal of design is (or should be) to improve the quality of life—to take what exists and make it better. In this activity you'll think about something irritating in your daily routine that you'd like to change, and then suggest creative ways to solve your problem.

DESCRIBE THE PROBLEM
At the top of a page in your journal, write in big letters "It really makes me mad when . . ." Then, using words and sketches, describe what's bugging you. Why is it a problem?

SOLVE THE PROBLEM
At the top of another page, write in big letters "What if I . . . ?" Then, using words and sketches, communicate as many ways as you can think of to solve the problem. Your solutions can be wild and crazy—anything that will work. For example, maybe you could get the neighbors to bring their dog inside if you got a louder dog, whose additional barking set off a chain reaction of all the dogs on the street. Or you could throw the dog a bone on a string and retrieve it each morning. Or, you could simply talk to your neighbors about the noise (novel thought!). Look around for ideas. Has nature solved a similar problem? Can you apply a solution from a different problem? Quantity is important, so try to generate lots of ideas.

TALK ABOUT IT
If you're doing this alone, get some people to give you feedback. Discuss your drawings, the irritating problem, and your proposed solutions, and see what they think about your ideas.

KEEP LOOKING
As you go through your day, keep your eyes open for things you think resulted from someone's attempt to correct an irritating problem. Make a list in your journal of the 10 best solutions you find.

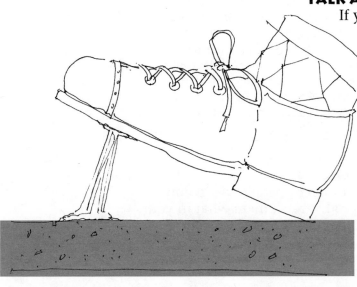

Does your problem affect your survival needs or emotional needs?

Does your solution affect the environment or other people, animals, or plants?

Would your solution be of interest to others?

Is your idea an improvement on an existing one?

Would you need to change a law, a behavior, or an attitude to make it a reality?

What does it mean when an advertiser says a design is "new and improved"?

Is the improvement worth the effort/resources it would take to make the change?

17

Satisfied customer

Design–when it works–is capable of improving your life.

MATERIALS
- Colored pens/ pencils
- Journal
- Paper
- Pen/pencil
- Photograph of you with your object (optional)
- Tape recorder (optional)
- Testimonial ads to examine
- Video camera (optional)

All of us can name a design we love—something that we just can't imagine living without. If we could live without it, life would not be nearly as good. It might be your rollerblades, the bus system that picks you up right in front of your house, the wheelchair that fits you just right, or a jacket with the perfect combination of fabric, fit, and color. This activity asks you to identify a designed object that works especially well for you and to convince others that they'd like it too.

TELL US ALL ABOUT IT
Think about the designs you value most. Is there an object about which you've said, "That was the best purchase I've ever made!"—something you would gladly recommend to your best friends? In your journal list your favorites. They can be graphics (posters, CD covers, signs, books), places (that corner table in the local coffeehouse, or the community garden), or products (a computer or your favorite T-shirt). Then select one and list the reasons you find it so valuable. Is it the quality of construction? Its reliability? Its durability? Is it easy to maintain and repair? Is it beautiful to look at? Does it feel good in your hands? Does it do exactly what you expected it to do? Is it easy to use? Do you like the way the materials, shape, and color work together?

SELL IT TO US
Advertisers, and the companies they represent, know one of the most effective ways to sell a product is to have a satisfied customer do the selling for them. It's easier to believe someone who is already a believer, especially if he or she isn't an actor. Design a magazine ad, radio ad, or television commercial in which you are the person who tries to convince the rest of us why this object is so special. First, examine real testimonial ads and determine what makes some more credible than others. How does the advertiser try to sell you on the product? What techniques are used? How do color, language, type size, and groupings of images work to catch your attention and persuade you? How about sound effects, camera angles, and what's inside the image area? Is the ad targeted to a specific group of people? How can you tell? Sketch your ideas first, then create the ad.

TEST YOUR POWERS OF PERSUASION
Does your ad work? Try it out on different people to see how effective you are in selling your product. Ask them what in your presentation made them trust you (and your product). Note their responses in your journal. Then, see if you can take that feedback and improve your ad.

Did you know this object was great before you purchased it? Did other people tell you about it?

Does what the design cost affect your attitude toward it?

Does the design's affect on other animals, plants, and the environment contribute to your attitude toward it?

How do advertisers convince us to buy things we don't need?

"Can't get no satisfaction"

Design is frustrating when it doesn't work.

MATERIALS
- Journal
- Pen/pencil
- Stationery
- Typewriter or word processor

You can do a number of things when your needs aren't being satisfied. If you're the Rolling Stones, you can vent your frustrations in a song. Even if songwriting isn't your thing, you can still make your voice heard by taking your frustrations directly to the people responsible for them. In this activity you'll do just that.

WHAT A LEMON!
What designs have failed to meet your expectations? In your journal, list and/or sketch five of them. These might be graphics (signs that you can't see), places (sports arena seats where your view is blocked), products (the pen that won't deliver a continuous flow of ink or that leaks all over you), and systems (badly coordinated traffic lights or potholes the city government never fills). Consider how and why they don't perform well for you. Then select one and describe several reasons it is unsuccessful in satisfying your needs. Is it something the ad, packaging, or literature promised but the goods didn't deliver? Is it poorly constructed? Is it unreliable? Is it difficult to maintain and repair? Are parts hard to find? Is it hard to use?

TO WHOM THIS MAY CONCERN
Find out who makes, owns, manufactures, or sells your design, and get their customer service address. Sometimes this information is on the thing itself, and sometimes it's found on the packaging. You may have to call the store where you purchased it to track this information down. Try calling information at 1-800-555-1212 to find out if the organization has a toll-free number. If it's a public service like transportation, a local, state, or federal government agency may be responsible. In this case, the phone book is a good place to start.

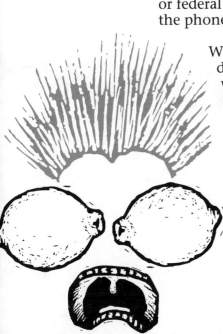

Write the organization a letter. In it, clearly describe the design, why you selected or used it, how you used it, what your expectations were, and how it failed to meet them. Describe yourself, your occupation, and the environment in which you used the product. Tell them what the object would need to do in order to fully meet your needs and how your life would be improved if it were better designed. Send the letter. You'll probably get a response. You may even get some satisfaction.

Were you satisfied with other designs from this company or organization?

How were you "counting on" this design?

How much does what the design cost affect your attitude toward it?

Are advertisers held responsible for creating ads that promise more than they deliver? If not, should they be?

What are legal solutions to dangerous or ineffective designs?

Can you do anything to make this bad design work better for you?

Town Meeting

Where to put the park

Design is a political process.

MATERIALS

- **Character props (as appropriate)**
- **Colored markers (as appropriate)**
- **Copies of the whole activity for each participant**
- **Easels or display areas (as appropriate)**
- **Friends**
- **Large meeting space**
- **Large surface to write on (chalkboard)**
- **Pens/pencils**

We don't usually spend much time thinking about the long-term impact of a specific design unless it affects us directly. It's usually when "somebody" wants to put a landfill in our neighborhood or run a major highway through it that we get actively involved. This kind of activism has even been given a name: NIMBY, or "not in my back-yard." Our society gives much design decision-making power to our elected representatives. These people must balance the social, economic, and aesthetic needs of many people. However, each of us can choose to be a part of the political process and make our opinions heard. In this group activity, you experience this political process firsthand by participating in a simulated town meeting. At least 16 participants are required to role-play the different characters in the town.

THE ISSUE

The issue on the floor is where to locate a new park that the town has funded through real estate and hotel taxes. Three sites are being considered (described on the fact sheet that follows). Three groups are particularly interested in the location: the School Board, the West End Neighborhood Association, and the East End Neighborhood Association. The town council will hear presentations from each group. It will then debate the issue before the whole audience and vote on the most appropriate site.

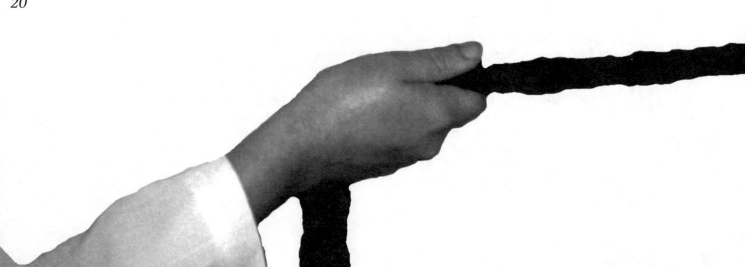

SETTING THE SCENE

Set up a space that resembles an official meeting room. Pass out copies of the complete, four-page activity, which includes a map and fact sheet about the town. Each person should select a character from those provided or make one up. The goal is to create a group of people with diverse needs and interests. Everyone can take some time to get into their role—using props can help—and read the information about the town and the issue. Then, each group meets to discuss its viewpoint, create a convincing argument, and develop a plan for making a presentation to the council.

Things to be considered: What are the concerns of the other groups? How will your group's solution address the others' needs? What makes your solution the most appropriate?

The town council also meets to create a list of criteria they will use to make the decision. Things to be considered here include economics, safety and liability issues, and the number of people served. The specific criteria can be shared with the groups.

CALL THE MEETING TO ORDER

After the mayor calls the meeting to order, each group has 10 minutes to present its position. Council members can question each group after its presentation. When all presentations are complete, the council debates privately, makes a decision, and explains its reasoning.

IT'S ALL OVER BUT THE SHOUTING

After the town council explains its decision, everyone can get out of character and discuss the following: What were the merits of each group's presentation? Did the council make the most appropriate decision? In making the decision, were any important factors forgotten or dismissed? Was anyone's perspective altered by playing the role of a different person? How important a factor is personality in the decision-making process?

Fact sheet

WELCOME TO YOUR TOWN
Here are some things you should know about the place you call home:

Approximately 60 percent of the city's population lives in the West End neighborhood. The population consists primarily of people with children of grade-school age. Some of the low-income housing for people in the area is partially paid for by taxes. The city's only school is located in West End. There is a small playground on the edge of the school property, and nature trails and wildlife preserves are located nearby.

The East End of town is populated by people whose children are grown and many senior citizens. The 40 percent of the city's population which lives here contributes more than half of the city's tax revenue. Most of the business owners and elected politicians live here.

A river bisects the city, separating West End from East End.

THREE SITES ARE BEING CONSIDERED FOR THE NEW PARK:
Site A is located in West End, near the school. There are nature trails and wildlife preserves near this location, and the school has a small playground.

Site B is located in West End adjacent to the river. West Enders could walk to this site by using any one of three overpasses.

Site C is located in East End and is adjacent to the city's only hospital. East Enders and downtown business people could walk to this site.

CREATE YOUR OWN CHARACTERS OR ENLARGE THE PERSONALITIES DESCRIBED BELOW:

TOWN COUNCIL
Mayor, 40, two teenagers, lives in East End.
Vice-mayor, 55, lives and operates landscaping business in East End.
Teacher, 30, lives in West End.
Parks and Recreation commissioner, 38, married, four children, lives in West End.
Antigrowth activist, 30, lives in West End.
Director of homeless shelter, 45, lives in West End.
Minister, 50, grandparent of six, lives in East End.

SCHOOL BOARD
President of school board, 53, computer programmer, three children, lives in East End.
PTA president, 34, chef, two children, lives in West End.
Medical doctor, 37, lives in West End.
McDonald's owner, 48, lives in East End.
Librarian, 55, three dogs, lives in West End.
Assistant principal, 39, science teacher and environmentalist, lives in West End.
Real estate broker, 45, owns property next to school, lives in East End.

WEST END NEIGHBORHOOD ASSOCIATION
President of association, 36, lawyer, uses wheelchair.
Parent who works in the home, 35, three children, two dogs and one boat.
Sporting goods store owner, 30, one child.
Expectant mother, 31, runs daycare center at home.
Unemployed hospital technician, 28, plays softball.
Minister, 40, parent of three (1 disabled), coaches Little League.
Retired teacher, 68, lives with daughter and grandchild, has difficulty walking, fourth generation West Ender.

EAST END NEIGHBORHOOD ASSOCIATION
President of association, 46, stockbroker, triathlete.
Retired Air Force colonel, 66, blind.
President of garden club, 53, naturalist.
Hospital administrator, 50, four children.
Newspaper publisher, 57, four grandchildren, plays golf.
Animal rights activist, 48, two children, avid bird watcher.
Retired teacher, 66, walks with cane, hard of hearing.

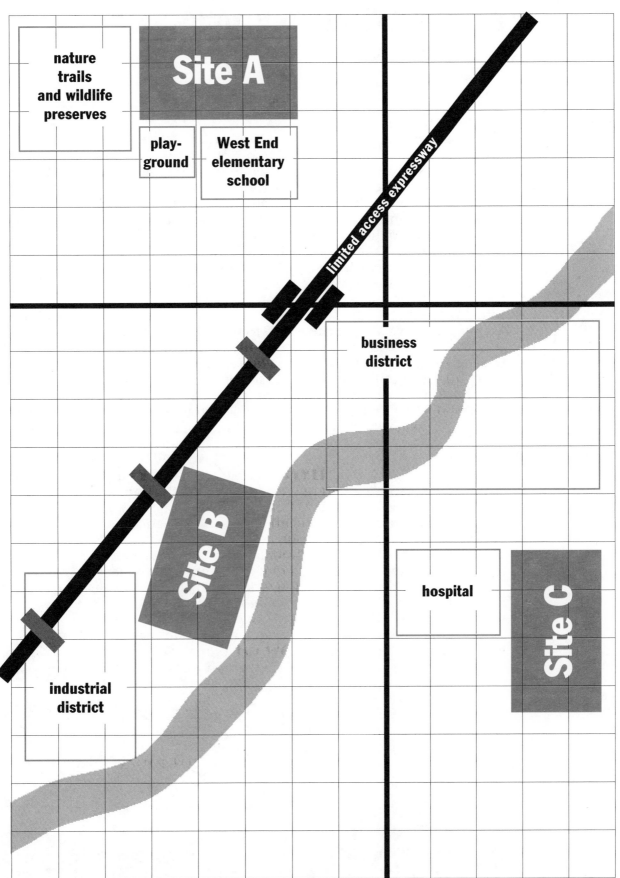

nature trails and wildlife preserves

Site A

play-ground

West End elementary school

limited access expressway

business district

Site B

hospital

Site C

industrial district

Mother Nature knows best

Design is natural.

MATERIALS
- Colored pens/ pencils
- Journal
- Magnifying glass (optional)

Ever hear the one about the Swiss engineer who returned from a walk and noticed cockleburs (seeds) stuck to his jacket and said, "Velcro!"? Well, the story's a little more complicated than that, but it's a great example of how nature probably already has a solution to every problem under the sun. Finding them just requires some clear and clever thinking on our part. In this example, after examining the cocklebur under a microscope, the engineer saw that it was really a maze of thin strands with hooks on the ends. This is one of nature's design solutions to the need to disperse seeds. The hooks enable the cockleburs to catch a ride on other things so they can grow in new places. The inventor saw new possibilities in this design. After eight years of work, this inspiration became the "hook-and-loop fastener" we know as Velcro.

In this activity you'll use your brain power and nature's solutions to solve human problems.

TAKE A MENTAL AND PHYSICAL HIKE
Choose one of the problems listed to the right under "Find nature's solutions to the need . . ." and identify at least three natural solutions. These solutions can be found in specific plants, animals, or systems (like the geologic process of erosion or the water cycle).

Go to the zoo, your backyard, the park, library, or botanical garden to see what possibilities exist. For example: natural solutions to the need for protection from predators are the chemical spray given off by skunks; the sensory organs frogs and toads have on their skin that let them sense pressure changes in the water made by moving objects; sharp spines on plants like the rose; alarm cries of squirrels; and the practice of zebra herds that assign one or two members to watch and sniff while the rest graze.

Sketch or diagram the solution in your journal. You can also photograph it, videotape it, or find images in magazines.

FIND NATURE'S SOLUTIONS TO THE NEED . . .
- for shelter
- for obtaining energy
- to attract a mate
- to identify territory
- to express social structure
- to minimize heat loss
- for waste disposal
- to stay cool
- to move efficiently through the atmosphere (aerodynamics)

IT'S AMAZING!

Find out as much as you can about the plants, animals, or systems you've selected. Thoroughly analyze each solution to discover how it works. What is it made of? How does its structure work? How does it grow? How does it function physically? How do its parts work as a system? What does it need to function? What must it do to work successfully for its user? What, specifically, enables it to be successful, and what are its limitations?

HOW DO THEY COMPARE?

Then compare the three solutions. Look at advantages and disadvantages of each.

AFTER ALL, THEY'RE OUR PROBLEMS TOO

The cocklebur is just like us. We must both adapt to a constantly changing environment. Now imagine and list ways humans can use these solutions as inspiration for solving the same problems. Like all species, humans have certain physical characteristics and ways of behaving that set us apart. Think about what makes us unique and create solutions that take advantage of those things. So, using the previous examples, you could bottle a spray that is offensive or dangerous to people; design clothing with special movement detectors; produce a spiny or sticky substance that can be activated when needed; design a loud whistle or alarm (think about house and car alarms); or get people together for a neighborhood watch. You might find that some of these ideas have already been discovered and are now making a lot of people happy.

Think about whether people in our culture would find your ideas acceptable. Would your solutions require attitude or behavior changes? If so, what might you need to do to convince people to try your ideas?

SHOW IT

Select one idea and sketch or build a model of it. Include a description of how it works to solve the problem. Then keep your eyes open for other ways we use natural resources and natural solutions to solve our problems, and keep an ongoing list of them in your journal.

How are we different from other animals? How are we the same?

How are we different from plants? How are we the same?

How many plants and animals have disappeared because humans have changed the environment?

How do our efforts to ensure the survival of a wide range of plants and animals (called biodiversity) help our own survival as a species?

Back to the future . . . again

Design is a tangible way to show how our society changes through time.

MATERIALS
- **Colored markers**
- **Journal**
- **Pen/pencil**
- **Selected design**

"Back when I was a kid, we had to . . ." We've all heard something like this from older people who want to let us know just how much harder life was in their day.

These kinds of conversations are probably as old as the human species itself. For over half a million years people have been changing things, trying to find better ways to meet our basic survival needs and our desires. We can't help it—it's human nature. You'll find you can trace a path from the designs we use today to ideas that date back thousands of years.

In this activity you will explore how graphic communications, places, products, and systems can be used to examine and better understand our past, present, and future.

PICK A LINK
Select a design from one of the categories that follow. In your journal, describe the need it satisfies.

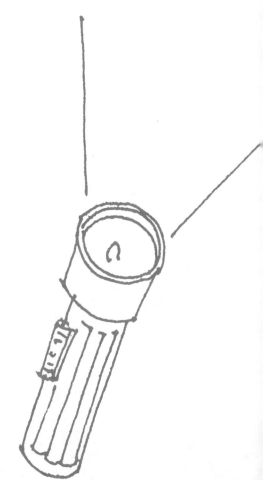

GRAPHIC COMMUNICATIONS

map
newspaper
product label
real estate ad

PLACES

apartment
grocery store
library
park

PRODUCTS

key
plastic lid for a cup
saucepan
toothpaste container

SYSTEMS

highway network
phone book
telephone system
town/city plan

TIME TRAVEL

Now find at least two examples of how the need was met during each of the following time periods:
20 years from now
50 years from now
100 years from now
1,000 years from now

Finding these examples will require some research. Make photocopies of any images you find of the examples and put them in your journal (or sketch them).

LOOK BACKWARD

Now see how much you can discover about how and why the design solution changed. Make notes beside each image in your journal that explain the answers to the following questions:

Why did the design solution change? Think about how people's needs, desires, technology, materials, economic system, values, attitudes, and behaviors changed.

When did the biggest change occur?

How did it change? Consider the amount and type of resources used to make and operate it, its energy efficiency, its complexity, and how it looks.

What combination of forces enabled it to change? Consider technology, other inventions, and information that happened to come along at just the right moment.

Find out what affect the change had on family life, social life, laws, the environment, technology, attitudes, or behaviors. Were these effects planned or unexpected?

LOOK FORWARD

Then, speculate how the need will be met:
20 years from now
50 years from now
100 years from now
1,000 years from now

How do you think things will change?

Over the years, how have our needs and desires changed? How have they stayed the same?

Is our society making choices with more thought about the long-range impact of our decisions? With about as much thought as in the past? With less thought?

Thank you, Mr. Gecko

Design is creative thinking, not necessarily making something new.

MATERIALS
- **Found images (optional)**
- **Journal**
- **Pen/pencil**
- **Polaroid camera (optional)**
- **Selected design**

They say that if you build a better mousetrap, the world will come marching to your door. Build a better cockroach trap and they'll come running! But what if you didn't have to design a solution because one already existed? What if the solution could go anywhere the cockroaches did and get there even faster? What if it automatically disposed of the remains and left only small amounts of recyclable waste? And what if the solution was kind of cute?

Enter Mr. Gecko. Or Ms. Gecko. House geckos, it turns out, love to eat cockroaches and other bugs violating your domestic shelter (mosquitoes are a particular favorite). Their Velcro-like feet allow them to travel across many surfaces, and because they're nocturnal, they go roach hunting at night when you're dreaming about better things. Like most design solutions, however, the geckos are not perfect. Their appetites keep them on the move, searching for someone else's problem to solve. The house gecko is just one of many potential solutions to this problem, and it's a good example of an idea that's right under our noses—if we only open our eyes and minds. In this activity, you'll stretch your creative mind by turning the ordinary into the extraordinary. And don't worry—your solutions don't have to be nocturnal.

CONSIDER THE ORDINARY
Find another use, or 75 or so uses, for something you use everyday. Choose an object from the list below or select your own. Fill up a page or two in your journal with ideas. If you're in a group, try it alone first for a few minutes, then try group brainstorming.

FIND 75 USES FOR A . . .
drinking glass
paper clip
television set

NOW LOOK FOR LEAPS
Select several design solutions (graphic designs, places, products, or systems) and trace the winding path that led to their invention. See if you can find all the related and unrelated connections that contributed to each design's creation. Was it the work of one genius in a flash of inspiration, or a long history of many people working in different places, doing different things? Put the solution in your journal using photographs, found images, or sketches. Next to each example, describe what makes the solution a creative response to the problem.

Were objects that were technologically complicated easier or harder to find uses for?

How wild were your ideas?

How practical?

How frivolous?

Did you need to handle the object in order to generate more ideas?

Did you manipulate the object in your mind?

Was the flow of ideas slower or faster when you were working alone?

Eye of the beholder

Design is capable of pleasing your senses.

MATERIALS
- **Colored pens/ pencils**
- **Journal**
- **Magazines**
- **Markers**
- **Polaroid camera (optional)**

Would summer really be summer without the steamy smell of water hitting hot pavement? What would life be like without the feel and sound of pebbles crunching under your feet as you walk a garden path? The way a mug filled with hot chocolate warms your hand on a cold day? Or the shadows the evening light casts on buildings as we make our way home after a long day? Everyone wants the designs we use to work well. We also want them to look and feel great. Sometimes we even tolerate poor performance just because of a design's look or the way it feels. We appreciate it just for its color, texture, shape, pattern, or the shadows it projects. This activity helps you explore how designers manipulate form in ways that catch your attention and make you feel good that they did.

COLLECT YOUR FAVORITES

Gather a group of your favorite designs—ones that you enjoy primarily because of the way they look or feel. Look for samples of graphic communication (posters, books, CD covers, or packaging), product design (vehicles, tools, sports equipment, or appliances), and places (buildings or parts of them, or parks). If you can't use the real thing, photograph it, make a sketch, or find an image in a magazine or other publication.

CURATE AN EXHIBITION

Curators are people who thoroughly study topics or objects that fascinate them. They want to know everything about the objects— from what they're made of to why they are important to society, both in the past and present. Curators turn this information into museum exhibitions based on different themes. Take a field trip to a local museum or art gallery and see if you can discover exhibition themes selected by the curators. Establish a theme for your exhibition. It might be why you like these designs, or how designers use color (or shape, line, texture, materials, light, or pattern) to appeal to our senses or convey a mood.

WRITE THE LABEL COPY

Research each design to discover its history, and make notes about it in your journal. For example, if your theme is why you like these designs, describe the choices the designer made that appeal to your senses. State why the choices caught your attention and

why you continue to enjoy them. Look for patterns in why you like certain things. Then rewrite and edit the descriptions so they say what you want people to know about your choices. Make them personal, and use interesting, engaging language. You could even write the labels as poems.

SELECT A DISPLAY AREA AND INSTALL THE EXHIBITION
Find a place where you can mount your exhibition. You'll need things to put the real objects on—either the floor or tables (called "exhibition furniture"). You may also want to display images on walls. Be sure to place the objects in a way that shows them off to their best advantage.

MAKE THE LABELS
Make the labels large and readable enough for people of all visual abilities, and place them near the object or image at a comfortable viewing height. Remember, eye level is lower if you use a wheelchair to get around.

HAVE AN OPENING
Invite friends and family. You can even make and send invitations. As the refreshments are served (don't forget the pretzels!), say a few words of welcome and fill the viewers in on some of the be-hind-the-scenes challenges you faced in creating your exhibition.

Are there materials and shapes you find particularly appealing?

Are these objects from a particular historical style (the way we group and classify similar designs) such as Art Nouveau or modern?

Do you have a favorite style?

Does your family feel similarly about these designs? Do your friends?

Need another trash can?

Design is most successful when the problem is fully analyzed.

WHY DESIGN? Activities and Projects from the National Building Museum

MATERIALS
- Journal
- Pen/pencil

Most of us might look at trash scattered along a street and think, "Problem: trash; Solution: trash can." Job done. But is the "problem" really being solved? Are trash cans the solution to the problem of trash? Or is the problem bigger than that? The individual pieces of trash certainly didn't start out as problems; they started out as solutions to problems.

What often appears to be a simple problem may be just the tip of the iceberg. This is an issue that simply can't be avoided or ignored because everything under the sun is interconnected. So all problems are the result of many independent pieces working together—intentionally and unintentionally. By breaking a problem down into its parts, you often find that the obvious problem and solution are really not so obvious. You may find more appropriate places to attack the problem. In this activity you'll look at the problem of trash as part of its bigger picture—kind of a family portrait. Just as a family tree illustrates the connections between relatives in a family, the family tree of trash will help you to discover its real root.

LOOK FOR SOME TRASH
First, do some detective work. Choose three sites in your neighborhood that have a trash problem. Then do a trash survey. In your journal create categories for types of trash: paper, glass, food, metals, plastics, and other. Note the location, quantity, and types of trash you see. Then spend some time observing the site to see if you can discover any reasons for the trash pileup. Who is bringing it and why? How long does it stay there?

LOOK BACKWARD
Now analyze the trash problem. Choose one specimen and draw its family tree in your journal. This will require starting with the raw materials and analyzing how they were acquired, processed, manufactured into a product, packaged and distributed. Then consider how the consumer used and disposed of the product. This may take some time and investigation. As you diagram the piece of trash's lineage, be sure to include people, businesses, manufacturers, designers, and transportation systems involved at each step. If you can't discover who the original "parents" are, speculate.

LOOK FORWARD
After you've traced the route from past to present, imagine the path the piece of trash will take to its ultimate end. Where will it go, and how long will it be there? Add that to your diagram. Since there are many possible routes in the future, draw all you can think of.

LOOK SIDEWAYS AND ALL AROUND IT
Now carefully examine the family tree of the piece of trash. Is there only one "problem," or are there more? Call on your imagination to try to figure out all the points along the route where a modification or a different choice could have been made so that the piece of trash didn't end up on the street. These could include changes in the material used to create the package, the use of a different processing technique to create the stuff inside the package, or more effective disposal methods.

FRAME YOUR FINDINGS
Use your findings to educate the rest of us. See if you can figure out a method to let other people know about the sources of trash and ways the problem could be solved—without creating more trash.

How complicated is the problem?

Is trash the only problem?

Is there only one solution?

How many points did you find where something could have been done differently?

Is trash always bad?

What can trash tell us about our society's attitudes toward energy and natural resource use? About our economy?

Wanted: The Design Gang

Design is affected by the decisions of many people.

MATERIALS

- Colored markers
- Journal
- Paper (11 x 17 inches)
- Pen/pencil
- Polaroid camera (optional)

When design solutions don't perform to your expectations, it seems easiest to blame the designer—and this may be justified. But designers are not usually the only culprits. Because design is a team effort by clients, writers, market researchers, managers, and manufacturers, it isn't always easy to point the finger at who is responsible. Nevertheless, someone, or some group, set the project's budget, chose the materials for it, and built it.

In this activity you'll identify an unsuccessful design that affects your daily life and find out all the people and/or groups responsible for it. You'll vent your frustration at the "Design Gang" by designing a "Wanted" poster like those used in the old West and still found in post offices across the country.

IDENTIFY THE WEAPON

Select a graphic design, product design, or place that just doesn't work as it should. Take a Polaroid photograph of it or draw it in your journal. Describe what the design is supposed to do, and how and why it fails to do it. For example, if it's a graphic design, is it hard to read? Is it boring? If it's a product, is it hard to hold? Does it break down a lot? If it's a building, is the entrance hard to find? Does it detract from its surroundings?

BE A DETECTIVE

Now, find out who the perpetrators are. This will take some investigation. The descriptions under "The Guilty Design Gang" on the next page give you a place to start your investigation. Your goal is to find out:
Who commissioned the design?
Who designed it?
Who printed, manufactured, or built it?

Once you have identified these gang members, interview each one to discover:
Did the project go as planned, but bad judgement was used? For example, type that is too small to read from a distance is used on a road sign.

Did the project go as planned, but things around it, or external to it, changed? For example, a large picture window that used to face a park now faces a brick wall.

Did one of the gang members not follow the rules or directions? For example, poor communication between an automobile designer and the manufacturer results in the construction of a faulty part that has to be recalled.

Did unrealistic restraints exist? For example, the budget a client sets for the construction of a building is too small, resulting in costs being cut in lighting and room size.

MAKE A WANTED POSTER

Think about how Wanted posters look. Check out one in your local post office. They often have a front view and a profile, so in your poster, use the image of your selected design or of the gang members in front and side views. Use text to explain why the design doesn't work and identify the responsible parties.

How often does "bad" design result from people's needs or perceptions changing over time?

THE GUILTY GRAPHIC DESIGN GANG

Graphic designers and their comrades create publications, advertisements, posters, billboards, logos, labels, packages, film titles, and many kinds of signs—the things that help us understand and navigate our environment.

To identify the responsible parties, check the printed material for a name and/or phone number of the advertiser or company that commissioned it or printed it, and work backward from there.

THE GUILTY PRODUCT DESIGN GANG

Product designers (also known as industrial designers) and their comrades create objects—everything from chairs to bicycles, airplanes to toothbrushes. These things help make living easier and more enjoyable.

To identify the responsible parties, check the object for a name and/or phone number of the company that commissioned it or manufactured it, and work backward from there.

THE GUILTY PLACE-MAKER GANG

Architects, landscape architects, interior designers, urban planners, and their gang create buildings, how they look inside, and the things around them—like gardens, plazas, and parks. They are responsible for how all these things and the roads that connect them work together to create a whole environment.

To identify the responsible parties: if it's a large office, apartment building, or shopping center, go into the management office; if it's a house or small apartment building, start at the local government planning office or county records office and work backward from there.

Zeitgeist objects

Design is an expression of cultural values.

WHY DESIGN? Activities and Projects from the National Building Museum

MATERIALS
- Journal
- Paper
- Pen/pencil

When you think of the 1960s, do bell bottoms, long hair, and psychedelic colors come to mind? Or maybe JFK, the Beatles, the Vietnam War, and the moon landing? These images stand for their time. Today, when we look at them as a whole, these flashbacks begin to tell us about the concerns, motivations, and values that dominated the 1960s. Each era has its own *zeitgeist*, the German word for "spirit of the times." Thirty years from now, what will come to mind about this decade? In this activity, you'll investigate American culture through some of the objects that represent it.

ENQUIRING MINDS WANT TO KNOW
Before you select the images that best represent our time, think about culture. Culture is something that helps us survive and cope with the natural environment and with other people. It is learned, changed, and passed on through education—you don't inherit genes to speak English, eat three times a day, use paper money, or get married to only one person. Anthropologists define culture as "a system of shared meanings people learn from their society." Basically, culture is our system of beliefs, attitudes, and customs, the social organizations we set up, our language and speech patterns, material possessions, tools, and industrial skills. Keep in mind that larger cultures can have subcultures (like identifying yourself as an African American or an attorney). So given all that, what characterizes American culture? What makes us unique?

FILL THE TIME CAPSULE
Fold a journal page in half vertically. Open it up. On the left-hand side, list in descending order the 10 designed objects you think best represent our culture right now. What's symbolic in politics, religion, economics, technology, recreation, work, entertainment, art, and communication? Look for objects that "say" America and this decade—and that will say it for years to come. If an object has been popular for more than a decade, reject it. Beside each entry, on the right-hand side, justify your choice.

TALK ABOUT IT, THEN JUST DO IT
Share your list to see if others agree with you. Then develop a list that represents a group consensus. Make a collage incorporating images representing all ten of your zeitgeist objects. Design the composition using the principle of hierarchy—so that the image on the top of your list is perceived as most important, and the image at the bottom as least important.

What makes an "average" American?

What is the difference between a trend and a fad?

What is currently trendy? Why?

Which of these trends, if any, represent current values? Which are nostalgic?

What are current fads?

How does the media influence our culture?

Which form of the media is most influential?

What a piece of junk!

Design is making responsible choices.

MATERIALS
- **Group of objects**
- **Pen/pencil**
- **Photocopy of worksheet**

Ever gotten sick from the smell of fresh paint? Walked on a floor made of Italian marble? Or wondered how to dispose of an aerosol can? If so, you are the happy or unhappy beneficiary of a choice made, in large part, by a designer. Choices that have the least negative impact on the health of people, the economy of an area, and the environment result in what is called "sustainable design." The goal of sustainable design is to meet the present generation's needs without compromising future generations' ability to meet their needs. But consumers can also affect sustainable design by the choices they make. If people don't buy a design, eventually it will no longer be made. In this activity you will analyze your design choices from the viewpoint of sustainability.

THINK ABOUT IT
Designers concerned with sustainability consider things like: Will the paint give off a lot of fumes? Which material will create the least waste when it's processed and disposed of? Does this wood have to be trucked across the country, or will a local wood be just as good (and help the local economy)? Consumers concerned with sustainability need to ask themselves questions too. Designer and teacher Victor Papanek has suggested that before making a purchase we ask ourselves the following six questions:

Do I really need it or am I being persuaded through advertising that I need or want it?
Will something else serve the purpose?
Are there substitutes I already own that will perform the same, or a similar, function?
Can I share, rent, borrow, or lease it?
Can I buy it used?
Can I make it from a plan or build it myself?

NOW CHOOSE
Take the list of questions above, and the worksheet titled "What a piece of junk!" into any store. Find a group of objects that are designed to meet the same basic need—things like pens. Pick two, and use the questions and worksheet to help you choose the one with the most sustainable design. Think of this list as a place from which to start—use the empty spaces near the bottom for your own criteria.

TAKE IT TO THE NEXT STAGE
Try using the worksheet the next time you make a purchase. Keep changing and adding criteria to make the worksheet meet your needs. You can also write different criteria for different types of designs, like buildings or magazines.

How do you balance environmental and economic concerns when you purchase things?

Is it an either or situation or is there a way for both the environment and the economy to benefit?

How easy is it to determine a product's sustainability?

Worksheet

Name of product on top half of line:

Name of product on bottom half of line:

As you evaluate each product, put an "X" closest to the word or phrase that best describes it. Use the top half of the line for one product and the bottom for the other.

parts are easy to get	parts are hard to get
safe	unsafe
accomplishes many tasks	accomplishes one task
requires little energy to operate	requires a lot of energy to operate
made from renewable/recycled materials	made from nonrenewable materials
recyclable or reusable	must be disposed of after one use
efficient packaging	excessive packaging
decomposes quickly	takes years to decompose
well made/durable	poorly made/falls apart easily
suited to person of any physical ability	suited to very specific user
manufactured close by	manufactured far away
easy to maintain/fix	hard to maintain/fix
works without additional purchases	requires other purchases to work well
materials required little processing	materials required a lot of processing
easy to understand and use	difficult to understand and use
meets my physical needs	doesn't meet my physical needs
meets my emotional needs	doesn't meet my emotional needs
overall, this design is worthwhile	overall, this design is a waste

Scrambled or over easy?

Design is a plan and a process.

MATERIALS
- Friend(s)
- Journal
- Paper (1 sheet, 8½ x 11 inches; and 1 sheet, approximately 20 x 30 inches)
- Pencil
- Standard-size rubber band
- Egg(s)
- Paper or plastic drop cloth (optional)

The packaging of delicate objects is critical to their survival. Your body is a good example of such a package. It uses skin and bones to protect your heart, lungs, and other vital innards. Imagine trying to carry a dozen eggs home from the store without their very important package. Now think about all the other moving and bumping those eggs had to endure before they landed in your protecting arms. Figuring out a design to solve this protection problem is only half the problem. The other, equally important half, is the design's actual construction. A good package design is only as good as its fabrication. So it's critical that the designer and manufacturer communicate clearly with each other.

If you've ever tried to assemble a do-it-yourself kit, you know this firsthand. You rely on the clarity of someone else's plan and the way he or she explains it. If the instructions are hard to understand, you get frustrated. And who knows what the final object will look like? In this activity you'll solve a challenging packaging problem. You'll discover firsthand how messy design can be if the process of solving the problem isn't well planned, and if those involved can't understand each other. This activity requires at least two people.

EGG DROP (SOUP?)
The challenge is to design in your head a "package" that uses only a single sheet of large paper and a single rubber band to protect an egg dropped from at least two stories. You are only the designer; a friend will produce your solution from the instructions you provide on the 8½ x 11–inch sheet of paper. You will not have the luxury of trying out your solution by building a prototype first, so it is important to anticipate and solve potential problems in your head. Before you start, make a list in your journal of the "performance criteria" (what your "package" must do in order to be successful). Make another performance criteria list for your instructions.

THERE'S NO SUCH THING AS A FAILURE
This is the most important thing to establish before you begin. As Thomas Edison said after the seemingly endless search to find a suitable filament for the lightbulb, "Now I know 118 things that don't work." The key to this project is fun and experimentation. Your egg may break, but you'll have lots of fun when it does, and you'll learn a lot about the capacities of paper and rubber bands.

GET TO KNOW YOUR EGG
Start by making sure you understand all there is to know about the egg, and the structural limitations and possibilities of paper and your rubber band. What are the advantages and disadvantages of paper as a building material? How can lightweight, flexible materials be made stronger? What are the advantages and disadvantages of rubber bands as a building material? Then consider existing solutions to similar problems. Also look for examples of good and bad instructions. Record the research in your journal.

IMAGINE YOUR SOLUTION

Review your performance criteria and all the information you collected. Then sketch in your journal a whole bunch of ways to solve the problem. Select the most promising solution, and make sure all the details are clear and potential problems resolved. Now "build it" in your head.

WRITE IT OUT

Next, develop your assembly instructions. Think about what makes printed instructions easy or hard to follow. The instructions may include words, diagrams, and scale drawings. They should be as specific as possible because your "manufacturer" will not be able to talk with you until after your solution is built. Don't take anything for granted.

PASS IT ON

Have your friend manufacture your eggceptional structure. Tell her or him not to improvise or try to correct what may seem to be design flaws—you will do the dropping and, if necessary, the cleaning up.

CRITIQUE YOUR SOLUTION

Gather the manufacturer and anyone else you can find around your package. If this is being done in a group, begin by sorting the solutions into similar categories. For example, do many of the solutions use the same structural idea? Discuss each one. First let the designer critique (analyze and offer helpful comments) the manufacturing. Was it built as you expected? Then let the manufacturer critique the design. How clear were the instructions? How could the instructions have been improved? After all this, think about how you might improve the basic design.

DO THE "DROP"

Before the drop takes place, select a site and prepare it so that cleanup will be quick and efficient (a paper or plastic drop cloth is great). If there are several packages, drop one egg at a time. Note carefully what happens in each drop. Sketch in your journal how the design moved through the air and how much time it took to drop relative to others.

CRITIQUE THE PERFORMANCE

Discuss what worked or didn't work. Analyze why. Which solutions made best use of the paper? Made best use of the rubber band? Were the most clever? Were simple yet accomplished a lot? Were complicated? Add your own questions to this list.

TRY IT AGAIN (OPTIONAL)

Now that you've seen what works or doesn't work, try solving the problem again. What changes would you make?

How does nature keep an egg from breaking?

What are some other solutions to similar packaging problems?

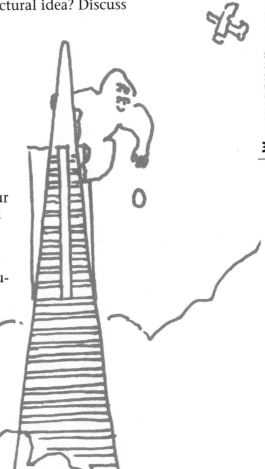

Hey bikers, take a hike!

Design is often a source of conflict.

MATERIALS
- **Flip chart or chalkboard for discussion**
- **Friends**
- **Markers**
- **Pen/pencil**
- **Photocopy of roles and fact sheets for each person**

One person's design solution often becomes another person's problem. Newspapers are filled with stories of conflicts over proposed or completed designs—whether the issue is building a shopping mall on an historic battlefield or building a road through a neighborhood. Every design represents a balance between economic, aesthetic, moral, social, technical, and political needs and desires. And, because these are different for each of us, design can become a focal point for conflict. Dealing with conflict requires compromise. This can be accomplished through negotiation, the goal of which is to allow all parties, through communication, to identify how to get what they need while ensuring that the others involved also get what they need.

In this group activity you will use negotiation to deal with a design solution that has become the focus of conflict. The design in question is the mountain bike, and the conflict is over its use in natural and recreational areas. Although the names have been changed, the conflict is based on a real one taking place nationwide.

HOW IT WORKS
This is a role-play that requires a minimum of three people—two to negotiate and one moderator to observe and lead a follow-up discussion. But the more participants the better. With a large group, a few moderators can be used.

Each negotiator serves as a representative of one of the groups affected by the conflict—either hiker B. G. Foote or biker P. D. Wheeler. They are given roles representing that specific point of view. These roles are not to be shared with anyone except the moderator(s), I. M. Neutral, chair of the city council. Everyone is given a fact sheet about recreational land in the area available to various interest groups.

It is the pair's task to resolve the conflict as best they can. It is the role of the moderator(s) to walk around and observe the pair(s) during their negotiation. He or she will lead a debriefing and discussion of the negotiation process that has taken place. The sheet titled "I. M. Neutral" provides instructions and suggestions for guiding the observation and discussion.

LET THE GAMES BEGIN!
Pass out all the roles. I. M. Neutral, the moderator, begins by briefly outlining the problem and the purpose of the activity to the whole group. After all the participants have had time to get into character, start the negotiation.

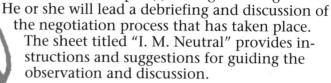

Fact sheet

HERE ARE SOME FACTS ABOUT RECREATIONAL LAND AVAILABLE IN THE RINMAR COUNTY, WISFORNIA, AREA:

STATE PARKS:
- 146 miles of total trails
- 146 miles available to hikers
- 47 miles available to bikers
- 65 miles available to horseback riders

METROPOLITAN WATER DISTRICT (MWD):
- 170 miles of total trails
- 170 miles for hikers
- 90 miles of fire roads available for bikers (no access to single-track paths)

COUNTY PARKS:
- 80 miles of total trails
- 80 miles available to hikers and horseback riders
- 40 miles available to bikers
- Hikers and horseback riders may go off trails

PEARLY GATE NATIONAL RECREATION AREA (PGNRA):
- 73 miles of total trails
- 73 miles available to hikers
- 53 miles available to horseback riders
- 42 miles available to bikers

PROBLEM SCENARIO

The peace of Rinmar County, Wisfornia, has been shattered by a controversy. Situated along the coast of northern Wisfornia, just north of Freswaukee, a major urban area, the county is considered one of the most beautiful areas in the world. It is known for its dramatic coastline with forest-covered hills that roll down to the sea. Many people choose to live in Rinmar County because of its pleasant year-round climate. Residents tend to be very concerned about the environment and proud of the more than 150,000 acres of public land set aside for recreation.

Rinmar County is considered the birthplace of the mountain bike. The bike was invented by a group of biking enthusiasts who wanted to enjoy the mountain trails on their bikes. At first, the mountain bike appeared to be a very positive force in the community because its wider, more stable design made it very comfortable, which encouraged many more people to use it around town. Its inventors considered it an environmentally friendly mode of transportation. But in the last few years, the mountain bike has become controversial. As the bikes have become more popular, more bikers go into the natural areas on the narrow trails, which are frequently used by hikers and horseback riders.

Hikers and horseback riders don't like bikes on the trails. They have been instrumental in getting laws passed that severely cut back on bike access. There is growing bitterness in the community. A lawsuit by the biking groups to regain trail access is now pending. Representatives of the major biking and hiking groups have been given full authority to negotiate a solution to the problem.

Role: B. G. Foote

PRESIDENT OF THE HIKING CLUB

MEET YOURSELF

You are B. G. Foote, president of the Hiking Club. You moved from Chicago to Rinmar County ten years ago because of its beauty, pro-environment government, and stress-free environment. You are an ardent environmentalist and you ride your bike to work in town.

You go hiking almost every weekend. You like the peace and quiet of the narrow trails. You are an avid bird-watcher and also like to stop along the trail to identify plants. You strongly believe that the only way to preserve the beauty of the wilderness for future generations is through limiting trail access to modes of transportation that do the least damage: hiking and horseback riding.

But the bikers have ruined your enjoyment of the area. It seems like they whiz by at really high speeds, frighten people and animals, and just expect everyone to get out of their way. They also spook horses and cause the riders to topple off. It had gotten to the point where you could no longer bird-watch in your favorite place because the birds were constantly frightened by the fast moving bikes. You have seen the damage bikes have done to the trails. Some riders like to go off trail, destroying vegetation and gouging holes. Because these new bikes can go anywhere in almost any weather, you are concerned about trail erosion, especially during the rainy season when bikers find it's more slippery and challenging.

Last year, your organization and the horseback riding groups got together and got a law passed that severely cut back on bike access to trails. Although allowed on the wide fire roads, bikers are now banned from all of the narrow, "single-track" trails that the riders really enjoy. But some bikers have been breaking the law by riding on the forbidden trails when the parks are closed at night.

You and your fellow hikers want even more restrictions put on bike access. It's a sport you believe will only destroy the area. You feel hiking is a more natural way to use the mountains. Bikers can use the wide roads, which are far more appropriate. Unfortunately, it's true that a few hikers have been acting violently towards bikers. Bikers have been hurt and their bikes wrecked by "traps," pieces of wood studded with large nails and hidden under leaves on the trail. Hikers have also been known to jam sticks into bike spokes and throw rocks at riders.

Anger has been building up. Although most of the trail users are courteous, growing bitterness between the bikers and hikers is affecting the spirit of the whole community.

Many meetings have taken place to resolve the problem. A lawsuit is pending by the bike groups. Because you are a representative of the major hiking enthusiasts group in the area, the city council has granted you full authority to meet with P. D. Wheeler, president of the Bicycle Club, to try to negotiate a solution. This is a critical meeting. There are tensions within your group between the hikers who also bike, and you are concerned that hiking on the trails that *do* remain open to bikers will be difficult because of the built-up anger. Also, the pending lawsuit is expensive and draining your group's treasury.

Role: P. D. Wheeler

PRESIDENT OF THE BICYCLE CLUB

MEET YOURSELF

You are P. D. Wheeler, president of the Bicycle Club. Your organization represents bike enthusiasts of all ages. You are a Rinmar native with a high-stress job in the financial district of Freswaukee. You are constantly surrounded by people during the day, so you really enjoy spending time in the outdoors. You like living here because you have access to so many natural areas. Although you enjoy hiking, your true passion is your mountain bike. Biking provides you a way to relax. You like to just hop on your bike and know that very quickly you can be in remote areas that would take hours to reach on foot. You enjoy the challenge of maneuvering your bike over the narrow, curving trails. You don't mind sharing the trails with hikers and horseback riders. Last year, however, bike access to trails was severely cut back due to political pressure by hikers and horseback riders. Although allowed on the wide fire roads, biking is now banned from all of the narrow, challenging, "single-track" trails in the area. These fire roads are OK, but they usually don't provide the same beautiful views, sense of isolation, and challenge. Most of the loop trails that used to let you go up one side of a mountain and down the other have been closed halfway up, so you have to turn around and come back without ever reaching the summit.

You and your fellow bikers are feeling persecuted. You pay the same taxes as everyone else, and you believe you have the same right to the trails. You know that people opposed to bikes exaggerate the damage the tires cause. You have heard that there are studies showing that bike tires do no more damage than hiking boots to plants and trails, and less than horses' hooves. And you have seen plenty of hikers and horseback riders go off the trail and destroy the vegetation. They probably do as much, if not more harm. You believe it's ridiculous to single out and exclude bike riders.

You feel the policing of the trails has become excessive. Park police have been known to hide in bushes, use radar, and write tickets for up to $200. Although you obey the law, many bikers have turned to "moon riding" (riding on the forbidden trails when the parks are closed at night), which is illegal.

Although most of the trail users are courteous, there is growing bitterness between bikers and hikers. On a couple of occasions bikers were hurt and their bikes wrecked by "traps," pieces of wood studded with large nails and hidden under leaves on the trail by hikers; a few bikers have also had sticks jammed into their bike spokes or rocks thrown at them. Although a few bikers are discourteous to others on the trail, you feel strongly that it's wrong to punish all bikers for the crimes of a few, especially when the other groups are not being punished for being discourteous.

Your organization wants to regain access to the trails. Many meetings have been held to resolve the problem. Your group, along with others, has filed a lawsuit. You believe that because trails are on public land they belong to everyone. Hikers can go wherever they want, why can't bikers? You feel that mountain biking can be a socially and environmentally responsible sport. Your organization has conducted voluntary patrols to watch for speeders, offered classes in bike use, and encouraged politeness on the trails. But your opponents don't seem to feel this is enough.

Since you are the representative of the major bicycle enthusiasts' group in the area, the city council has granted you full authority to meet with B. G. Foote, president of the Hiking Club, to try to negotiate a solution. This is a critical meeting. You are concerned about the bad image bikers are getting, and the pending lawsuit is draining your group's treasury.

Role: I. M. Neutral

CHAIR OF THE RINMAR CITY COUNCIL AND MODERATOR

MEET YOURSELF

You are I. M. Neutral, chair of the Rinmar City Council, and moderator. You are very concerned about the effect of this conflict on your community. People are angry, and Rinmar's reputation is suffering. You are very worried about losing critical tourist dollars. It is extremely important to you that the negotiators reach an agreement.

Your task is to be a neutral observer of the teams and gather information that will help you lead a follow-up discussion about the negotiation process. The goal of negotiation is for parties with different wants, needs, and perspectives to reach a "win/win" solution—that is, one in which all parties get what they need, if not everything they want. However, as you may discover, what often happens is that people get so embedded in the argument, they lose sight of what they are arguing for.

YOUR JOB

Start the negotiation by reading the "Problem scenario" to the whole group. When the negotiation begins, walk around, observing and making notes about each team's interaction. About 15 minutes or so after the negotiation begins, stop the teams. Some will have reached agreement, some won't.

Then call everyone together and initiate a discussion. The purpose of the discussion is for the negotiators to examine the factors that affected whether they were successful in reaching an agreement, and to decide how the interaction could be improved in order for both parties to get some of what they want. After the discussion, you may choose to let the negotiators return to their teams and see if they can reach a settlement. A discussion about the various agreements can then be held.

FACTS THAT ONLY YOU HAVE (OFFER ONLY IF ASKED)

Studies done by Los Padres National Forest, San Mateo County Parks, and the University of Montana have shown that bicycle tires cause no discernible erosion and that horses' hooves are more damaging—in fact, they are the equivalent of motorcycle tires. Informal user studies by bikers show that in MWD 60 percent of use is by bikers, 20 percent by hikers, 20 percent by joggers, and 1 percent by horses. Only hikers may go off the trails.

WHAT TO LOOK FOR AS YOU OBSERVE

Walk around and make notes on the negotiation styles of the different teams. Clues to these styles can be found in the language, behaviors, and attitudes of the members. What follows are questions to help guide your observation and points about negotiation that you can use when leading the follow-up discussion. These are not in any particular order. When it's time to start the discussion, one way to begin is to ask how many teams reached agreement. Then follow up by finding out why or why not, and use the questions and points below to enlarge the discussion.

QUESTIONS TO GUIDE YOUR OBSERVATION

Are they competing or cooperating with each other?
Point: Because we want to get as much as possible of what we need and want, negotiators often start out competing. But you can often get more for yourself by helping the other person get what he or she needs. People usually become more relaxed and open to compromise when they are cooperating. One way to move from competition to cooperation is to establish mutual understanding—not simply problem solving—as a goal. This helps establish trust. Understanding why someone feels a certain way doesn't mean you have to agree. One way to achieve mutual understanding is by restating the other person's views and concerns in your own words. This doesn't mean simply repeating the views like a parrot, but saying them in a way that shows you truly understand the other person's concerns. Then ask the other

person to let you know if what you have said is an accurate interpretation. Do this whenever a complex or emotionally difficult issue comes up.

How much information are the teams gathering about each other's wants and needs, in addition to the other facts of the problem?
Point: Knowledge is power, so gather information. Both groups have valid concerns that are extremely important to them. Ask a lot of questions and listen carefully, even if you don't agree. Ask for the other group's viewpoint—their thoughts, feelings, and desires. What does the other side *really* want? Try putting yourself in their shoes (or boots). Also find out about the physical aspects of the site under discussion: How much land is currently available for all recreation use? Is it known who is the biggest user of this land? Is it proven that bikes cause severe erosion, or is it just assumed?

Point: Try joint fact finding. When information that would be helpful in solving the problem is not available, parties can often agree on a way that the information can be collected so that both groups trust its accuracy.

How much is one group assuming about what the other wants, needs, and knows about the issue?
Point: Never assume you know what the other person wants or will do. Each of us has misconceptions, preconceptions, and suspicions about other people. But you aren't a mind reader. Always ask questions. If your assumption is confirmed, you haven't lost anything.

Are personal feelings being considered separate from, or as part of, the facts of the problem?
Point: Be sensitive to emotions, perceptions, attitudes, and feelings about the issue—both yours and the other side's. These are as valid as the facts in any negotiation. Get them out in the open. Share yours and acknowledge theirs.

Is either side appearing defensive?
Point: It's natural to want to defend yourself when you feel attacked. Feelings often run high when we're discussing something that is very

important to us. Try not to put the other person on the defensive by aggressively disagreeing, asking questions, or making statements in a critical or judgmental manner (language and tone of voice is a clue). For example, when you have facts that help make your case, present them in a way that lets the other person "save face." Phrase them as questions, open to correction.

Point: Try not to be defensive. Listen quietly to the other person's criticism and try not to react with blame and self-defense. Keep in mind that the goal is mutual understanding. Try putting the other person in *your* shoes and ask for advice. For example, "What would you do if you were not allowed to hike in the mountains?"

Is a verbal attack taking place?
Point: Be sure you are addressing the problem and not making statements about the other negotiator. Keep focused on the problem you share.

Point: Everyone has difficulty handling strong feelings. People who feel threatened, insecure, or unheard often go on the verbal attack. They stop listening for understanding and start looking for weak points in the other person's argument. Language can be very important. Instead of accusing someone by saying, "You guys have ruined my visits to the mountains," start with "I feel" and describe your experience. For example, "I feel really frightened when I'm stopping to look at a flower and a bicycle comes up quickly behind me."

If a verbal attack *is* made, you gain power and authority by listening quietly to what is said and then restating it in a way that shows you understand the underlying concern. This can be very difficult because your initial reaction is to defend yourself. But try to calmly recast hostile comments as an attack on the problem in general. For example, "When you say that bikers are just speed freaks who don't care about the environment, I understand that comes from the concern you feel for the mountains. We also care about the area. That's why we want to be there, along with you. We don't want to break any laws. How can we work together to solve the problem?"

Are both negotiators focused narrowly on a specific position, or are they keeping in mind the underlying concern?

Point: Negotiate over interests, not positions. Often, we start out stating a position ("I want no bikes on the trail") that is not our primary interest ("As a hiker, I want to be able to enjoy the peace of the mountains"). A position is something you have decided on. An interest is why you decided. Interests can be very intangible, and there may be many in any issue. But once you find out what each person is really interested in, it may be easier to find areas of agreement. A good technique is to identify your shared interests and conflicting interests. Asking questions is a critical way to get from positions to interests. Again, put yourself in the other person's shoes.

Are the negotiators thinking creatively and generating a lot of options in trying to resolve the problem?

Point: There is no one right answer. There are many ways to solve a problem—ways that neither side may have imagined. Generate a lot of ideas and don't criticize them too quickly—that can put a real damper on creative thinking. You can analyze the options later.

Did the negotiators use any objective criteria in developing a solution?

Point: Using objective criteria takes the discussion out of the personal realm. If you have a tendency to be "nice" or try to please others, this can be an especially helpful technique because you don't have to worry as much about giving in to pressure. And you spend less time attacking the other person's ideas and defending your own. Find criteria that are indepen-

dent of each side. For example, identifying those trails with the lowest potential for erosion, or identifying the times of day or year that potential trails are busiest with hikers might lead to a solution that minimizes conflict.

**FOR THOSE TEAMS
WHO REACHED AGREEMENT**

An agreement is just the first step—it often breaks down later because an implementation plan was either not developed or not adequately developed. Did the two sides go further than simply agreeing and consider what it's going to take to implement the solution? Did they think about issues that might arise later and develop a plan to deal with them? How will the agreement be enforced? How can troublemakers on both sides be dealt with? Where objective criteria are used, how will data be gathered and collected?

**FOR THOSE TEAMS
WHO DIDN'T REACH AGREEMENT**

Ask if they believe they are in a better situation without an agreement, or would they be inclined to continue trying to reach an agreement? Why or why not?

Why design?

To meet our needs.

The activities in this chapter examine one of the main reasons we design—as a response to our needs and desires.

We need shelter, health, meaning, social interaction, food, beauty, and a sense of community, to name just a few.

To meet these needs we design graphic communications—like bumper stickers and magazines; places—like rest rooms, theaters, and parks; products—like paper clips and tissue boxes; and systems—like trash disposal and transportation.

CHAPTER

2

One-way bridge

How do you decide which designs you need and which you desire?

MATERIALS
- Journal
- Pen/pencil

It's often not until a tragedy strikes, like a fire or flood that destroys our home, that we are forced to think about the material possessions that are most important to us. How much of what we have are things we really need? How much are things we want? How much is just junk we've collected over the years—that we aren't even sure why we bought in the first place? This activity asks you to take some time to think about the designed objects you could and couldn't live without.

START PACKING

Imagine the following: You are making a journey across a one-way bridge to a place without objects where you will spend the rest of your life. You may take 20 objects with you: ten to satisfy your survival needs and 10 to satisfy your desires. Think carefully about your choices and the values they represent. What do you consider a need? What is a desire? Do you need to be entertained? Do you need to be intellectually stimulated? Do you need joy? Consider your body *and* mind. Do any objects satisfy both needs and desires? Remember, there's no going back. Write your choices in your journal.

Now edit your list of 20 objects down to 10. Again, write your choices in your journal. This time, explain why you kept some and deleted others. Bon voyage!

DESCRIBE THE OTHER SIDE

Now you're on the other side of the bridge. In your journal describe what it's like there. You can use words, images, or both. Begin by describing the first few days in your new environment. Then describe your life a few years later. Consider how your new life is different from what you left behind.

TALK ABOUT IT

Share your description with others. Justify your choices and note your listeners' reactions in your journal. Would you now consider different choices?

How might your needs change in the future?

What are the energy requirements of your objects? Did you plan for these requirements?

How have you solved the problem of boredom?

What would your life be like if you bought only what you truly needed? What would happen to our economy? To our laws?

How does our society create need?

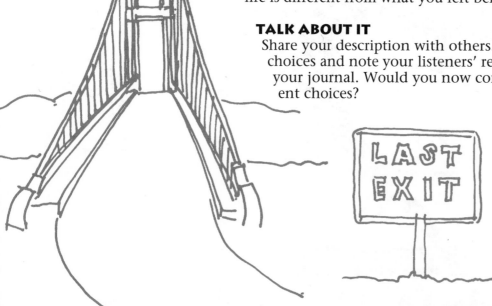

Checking out the neighborhood

How does the design of your neighborhood meet community needs?

MATERIALS

- City/neighborhood map
- Clipboard
- Colored pens/ pencils
- Pencil
- Photocopy of each worksheet
- Tracing paper

Quick, what color is the house or apartment three doors down from your home? How many children live on your block? Most of us aren't too observant when it comes to our neighborhood. It's kind of like asking a fish to think about the water it swims in. Urban planners, however, make it a point to be very observant about communities. They use information gathered by observation and research to improve the way a community functions for the people who live there. One of the things they do is a field study: they inventory the physical makeup of the natural and built environments; they also investigate the residents and their culture—to discover things like, who has power (officially and unofficially), the social systems people have set up to take care of themselves, and the goods and services the community produces and uses. In this activity you'll become an urban planner in your own neighborhood and compare it with another in order to discover what's great and not so great about the place you call home.

PREPARING FOR THE FIELD STUDY OF YOUR OWN NEIGHBORHOOD

Decide how large an area you want to examine—several blocks is large enough for a detailed study by one or two people. You'll need an outline of your neighborhood (traced from a map) on which to roughly sketch the things you find. You'll also need Worksheet 1, which provides a way to inventory the physical makeup of your neighborhood—things like buildings and parks. Design a pattern—stripes, dots, or shading—that can be used to note the location of each of the major categories listed on the worksheet (residential, commercial, etc.). You may also want to create symbols to note certain features (like hospitals) that are significant to the residents.

Worksheet 2 provides you a way to study the people and groups in your neighborhood. You can gather these facts by observing people, talking to them, reading the local newspaper, or going to the local historical society or library.

TAKE A HIKE

Take the map, outline, and Worksheets 1 and 2 into the field. Count the numbers of things you see and put the tallies on the worksheets. These numbers will be used when you're ready to do your analysis. Use the outline and the patterns you've created to sketch clusters of things like houses or shops. While you're out there, keep your eyes and ears open for any unusual sites or any problems you find.

WHAT DOES IT ALL MEAN?

When you've completed the field study, look for patterns in the data you've col-

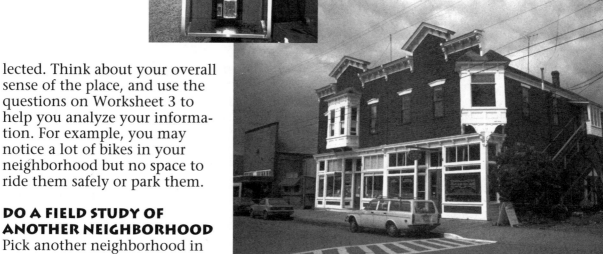

lected. Think about your overall sense of the place, and use the questions on Worksheet 3 to help you analyze your information. For example, you may notice a lot of bikes in your neighborhood but no space to ride them safely or park them.

DO A FIELD STUDY OF ANOTHER NEIGHBORHOOD

Pick another neighborhood in your community that is approximately the same size and has a similar number of people. Investigate it just as you did your own. Again, while you're out there, keep your eyes and ears open.

HOW COME THEY'VE GOT . . .

Now compare your neighborhood data to that of the other neighborhood: What does the other neighborhood have that yours doesn't? What do you like about the other neighborhood? What do you dislike about the other neighborhood?
On a scale of 1 to 10 (1 being lousy), how would you rate your neighborhood overall? On a scale of 1 to 10 (1 being lousy), how would you rate the other neighborhood overall? How can you get the things you like for your neighborhood?
How can you get rid of the things you don't like in your neighborhood? Why might the differences between the two neighborhoods exist?

What pleased you about your neighborhood? Disappointed you? Surprised you?

What problems did you notice that design could solve?

What problems needed political or social solutions?

How do you know when you're in a different neighborhood?

Worksheet 1

NAME OF NEIGHBORHOOD OR DEFINING STREETS:

Make a tally mark for each of the
following:

Residential
single family (houses, trailers)

multiple family (apartment buildings, townhouses)

porches/balconies

yards

Commercial
offices
shops
restaurants/fast food
banks
gas stations
entertainment (theaters, video arcades)
chains or franchises
other

Industrial
manufacturing plants
warehouses
power plants
water treatment facilities
dump/trash disposal sites
farms
other

Public institutions (paid for by taxes)
libraries
town hall
post offices
police stations
fire stations
other

Community institutions (some may be paid for with taxes)
places of worship
hospitals
schools
museums
other

Animals
pets
livestock
wildlife

Green space/natural features/recreation
parks
sports facilities
private gardens
community gardens
bodies of water
forests
other

Transportation/circulation
bicycles
bike lanes
cars
parking lots
mass transit
bus stops
other

Sites of historic/community significance
(homes of historical figures, restored historic buildings, the place where everyone "meets")

Other community needs
public telephones
public rest rooms
benches
trash cans
fire hydrants
streetlights
other

Clues to potential problems
broken windows
boarded up buildings
vacant lots
barbed wire fences
burglar alarms
uneven pavement or potholes
litter
poorly maintained areas (overgrown landscapes, trash cans not emptied)
other

Worksheet 2

Name of neighborhood or defining streets:

Make a tally mark for each of the following (or fill in the appropriate responses):

Who lives in the neighborhood?

people under 5

people 6–12

people 13–18

people 19–40

people 41–65

people over 65

couples

singles

ethnic groups

people with disabilities

gender distribution

Income range:

0–$15,000

$16,000–$25,000

$26,000–$35,000

$36,000–$50,000

$50,000+

What kind of work do people in the neighborhood do?

Who are the people active in shaping the neighborhood?

elected representatives

private citizens

What groups affect the neighborhood's quality of life? (school board, religious institutions, historical associations)

Worksheet 3

Questions for Worksheet 1

Are the buildings appropriately sized for the neighborhood?

Are most of the buildings close together or far apart?

What places are symbolic in the community?

Where do people go to meet?

to be alone?

to play?

Are most natural areas publicly or privately owned?

What is the mix (percentages) of residential, commercial, industrial, and natural areas?

Can you buy what you need?

Do people who live in the neighborhood work there or elsewhere?

Things that make this neighborhood a great place to live:

Things that make this neighborhood an unpleasant place to live:

Things that could make this neighborhood better:

Questions for Worksheet 2

If there were problems, how could they be solved?

Do most people own or rent their homes?

Is it easy to get where one needs to by mass transportation?

Do things get fixed in the neighborhood? How long does it take? Why?

How much of the neighborhood is maintained by government?

How much is privately maintained (neighborhood groups, store owners)?

What is the mix (percentages) of people (age, gender, race, income)?

How would one become influential?

Do people in the neighborhood care about it? How do you know?

Making the grade

How successfully do components work as a system?

MATERIALS
- Journal
- Markers
- Pen/pencil

Would your perceptions be different if you looked at your home, community, and nation as a system of tools designed to get various jobs done? This activity asks you to look at them in just that way. Systems are made of independent parts that work together to accomplish a task. Systems are funny things—you can consciously create them, like when manufacturers call in efficiency experts to develop the most time- and cost-effective way for people and machines to work together. Or they can develop naturally—people can be very good at finding the most effective way to get a task done, especially if it's a boring one. For example, at home, have you ever found yourself rearranging the things on your desk so you can easily get at the papers, scissors, tape, pens, and pencils? You consider where you place them in order to have easiest access. Communities also develop systems that perform tasks that are too much for an individual to handle. These can include trash pickup, sewage disposal, transportation, emergency planning, and fire protection. In this activity you'll examine a system in your home and a comparable one in your community to identify the needs they are satisfying and how well they work.

BE SYSTEMATIC
Choose one of the three following systems to analyze.
You'll be comparing a system that works in your home with a system that performs a similar task on the larger, community level.

System 1: Preparing food at home and preparing food at a fast-food restaurant.
System 2: Waste disposal at home and waste disposal in your community.
System 3: Maintaining your home garden and maintaining a public park.

BE A SYSTEMS ANALYST
In order to judge the effectiveness of an existing system, you've got to figure out how it works. First, draw a map in your journal of the site you will be analyzing. At the home level this might be a room or several rooms. At the community level it might be a building, an area like your neighborhood, or the whole town.

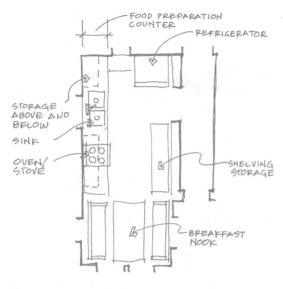

FOOD PREPARATION COUNTER
REFRIGERATOR
STORAGE ABOVE AND BELOW
SINK
OVEN/ STOVE
SHELVING STORAGE
BREAKFAST NOOK

Second, list all the things necessary to complete the task. Draw these things on the map and label them. Depending on whether it's your home or community this might include objects, furniture, streets, or vehicles.

Then list the criteria you decide are necessary for the system to be considered successful. This might include things like the time it takes, the pleasure received while doing the task, or its effect on the environment and other people.

BE A SILENT OBSERVER

For the system in your home, watch how someone performs the task. How do they use the site? What do they do? What do they say? What do they interact with? How long does it take? What movements and actions are necessary or unnecessary? On your map, trace their movements. Put arrows showing the path that they follow, and circle the objects they use. Be as specific as you can. Use a stopwatch and time them. Did they use the objects you thought or move in the path you thought they might?

For the system in your community identify the mode of movement. Is it by foot or vehicle? Trace the path. Count the number of different operations required to do the task, and the number of people involved. What are the processes—like sorting or storing—used?

GRADE THE SYSTEM

When you're done, grade the system on its performance—an A+ if it perfectly meets your needs, a C if it does an adequate job, and so on. Note any items that were particularly helpful in accomplishing the task or made it a real pain. Indicate if objects were intentionally designed to work together, or if the system was un-planned, and grade each for its ability to work as a team. In a sentence or two, state your reasons for the grade.

Were the objects or components in your home selected by your family or did they "come with the house"?

How many different people or groups were involved in creating the community system?

What role do you play in affecting the community system? What role can you play?

What makes each component a "good worker"?

Forms following functions?

How can forms suggest a response to different needs?

MATERIALS
- Pencil
- Worksheets

The architect Louis Sullivan, working in Chicago in the late 1800s, made the saying "Form follows function" into a battle cry for the generations of architects that followed him. But does something always look like what it does? Or should it? And is it really that simple? This issue has been debated for many years, and that debate is visible in the buildings around us.

The creation of a building is the result of many forces—our culture, the available budget, and technology, to name just a few. In this activity you'll take a walk through your community and look at how architects and builders use form and function to satisfy needs. But be careful, looks are often deceiving. . . .

SEE IT IN 2-D
On the following six worksheets are illustrations of building parts such as roofs, doors, or windows. Before you go outside, compare the examples within each category to determine the advantages and disadvantages of the forms. For example, do some roofs appear better able to handle a heavy snowfall? Do others provide more space?

SEE IT IN 3-D
Then go out into your community to find actual examples of buildings with these parts. Look at a variety, including banks, government buildings, schools, and stores. As you study the real building, try to figure out why these design choices were made. It might have been for structural reasons (to hold the building up and protect it from the weather), decorative (to add beauty), or symbolic (to express ideals, attitudes, or status). It may be more than one. Put a check mark next to all you think apply.

WERE YOU CLOSE?
After you've completed your worksheets, show them to other people who know the buildings and see if they agree. If not, how and why were their views different? Then see how many of your guesses were close to the designer's intent. For relatively new buildings, try to find the architect who designed them; you might also do a little architectural history and research the origin of the forms.

*How might these forms be responses to environmental needs?
To personal taste?
To laws?
To cultural values?*

Worksheet 1

Roofs

flat

☐ **Is this design structural?**

☐ **decorative?**

☐ **symbolic?**

Building's primary use:

_____

_____

_____

gambrel

☐ **Is this design structural?**

☐ **decorative?**

☐ **symbolic?**

Building's primary use:

_____

_____

_____

gable

☐ **Is this design structural?**

☐ **decorative?**

☐ **symbolic?**

Building's primary use:

_____

_____

_____

shed

☐ **Is this design structural?**

☐ **decorative?**

☐ **symbolic?**

Building's primary use:

_____

_____

_____

mansard

☐ **Is this design structural?**

☐ **decorative?**

☐ **symbolic?**

Building's primary use:

_____

_____

_____

salt box

☐ **Is this design structural?**

☐ **decorative?**

☐ **symbolic?**

Building's primary use:

_____

_____

_____

pyramid

☐ **Is this design structural?**

☐ **decorative?**

☐ **symbolic?**

Building's primary use:

_____

_____

_____

hipped

☐ **Is this design structural?**

☐ **decorative?**

☐ **symbolic?**

Building's primary use:

_____

_____

_____

Worksheet 2

Roof details

cupola

- [ ] Is this design structural?
- [ ] decorative?
- [ ] symbolic?

Building's primary use:

_____

_____

_____

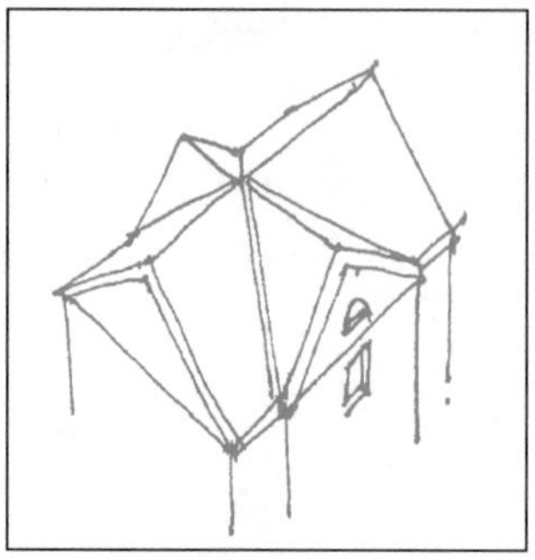

cross gable

- [ ] Is this design structural?
- [ ] decorative?
- [ ] symbolic?

Building's primary use:

_____

_____

_____

steeple

- [ ] Is this design structural?
- [ ] decorative?
- [ ] symbolic?

Building's primary use:

_____

_____

_____

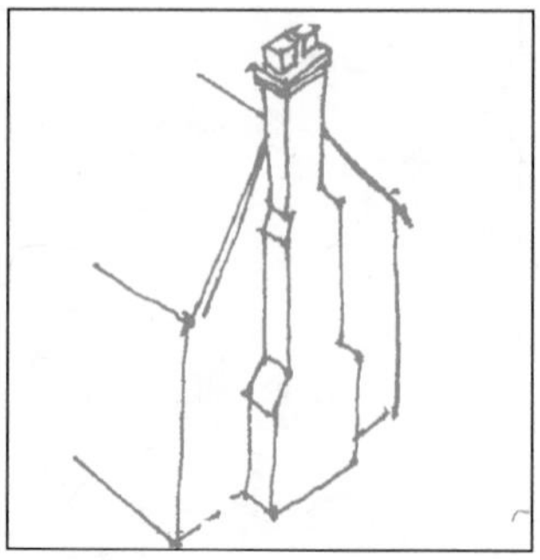

chimney

- [ ] Is this design structural?
- [ ] decorative?
- [ ] symbolic?

Building's primary use:

_____

_____

_____

Windows

double-hung

- [ ] Is this design structural?
- [ ] decorative?
- [ ] symbolic?

Building's primary use:

_____

_____

_____

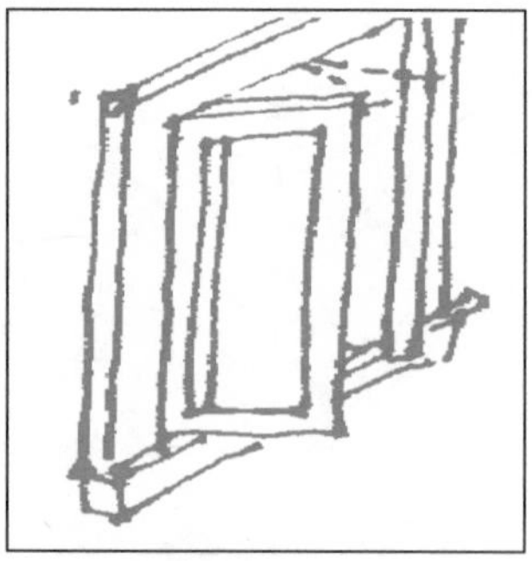

casement

- [ ] Is this design structural?
- [ ] decorative?
- [ ] symbolic?

Building's primary use:

_____

_____

_____

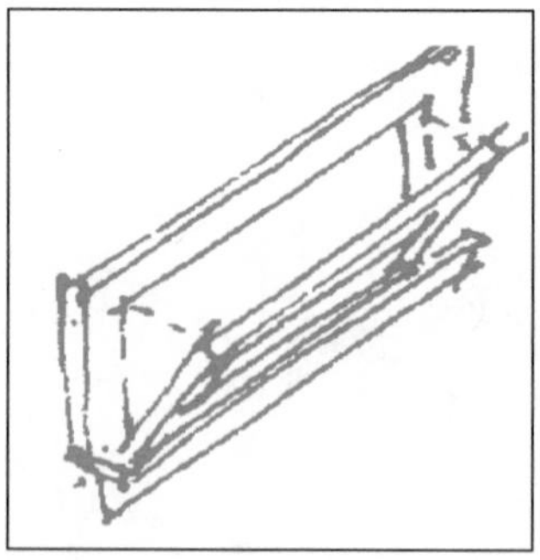

hopper

- [ ] Is this design structural?
- [ ] decorative?
- [ ] symbolic?

Building's primary use:

_____

_____

_____

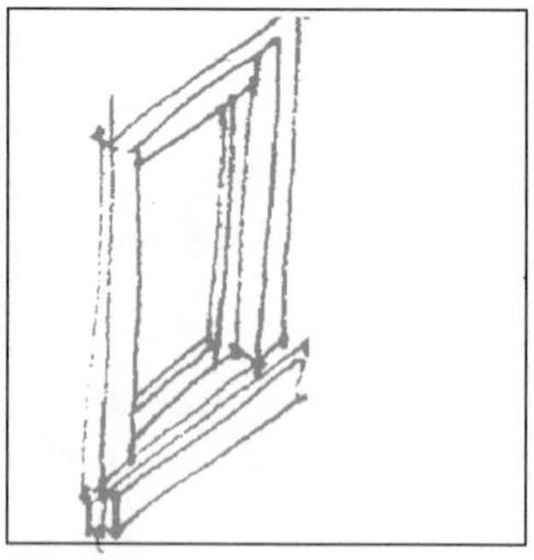

fixed

- [ ] Is this design structural?
- [ ] decorative?
- [ ] symbolic?

Building's primary use:

_____

_____

_____

Worksheet 3

Windows

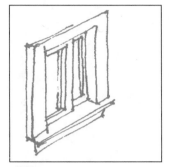

sliding

☐ **Is this design structural?**

☐ **decorative?**

☐ **symbolic?**

Building's primary use:

_____

_____

_____

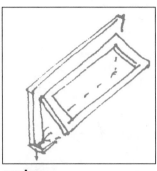

awning

☐ **Is this design structural?**

☐ **decorative?**

☐ **symbolic?**

Building's primary use:

_____

_____

_____

louver

☐ **Is this design structural?**

☐ **decorative?**

☐ **symbolic?**

Building's primary use:

_____

_____

_____

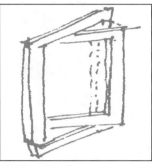

pivot

☐ **Is this design structural?**

☐ **decorative?**

☐ **symbolic?**

Building's primary use:

_____

_____

_____

dormer

☐ **Is this design structural?**

☐ **decorative?**

☐ **symbolic?**

Building's primary use:

_____

_____

_____

stained glass

☐ **Is this design structural?**

☐ **decorative?**

☐ **symbolic?**

Building's primary use:

_____

_____

_____

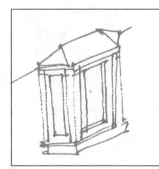

bay

☐ **Is this design structural?**

☐ **decorative?**

☐ **symbolic?**

Building's primary use:

_____

_____

_____

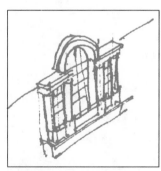

Palladian

☐ **Is this design structural?**

☐ **decorative?**

☐ **symbolic?**

Building's primary use:

_____

_____

_____

WHY DESIGN? Activities and Projects from the National Building Museum

Worksheet 4

Wall surfaces

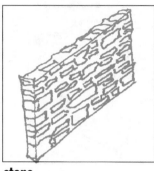

stone

☐ Is this design structural?
☐ decorative?
☐ symbolic?

Building's primary use:

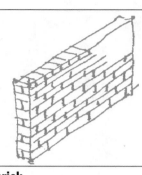

brick

☐ Is this design structural?
☐ decorative?
☐ symbolic?

Building's primary use:

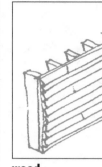

wood

☐ Is this design structural?
☐ decorative?
☐ symbolic?

Building's primary use:

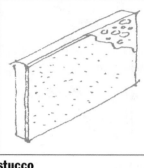

stucco

☐ Is this design structural?
☐ decorative?
☐ symbolic?

Building's primary use:

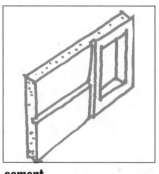

cement

☐ Is this design structural?
☐ decorative?
☐ symbolic?

Building's primary use:

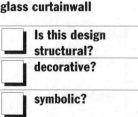

glass curtainwall

☐ Is this design structural?
☐ decorative?
☐ symbolic?

Building's primary use:

metal panel

☐ Is this design structural?
☐ decorative?
☐ symbolic?

Building's primary use:

precast concrete

☐ Is this design structural?
☐ decorative?
☐ symbolic?

Building's primary use:

Worksheet 5

Attachments

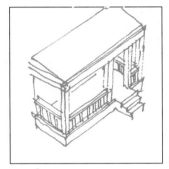

porch

☐ **Is this design structural?** _____
☐ **decorative?** _____
☐ **symbolic?** _____

Building's primary use:

_____
_____
_____

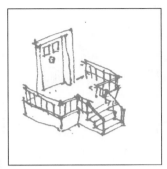

entry stoop

☐ **Is this design structural?** _____
☐ **decorative?** _____
☐ **symbolic?** _____

Building's primary use:

_____
_____
_____

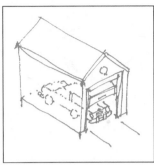

garage

☐ **Is this design structural?** _____
☐ **decorative?** _____
☐ **symbolic?** _____

Building's primary use:

_____
_____
_____

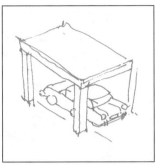

carport

☐ **Is this design structural?** _____
☐ **decorative?** _____
☐ **symbolic?** _____

Building's primary use:

_____
_____
_____

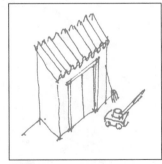

shed

☐ **Is this design structural?** _____
☐ **decorative?** _____
☐ **symbolic?** _____

Building's primary use:

_____
_____
_____

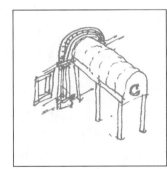

canopy

☐ **Is this design structural?** _____
☐ **decorative?** _____
☐ **symbolic?** _____

Building's primary use:

_____
_____
_____

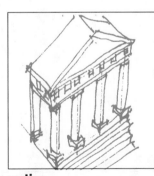

portico

☐ **Is this design structural?** _____
☐ **decorative?** _____
☐ **symbolic?** _____

Building's primary use:

_____
_____
_____

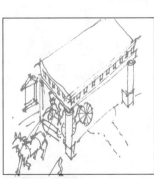

carriage porch

☐ **Is this design structural?** _____
☐ **decorative?** _____
☐ **symbolic?** _____

Building's primary use:

_____
_____
_____

Worksheet 6

Attachments

shutters

	Is this design structural?
	decorative?
	symbolic?

Building's primary use:

pediment

	Is this design structural?
	decorative?
	symbolic?

Building's primary use:

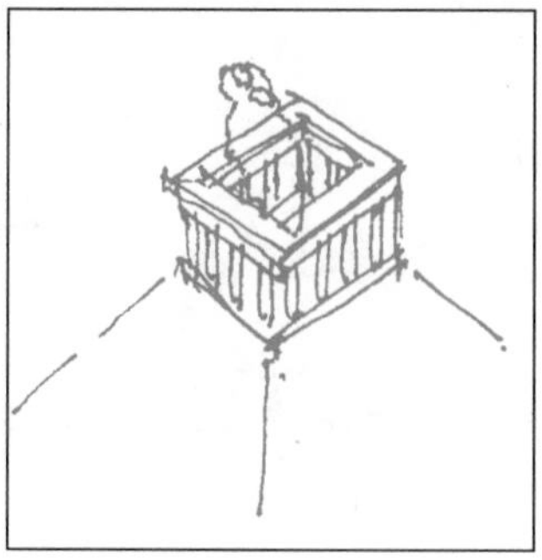

widow's walk

	Is this design structural?
	decorative?
	symbolic?

Building's primary use:

tower

	Is this design structural?
	decorative?
	symbolic?

Building's primary use:

Doors

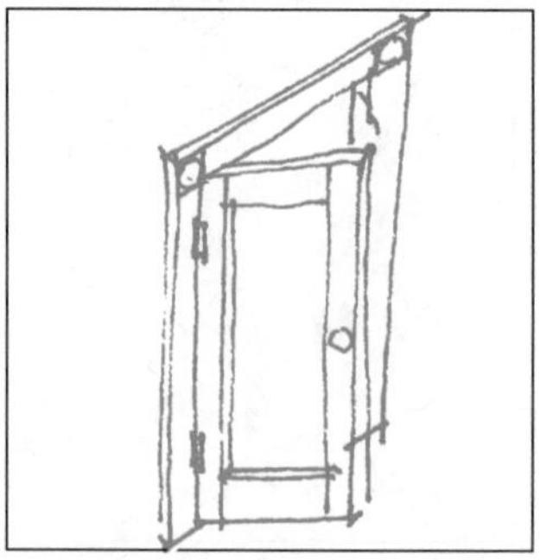

single

	Is this design structural?
	decorative?
	symbolic?

Building's primary use:

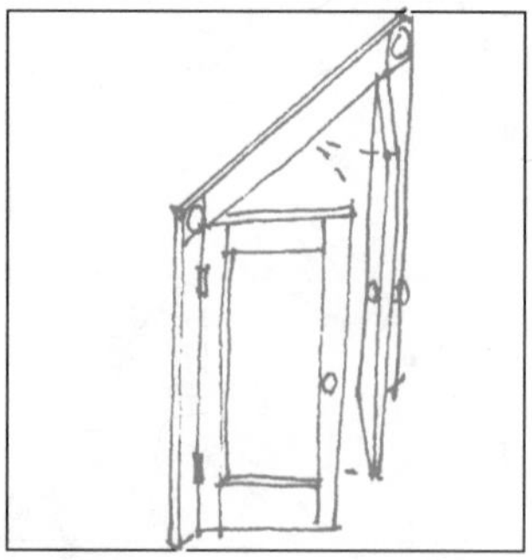

double

	Is this design structural?
	decorative?
	symbolic?

Building's primary use:

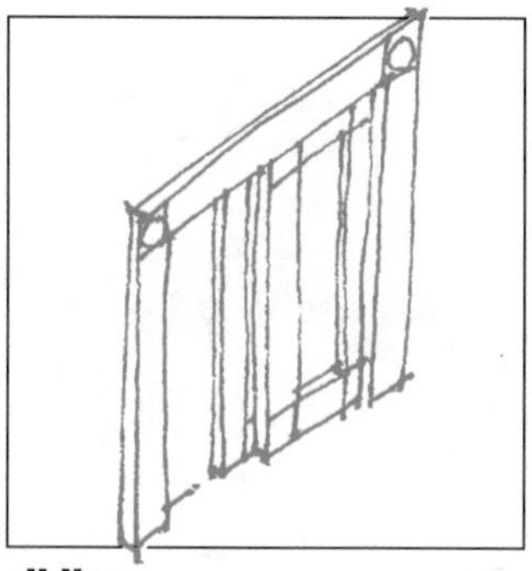

sliding

	Is this design structural?
	decorative?
	symbolic?

Building's primary use:

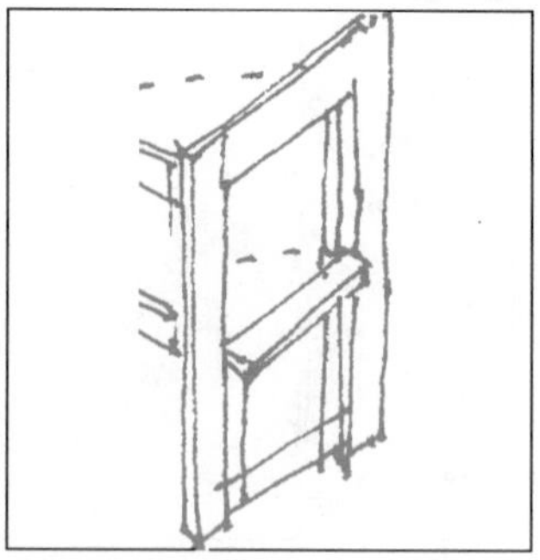

Dutch

	Is this design structural?
	decorative?
	symbolic?

Building's primary use:

Feeling spaces

How can listening to inanimate objects tell us something about our needs?

MATERIALS
- Friends
- Performance space
- Photocopies of worksheet
- Props (appropriate to place)

You've probably heard someone say, "Wow, if this room could talk. . . ." In this activity you'll imagine that rooms can. Through group role-playing, you'll hear what inanimate objects from the built environment have to say. If you listen closely, they may tell you why they work well. And why they don't.

CREATE THE SCENARIO
First, determine the location in which the action will take place (airport, restaurant, subway train, dentist's office, etc.). Then cast the characters. Each participant becomes one of the objects normally found in that environment. They all come alive after the humans go home.

DEVELOP YOUR CHARACTER
Before "becoming" your object, get to know it better by interviewing it. Ask the object the questions found on the worksheet titled "Feeling spaces," and, when you've settled on the answers, get in character.

CREATE A PLAY
Assemble the characters and collaborate on the story. This activity can be either scripted or improvised. Incorporate as many props as possible. Although the type of story may vary (mystery, comedy, etc.), the dialogue should focus on the normal interaction that takes place between humans and objects during the day. Remember, all the humans have gone home, and this is the time when the objects can talk without being overheard. Make sure each object has plenty to say.

GET THE MESSAGE
After the play is over, discuss what the objects had to say. Consider how the setting and objects used in the play might be redesigned to resolve some of the issues raised when we let objects have their say.

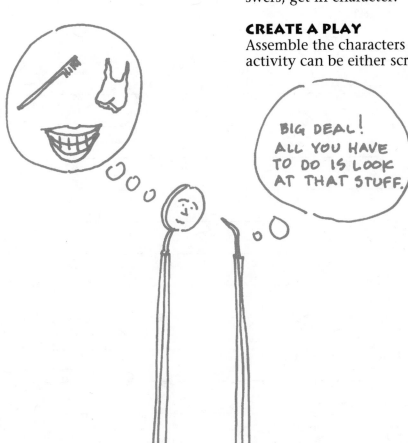

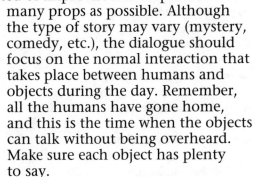

BIG DEAL! ALL YOU HAVE TO DO IS LOOK AT THAT STUFF.

Worksheet

Object: _____

What is your name?
_____

Do you have any nicknames?
_____

When, where, and how were you born?
_____

How have you grown?
_____

Who were your parents?
_____

Who are you related to?
_____

How old are you?
_____

How do you like where you live and work?
_____

Do you have any friends? If so, who are they? If not, why not?
_____

Do you have any enemies? If so, who are they? If not, why not?
_____

Do you like children? Why?
_____

Do you like adults? Why?
_____

Do you like to be alone? Why?
_____

What kind of attitude do you project? Why?
_____

How do you feel most of the time?
_____

What makes you happy?
_____

Do you like a lot of company?
_____

Are you polite to people?
_____

Are you mistreated? Respected? By whom?
_____

When is your favorite time of day?
_____

When is your favorite time of year?
_____

What is your favorite thing to do?
_____

What is your least favorite thing to do?
_____

Disabled by your environment

How does the designed environment work for people with special needs?

MATERIALS

- Backpack or pillowcase, and 5-pound bag of sugar
- Camera
- Earplugs
- Eyeglasses and petroleum jelly
- Friend
- Journal or notepad
- Tape or thin gloves

Many of us have physical conditions that limit our ability to easily navigate our towns. We have impaired vision, a bad knee, or we use a wheelchair. As a society, we are finally designing to meet everyone's needs. This improves the quality of life for all people because we'll all experience limited mobility at some point, even if only temporarily.

In this activity you'll experience how the designed environment functions for people with a variety of impairments.

EXPERIENCE AN ALTERED STATE

Choose one or more of the four activities on the next page to get a limited idea of what it's like to negotiate the designed environment with a physical disability. WARNING: Some of your routine experiences may become dangerous, so pair up with a friend to make sure you don't hurt yourself or others. To best understand the complete day of a person with a disability, try to experience the disability from the moment you get out of bed until your day is over.

Keep your journal or a notepad handy and record difficult interactions with the designs you encounter (even this may be harder than you think). Note how the experiences make you feel, physically and emotionally. Also note how much longer it takes to accomplish simple tasks. Have your friend photograph "barriers" (things like high curbs without curb cuts, heavy glass doors without electronic openers, elevators that don't signal what floor you're on) that make getting around especially difficult for you. And be careful, it's a jungle out there!

LOOK OUT!

If you choose to experience a visual impairment, you'll need a pair of glasses (glasses with magnifying lenses are available at a drug store, or safety glasses from a hardware store). Cover the lenses with petroleum jelly or another substance that allows you to see basic shapes but without much detail. Or wear a pair of dark sunglasses all day.

SAY WHAT?

If you choose to experience a hearing impairment, you'll need a pair of earplugs (available at most drug or hardware stores).

GET A GRIP ON IT!

If you choose to experience an impairment of your ability to feel things with your fingers or your ability to use all of your fingers, you can use tape. Wrap a few or all of your fingers together with the tape, or wear a pair of thin gloves.

OH, MOTHER!

Half the population may experience the altered state of pregnancy. Although it may seem to last forever, it is a temporary condition affecting mobility. To experience how pregnancy affects mobility, put a 5-pound bag of sugar in a backpack or pillowcase and tie it around your waist.

Even after delivery, being a parent of a young child can make it difficult to get around. Think about unloading groceries from a vehicle while carrying a sleeping (or crying) infant. To experience some of what it's like, borrow a stroller and try taking it everywhere.

Should the designed environment be accessible to everyone regardless of cost?

What are the costs to our society if everyone isn't able to make a contribution because the designed environment isn't accessible?

What new technologies are making the world more accessible to all people?

Are you familiar with the Americans with Disabilities Act (ADA) and its role in making the designed environment usable by more people? You can learn about the ADA in the **Resources** *section of this book.*

The Goldilocks Syndrome

How well do objects fit your needs physically?

MATERIALS
- Pencil
- Selected objects
- Tape measure

Goldilocks discovered firsthand the importance of a good fit. Like the chairs in the classic Goldilocks story, the objects and places you use every day are designed to do specific tasks. Some objects are designed for everyone to use, and others to satisfy the sizes and needs of a specific group of people.

The term "anthropometrics" describes the size relationships between the human form and designed objects and places. Designers use charts of typical user measurements (height, reach, leg length, viewing height and distance, grasp size) in seated and standing positions to ensure their solutions fit well with the targeted user. In this activity you'll see how well you fit the objects and spaces you use. And how well they fit you.

INVESTIGATE BAD FITS
Find five familiar objects that don't fit you as well as they should because of their size relative to yours. On the worksheet titled "The Goldilocks Syndrome," describe the bad fits. Measure the parts that seem wrong and suggest solutions. For example, do your knees hit the dining-room table? Is the problem with the height of the table? With the height of the chair? Is there a solution less drastic than leg surgery? What physical factors make an object a bad fit for you?

INVESTIGATE GOOD FITS
Now find five familiar objects that fit you really well. Describe, relative to your size, why they work. For example, a mountain bike with a custom 28-inch frame and extended seat may be the perfect fit for your 6-foot 5-inch body. What physical factors make an object a good fit for you?

Do most of the things you own fit you "like a glove"?

What type of objects tend to fit you best? Worst? Why might that be?

What would happen to our economic system if we insisted that everything be custom-made?

Worksheet

Bad fits (Objects that don't fit and why)   **Solution**

1

2

3

4

5

Good fits (Objects that fit and why)

1

2

3

4

5

Utopia

What would your perfect world be like?

Throughout time, people have tried to develop perfect places where they could live in harmony with each other. They have also tried to live in harmony with nature. Most of these visionary utopias had to partially isolate themselves from the rest of society. As our world gets smaller and more interconnected, we realize it's almost impossible to exist in isolation.

What keeps people from thinking about a better world? From creating one?

Today, many of us are so driven by the details of daily life that we don't stop to dream of a better life in a better place. In this activity you'll slow down to reflect on what it takes to get from our existing to your preferred world.

IMAGINE A PERFECT WORLD
To envision a perfect world, you'll need to identify what's wrong with the one you're in. In your journal, make a list of local and global situations that need changing and title the list "What's wrong with my world." Find out how long these situations have been problems? What caused them? Who else thinks they are problems? Write these answers in your journal.

WHO'S WORKING FOR YOUR UTOPIA?
There's a good chance that other people share some of your goals and may even be doing something to make them happen. Research and list in your journal organizations that are working to change the global situations you identified.

WHO MIGHT DISAGREE?
Consider who and what might keep your utopian vision from becoming reality. Consider also who and what might not benefit from your perfect world. What social, political, and economic forces are involved? Are any natural resources involved?

PROMOTE YOUR UTOPIA
Design a poster that promotes your idea of a perfect world. Include in it your list of the organizations that support your vision, their addresses, phone numbers, and how other interested people can become involved. Consider who is the audience for the poster? How do you want people to react to it? How much time do you think they will spend looking at it? Where should the poster be placed? What words, images, colors, and style would best communicate your ideas to this audience?

What affects design

and what design affects.

*Our needs don't exist in a vacuum.
So in order to truly understand what we design,
it's important to look at all the things that affect
our needs and the things that our design
solutions affect.*

*These "things" can be our culture—the laws,
attitudes, values, and meaning we bring to our
perceptions. They can be other people. They can be
environmental—the laws of nature, the climate
and topography of the place where we live, and
other animals, plants, and natural systems. They
can be physical—our sensory perceptions, and our
reactions to things like color and scale.*

*Activities in this chapter enable you to take a closer
look at these factors.*

CHAPTER

Learning how you learn

How does your learning style affect your perception?

MATERIALS
- Friends
- Colored pens/ pencils
- Photocopies of worksheet

When faced with a 10-page instruction manual for your VCR, do you (a) faint dead away, (b) rub your hands excitedly, looking forward to a stimulating evening, or (c) toss it out the window, grab the remote, and roll up your sleeves? We all know people who would do each of the above. It is the designer's ultimate challenge to create something that is easy for a variety of people to understand and use. Now this becomes quite a challenge because each of us is unique in how we learn—that is, how we perceive and process information.

Some people, for example, like to learn by first watching others, thinking about what they've seen, and then trying it themselves. Some people, on the other hand, like to jump in, try it, and then think about it. Your preference is a result of many things: genetics, the environment in which you grew up, friends, your education, and lots of other influences. It can also depend on what you are learning at any given time. In this group activity you'll learn more about the needs of different people and how learning style can affect a design solution. You'll also see where your strengths are as a learner and find out where you can stretch yourself.

IDENTIFY YOUR LEARNING STYLE
You'll need a large enough group so that you have *at least* one person representing each style. The four learning styles described on the worksheet on the next page were identified by Dr. Bernice McCarthy. (She is one of many people researching how people learn.) Everyone reads all the descriptions and picks the one that best describes him or her. Keep in mind that these are pure types and people are not, so you may find elements you identify with in each. For this activity, however, choose only one category.

IMAGINE YOUR PERFECT WORKSPACE
Then get together with those who have the same learning style. There should be four groups—ones, twos, threes, and fours. Each group (or individual) generates a "wish list" of what should be included in their perfect personal workspace. Be sure to be as thorough as possible in listing your needs and desires.

DESIGN ONE FOR SOMEONE ELSE
Now trade lists with another style group and interview them. Get to know more about them and what's on their list. Each group then designs a workspace for the "client" group. The design should include sketches, pictures, and/or models. Conclude by presenting the design to the clients and asking for feedback to determine how well this satisfies their needs. If there's time, modify your design and make a model for presentation to your clients.

How can you use an understanding of learning styles to help you solve problems? Set goals? Deal with new situations? Work with others?

What disadvantages can you see in using this information?

How well did the designers meet your needs and desires?

Did they meet your minimum needs?

Did they go beyond what was on your list?

1

The Learning Styles

YOU ARE A TYPE ONE LEARNER IF . . .

You try to make new information relate to your own experiences so that it becomes personally meaningful. You prefer to think about information before taking action. You are people oriented—you learn by observing others and hearing about their experiences, and you tend to be concerned about their feelings. It is important to you that people get along. In solving problems you like to work in groups, get opinions, and work toward consensus.

You get passionate about issues that are important to you and like to be personally involved. You often don't work well under pressure, and you dislike risks. People consider you caring and imaginative, but you often appear to worry too much and are thought to be too easy on people. One of your favorite questions is "Why?"

YOU ARE A TYPE TWO LEARNER IF . . .

You learn best when given facts, details, and the opinions of experts. You are good at understanding abstract information and like to think things through carefully before taking action. You can take what you see in the world and fit it into existing theories—reexamining the facts if they don't fit. You are thorough, well organized, and tackle problems with rationality and logic. You don't trust intuitive decisions.

You tend to be more interested in ideas than in people. Intellectual recognition is important to you. You follow the rules, can be rigid, and sometimes discourage original thinking. People consider you organized, logical, precise, and knowledgeable. One of your favorite questions is "What?"

YOU ARE A TYPE THREE LEARNER IF . . .

You like to get right in and try things out. You are a hands-on person, preferring to experiment and tinker with things. Reading instructions is something you'd rather not do. You prefer to deal with real objects and choices and are interested in technical skills.

You are good at taking what you see in the world and creating theories and concepts to fit it. You like problem solving and figuring things out on your own—teamwork can seem like a waste of time. You like clarity and usually get right to the point. You like to learn new skills. People consider you very practical and down to earth, but sometimes you are thought to be bossy, inflexible, and impersonal. One of your favorite questions is "How does this work?"

YOU ARE A TYPE FOUR LEARNER IF . . .

You are action oriented and enjoy change. You are enthusiastic about new things and fairly adaptable. You like to discover things for yourself and learn by trial and error. You thrive on challenge and deal imaginatively and intuitively with decisions and problems. You are a risk-taker. When solving problems, you look for patterns, look at all sides of an issue, and see possibility in everything.

You are an idea person who enjoys working with people and is at ease with different personalities. People consider you enthusiastic, flexible, and someone who makes things happen. Sometimes, however, you can appear manipulative and pushy and can make rash decisions. One of your favorite questions is "What if . . . ?"

These descriptions are taken from *The 4Mat System: Teaching to Learning Styles with Right/Left Mode Techniques*, by Bernice McCarthy, ©1980, 1987 by Excel, Inc. Those desiring a copy of the complete work for further reading may acquire it from the publisher, Excel Inc., 23385 Old Barrington Road, Barrington, IL 60010, 708-382-7272. Used by permission.

An apple isn't just an apple

How does culture affect our understanding of symbols?

WHY DESIGN? Activities and Projects from the National Building Museum

MATERIALS
- **Colored pens/ pencils**
- **Worksheet**

When we communicate, we tend to assume that people understand all the words and images we use. But good communication takes place only when people are in agreement with the symbolic meanings of the words and images. For example, you may see someone dressed in black and think it's a fashion statement. Add a hearse to the picture and the meaning of black changes to mourning. This is true, however, only if your culture teaches you that black is the appropriate color for mourning.

In this activity you'll see how words and images can be manipulated to change meaning. You'll also question how culture influences meaning.

COMPARE APPLES TO APPLES

On the worksheet titled "An apple isn't just an apple" are pictures of apples. But you can change their meaning to something other than just *apple* by making them symbols (something that stands for something else). Do this by adding a different word or image to each, as illustrated in the first box. Jog your mind by thinking about any cultures, companies, professions, places, legends, or sayings you associate with apples.

COMPARE RED'S SHADES OF MEANING

Now add images or additional words to the word "red" to change its meaning to something other than just a color. Consider how the word is used to describe people or environments. Do you associate the word red with any cultures, companies, professions, places, legends, or sayings?

IS IT UNDERSTANDABLE?

After you've made your additions, ask some friends if they "get" your meaning. List their comments in the space below the image. Then ask people from other cultures what they think the combinations mean. Then choose one image and investigate its history—how did it come to mean what you think it means?

Why does an apple symbolize so many things?

Why does the color red symbolize so many things?

Why do people recognize the meaning of some symbols and not others?

73

Worksheet

New meaning:

Biblical
references
—original
sin

New meaning:

New meaning:

New meaning:

red

New meaning:

red

New meaning:

red

New meaning:

red

New meaning:

Rethinking your primary sense

How does our reliance on sight influence the designed environment?

MATERIALS
- Journal
- Pen/pencil

Ever notice how nosy dogs can be? Unlike humans, dogs perceive their surroundings primarily through their noses. They store memories of smells like we remember words. Watch any dog in a new environment and see how it explores through its sense of smell. It is that keen ability to sniff that makes our canine friends so useful in helping us find what we're looking for. What other animals have different primary senses? How do those senses meet their needs?

Human animals, on the other hand, use sight as our primary sense. When we visit a new environment, our discoveries are most often based on what we see. Our world is so visual that we even have sayings like "See what I mean?" and "Seeing is believing." What are the advantages and disadvantages of having sight as our primary sense? In this activity you'll find out by reducing your reliance on sight and increasing your sensitivity to your other four senses.

IMAGINE A NEW WORLD
Each of the four scenarios on the next page asks you to imagine a world in which people's primary sense is not vision, but one of the other four senses. All the designs in this "new" world have been created around the needs of that sense. The task is to describe in your journal a day in your life as an inhabitant of this new world. First, describe how the people have evolved physically to adapt to their primary sense—do they still need eyes? Can they sing? Are their ears larger or shaped differently than those of humans on planet Earth?

Then, think about your current daily routine and your interactions with people, graphic communications, objects, places, and systems. How would all these things change? Consider how you would socialize, what you would do for entertainment, how you would communicate, what type of house you would want, and how you would get around. It might help to think about the role your senses play in your current life. For example, what human occupations require a special "sensitivity" to sound? What pleasure does your sense of touch bring to your daily experience? What sayings ("See what I mean?") do we have that relate to our sense of taste?

Think about whether the design solutions necessary to meet your new needs in this world would be very different from those used on Earth. If you returned to Earth for a visit, would the designed environment accommodate your primary sense, allowing you to do everything Earthlings do? Describe the design solutions that would meet these needs. Use words and images to illustrate your ideas.

SCENARIO 1: WHO "NOSE" WHERE I LIVE?
Imagine a world in which you "follow your nose," a world in which your brain depends on your smelling ability to navigate, communicate, and survive.

SCENARIO 2: DO I LIVE "HEAR"?
Imagine a world in which your ears rule, a world in which your brain depends on your hearing ability to navigate, communicate, and survive.

SCENARIO 3: HOW DO I STAY IN "TOUCH"?
Imagine a world in which your fingers do the walking and talking (you can hear but you cannot speak), a world in which your brain depends on your ability to touch and feel to navigate, communicate, and survive.

SCENARIO 4: "TASTES" JUST LIKE HOME!
Imagine a world in which your tastebuds are in charge, a world in which your brain depends on your ability to taste to navigate, communicate, and survive.

Are your needs different when a different sense becomes primary?

Was one world harder to imagine than another? Why?

Did one primary sense require more design solution (products, environments, graphics, or systems) changes than another?

How does our world meet the needs of people whose primary sense may not be sight, or people who have varying degrees of physical and mental abilities?

Are you familiar with the Americans with Disabilities Act (ADA) and its role in making the designed environment usable by more people? To learn about the ADA refer to the **Resources** *section of this book.*

Sensory treasure map

How can using all your senses affect the quality of an experience?

MATERIALS

- Colored pens/pencils
- Friend
- Objects that appeal to your senses and will help someone get to your special place (you will need a way to store and transport these objects)
- Paper

We are used to thinking of a map as something with images and words that is flat and foldable. But who says a map has to be that way? Communicating the three-dimensional world in a two-dimensional way is a challenging task, and many people find maps difficult to use.

In this activity, you'll design a way for someone to find a special place—a place you think others might enjoy as much as you do. But this map is not going to be an ordinary flat map. Your map will be multidimensional and appeal to all the senses!

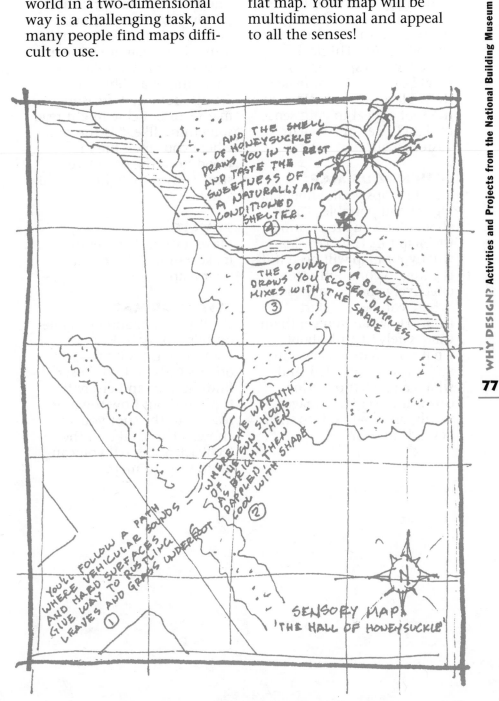

SELECT A SPOT

First, find the right spot. Select a place you think most people don't know about but would enjoy experiencing. The spot should be reasonably hard to find, enjoyable by all the senses, and reached using all the senses. And getting there should be fun. Think about some favored spots in your neighborhood. What makes these places special? How does the spot appeal to your sense of sight? Hearing? Touch? Taste? Smell?

DESIGN YOUR MAP

Like all maps yours should be logical and portable. Think about who you are creating the map for. Then consider what your map will need if it is going to communicate effectively and be easy to use. Where will people start from? How can you get them there safely? Think about what information is essential and must be included, and what can be left out. How can you use colors, images, words, and materials to their best advantage?

HOW CAN YOU GET PEOPLE THERE USING ALL THEIR SENSES?

How will you use senses other than sight? You may want the user to smell things in order to find the way, find or create rubbings of architectural details, collect edible samples (only those that are known to be safe!), or listen to a tape recording of audible clues. Think about how treasure maps work. A clue might read something like: "At the spot where you smell the musty wood from the dead tree struck down by lightning, take a right."

PLAN IT

Make several sketches or make a model, then create your map.

TEST YOUR MAP

Try it yourself, and ask someone else to try it. Evaluate your map. Does it work? In other words, did your user find the spot and enjoy the trip? Find out how the users reacted to the spot you've chosen. Then, take all the feedback and see if you can improve your map.

How do the maps we use every day reflect the people and cultures who create them?

Do you find maps easy or difficult to use? Why?

What makes a good treasure map?

How difficult was designing the map?

Does this activity change your evaluation of traditional maps?

They're such a pain to work with!

How do diverse personalities affect communication?

MATERIALS
- Large meeting space
- Pens/pencils
- Photocopies of the complete set of worksheets for each person
- Photocopy of Worksheet 1, cut up, and 2 containers to put the pieces in
- Props as appropriate

Have you ever been accused of being too bossy? Been told you did a great job organizing the group? Or had someone comment on your enthusiastic outlook? Design is a social activity that requires people to work together to change and improve the world. Obviously, the way you work in a group can help or hinder this process. In this group activity, you'll role-play a specific personality in a group that is trying to solve a problem. You'll experience the productive and nonproductive ways people behave and practice ways to deal effectively with specific personality traits.

HOW THE ROLE-PLAY WORKS
This requires a group—the more the merrier. Ten or more is good. Some people will play the town council (five to seven members) whose task is to solve the problem. Others will be the residents of the town. It is their job to watch the council discussion and, using the two worksheets that follow, identify the different personality types being played, as well as the productive and nonproductive behavior and language used. One person serves as moderator.

Cut up the roles on the photocopy of Worksheet 1. Put the "productive" roles in one container, and the "nonproductive" roles in another. Have each town council member draw one that only he or she sees (the moderator is responsible for making sure there is a balance between productive and nonproductive roles on the council). One council member serves as the chair. He or she is responsible for opening the meeting and beginning the discussion. The members should first take time to get into character by thinking about the issue under discussion and developing their characters' attitudes. Props can help.

CALL THE MEETING TO ORDER
The activity begins with the council chair introducing the problem (see scenario) to the whole group and passing out Worksheets 1 and 2. At several points during the discussion, the moderator freezes the action. Using the "Guidelines for moderator" questions, he or she helps the group identify the personality types on the council, analyze the action to determine the productive and nonproductive behaviors, and suggest methods for dealing with difficult personalities. After each freeze, new council members can rotate in, taking a new personality; old and new members can be mixed; or a completely new council can be selected. The council then resumes its discussion until the next freeze-frame.

Guidelines for moderator

SCENARIO

You live in an old frontier town that sits in a small valley protected by hilly, rough terrain. There is a single entrance to the town through a huge stone pass in the cliffs. More than 150 years ago, the town's founders built a gate into the entrance that served to protect the settlers. Over the years the stone entrance and gate have become a landmark and a meeting place for the community, as well as a tourist attraction. But the entrance has eroded and is becoming a hazard. Cracks indicate that it could crumble at any moment. This entrance is still the only way in and out of the valley. What should you, the town council, do?

ACTIVITY EXTENSION

Use the worksheets to examine real-life problem-solving situations. Or watch a TV show (sitcoms work really well) to see how personality affects the way conflicts are handled.

QUESTIONS TO USE IN GUIDING THE DISCUSSION:

Who was playing which role? How could you tell?
Is the group solving the problem in a positive way?
Why or why not?
Who is hindering the process?
Who is helping the process?
Which roles were easiest to identify? Why?
Which roles were easiest to play? Why?
Were people listening to each other? How could you tell?
How can (could) the group come up with a list of solutions?
What's in the way?

IF NONPRODUCTIVE CONFLICT ARISES IN THE COUNCIL . . .

Are people angry?
How can you tell (voice, body language, eye contact)?
Were they listening?
What makes it hard to listen when you are in an argument?

DO YOU SEE ANY OF THE FOLLOWING COMMUNICATION CLOSERS . . .

Criticizing? Name-calling? Diagnosing? Ordering? Threatening? Moralizing? Advising? Diverting? Diminishing?
Which personalities are using them?
How are these affecting the group and its ability to solve the problem?

WHAT TECHNIQUES CAN HELP NEUTRALIZE THE NONPRODUCTIVE ROLES IN THE GROUP? FOR EXAMPLE:

With the Boss: Try to open up the discussion to other people by saying, "I'd be interested in knowing what . . . thinks."
With the Unconnected: Try to get him or her to focus on a question.
With the Blocker: Get him or her to address the specific question by saying, "Can you offer a suggestion for solving the problem?"

HOW CAN ANY OF THE FOLLOWING COMMUNICATION OPENERS BE USED . . .

Encouraging? Clarifying? Restating? Reflecting? Summarizing? Validating?
Is any personality using them?
How are these affecting the group and its ability to solve the problem?

Worksheet 1

*As you watch the group solve the problem,
look for the following personalities.
Put a check mark by every one you see.*

PRODUCTIVE ROLES

Do-er—You are very practical and action oriented, always suggesting ideas, and proposing realistic solutions.

Energizer—You are enthusiastic and help move the group to make a decision or find a solution. You remind people why they're all there in the first place.

Information seeker—You ask the questions needed to get the facts and information that are important in finding a solution.

Orienter—You make sure the group stays on course toward the goal of solving the problem.

Encourager—You praise ideas. You are peppy and make the group fun and friendly.

Harmonizer—You keep the group looking at the problem and solutions, not at personalities. You show how different solutions have merit and may contain similar ideas.

Peacemaker—You try to make the group discussion go more smoothly, especially when people get angry.

Summarizer—You pull together the ideas, suggestions, comments, or information to help the group know where it stands on the road to the goal.

NONPRODUCTIVE ROLES

Boss—You try to get your own way without regard for the others in your group. You use flattery, sarcasm, and commands. You make fun of other people's ideas.

Blocker—You find a problem with every solution offered. It seems you just don't want any solution. You never offer an idea of your own. You aren't helpful; you only stop things.

Special-interest pleader—You have your own plan, so what the group wants is not important. You refuse to compromise.

Unconnected—You go out of your way not to be a member of the group. You will do anything during the meeting to show you are not interested. You listen to your tape player, crack your gum, whistle, and do other things that distract the group. You participate only when forced.

Attacker—You think everybody's ideas are dumb. You attack any idea that comes along in a negative and mean-spirited manner.

Follower—You just go with the flow, agreeing with everybody, not suggesting ideas of your own.

Moralizer—You are always telling other people what they should or shouldn't do. You act superior, as though you're the only one who knows what's right.

Worksheet 2

COMMUNICATION CLOSERS

As you watch the discussion, listen for language that encourages and discourages productive communication. Put a mark beside each one you see. Then use "Communication openers" to come up with strategies for difficult personalities.

☐ **CRITICIZING**
Negative evaluation of another person's actions or attitudes: "Well, you certainly brought that on yourself."

☐ **NAME-CALLING**
Putting down or stereotyping the other person: "Just like a girl" or "What a jerk."

☐ **DIAGNOSING**
Playing amateur psychiatrist: "I know why you did that. You're just trying to irritate me."

☐ **ORDERING**
Commanding what you want done: "I'm in charge and I want you to do it now!"

☐ **THREATENING**
Trying to control by warning of negative consequences: "You'll do it or else I'll . . ."

☐ **MORALIZING**
Telling others what they should do: "You ought to tell her your sorry" or "Shouldn't you consider . . ."

☐ **ADVISING**
Giving the other person a solution to the problem when not asked: "If I were you, I'd . . ." or "That's an easy one to solve. First . . ."

☐ **DIVERTING**
Trying to distract the person from the problem: "Don't dwell on it" or "Think you've got it bad? Let me tell you . . ."

☐ **DIMINISHING**
Trying to stop the other person from feeling negative emotions: "Don't worry, it will all work out in the end" or "There's no reason to feel that way . . ."

COMMUNICATION OPENERS

☐ **ENCOURAGING**
Showing interest in what the other person is saying by supporting his or her ideas or comments: "That sounds really interesting" or "Wow, I wish I were able to do that!"

☐ **CLARIFYING**
Trying to gain more information to understand what the person wants, needs, feels, and thinks: "Tell me more about . . ." or "Why do you think . . . ?"

☐ **RESTATING**
Repeating the other person's words in a way that shows you are listening and trying to understand. Checking your interpretation by paraphrasing basic ideas and facts: "Am I right that you want me to . . ."

☐ **REFLECTING**
Showing you recognize the other person's feelings: "You seem very discouraged."

☐ **SUMMARIZING**
Concisely pulling together all the important ideas, facts, and feelings in an effort to establish a basis for further discussion: "You are concerned because I don't want you to do . . . and you feel I don't value your opinion."

☐ **VALIDATING**
Acknowledging and showing appreciation for (but not necessarily agreeing with) the other person's issues and feelings: "I can see why you are angry because . . ."

Routine or special

How can design influence your quality of life?

MATERIALS
- Journal
- Pen/pencil

Picture in your mind all the kinds of cups for drinking coffee. There are Styrofoam cups, cups designed to stay attached to the dashboard during morning commutes, and insulated cups. All of these, and many others, get the job done. They contain the coffee, keep it warm, and can be held and lifted to the mouths of their users. Yet some cups do more. There is something about their form that says this cup and what's inside it are special. Their job isn't just to hold liquid; it is also to celebrate the act of drinking it. These cups become special objects. In this activity you'll use design to turn an ordinary routine into a special experience.

REFLECT ON YOUR DAILY ROUTINE

Start by making a list in your journal of all the activities that make up your daily routine. Identify all the objects and spaces that are key to each activity. Note that an activity may involve more than one object. For example, drinking coffee can include, in addition to the coffee cup, a coffee grinder, a coffee pot, a coffee decanter, a coffee filter, a sugar bowl, a sugar spoon, and a cream pitcher.

ROUTINE TO SPECIAL

Select one activity from your list and design a way to make it special. On a separate page in your journal, use words and images you draw, find, or photograph, to describe how you could increase the activity's meaning. This should include not only objects, but a plan. For example, think about your routine before you go to sleep. Do you just rush in the room, throw your clothes somewhere, and fall into bed? This routine could be made special by lighting a scented candle, using sheets that feel good on your skin (flannel, natural cotton, or even silk!), snuggling into a featherbed that hugs you or under a homemade quilt that brings back family memories, or playing some soothing music before you get in bed. Consider how you can satisfy all five of your senses. Feel free to invent new objects and spaces if the appropriate ones don't already exist.

MAKE IT HAPPEN

Which of the things you listed can you actually do? Some things will be free, some you can make (the candle), and some might cost something—but if they make you feel great, maybe they're worth it!

What gives an object a special meaning:

The person who designed it?

The raw material from which it was made?

The place in which it was made?

The decoration on it?

The emotions and memories you associate with it?

Its size?

Its age?

Its cost?

How might an object you routinely use differ from one you save for special occasions or uses?

How does the design of an object improve the quality of your life?

83

You're not my type

How do communication needs affect typeface selection?

MATERIALS
- Book of typefaces from library (optional)
- Designs selected from list (see below)
- Journal
- Personal computer with multiple typefaces

Think about the last time you wore a bathing suit to a wedding. Typefaces, like clothing, fit some situations better than others—that is, they look like we expect them to look. Some typefaces are formal, some are casual. Some are classic, some are trendy. The style of type is a critical component of graphic communication because it affects both readability and the emotional response of the reader. In this activity you'll locate documents illustrating the many different fashion statements type can make, and then you'll have some fun redesigning some of them.

DOCUMENT THE DOCUMENTS

Find as many of the items listed below as you can. Finding multiple samples of the same kind of item is even better because it will help you see patterns and similarities.

Ad for an alternative rock music performance
Ad for a classical music performance
Ad for a jazz music performance
Ad for a new age music performance
Book jacket for a mystery novel
Book jacket for a religious text
Book jacket for a romance novel
Book jacket for a science fiction novel
Driver's license
Graduation announcement
Wedding invitation

In your journal describe the visual characteristics of the typefaces in each situation. For example, the wedding invitation type might be described as "elegant, formal, and like calligraphy." Then try to identify the name of the typeface by finding it on the following pages or on your computer. You may need to find a book of typefaces at the library. If you can't find the exact typeface, pick one that is most like it.

DON'T WORRY WHAT THE WEDDING GUESTS THINK

After you've done your research, pick a few of the items and redesign them using the most inappropriate typefaces you can find. Try to keep everything the same (size, color, placement, etc.) except for the typestyles. Show them to other people to see what they think without mentioning the change in typefaces. Do they notice?

What makes a typeface seem appropriate? Inappropriate?

How often do you think a typeface is inappropriate?

Do the type choices in this book seem appropriate?

Garamond

ABCDEFGHIJKLMNOPQRSTUVWXYZ
abcdefghijklmnopqrstuvwxyz123456789

Garamond italic

ABCDEFGHIJKLMNOPQRSTUVWXYZ
abcdefghijklmnopqrstuvwxyz123456789

Bodoni

ABCDEFGHIJKLMNOPQRSTUVWXYZ
abcdefghijklmnopqrstuvwxyz123456789

Elektrix bold

ABCDEFGHIJKLMNOPQRSTUVWXYZ
abcdefghijklmnopqrstuvwxyz123456789

Franklin Gothic Condensed

ABCDEFGHIJKLMNOPQRSTUVWXYZ
abcdefghijklmnopqrstuvwxyz123456789

Optima

ABCDEFGHIJKLMNOPQRSTUVWXYZ
abcdefghijklmnopqrstuvwxyz123456789

Palatino

ABCDEFGHIJKLMNOPQRSTUVWXYZ
abcdefghijklmnopqrstuvwxyz123456789

Senator demi

ABCDEFGHIJKLMNOPQRSTUVWXYZ
abcdefghijklmnopqrstuvwxyz123456789

Stone Sans

ABCDEFGHIJKLMNOPQRSTUVWXYZ
abcdefghijklmnopqrstuvwxyz123456789

Stone Serif

ABCDEFGHIJKLMNOPQRSTUVWXYZ
abcdefghijklmnopqrstuvwxyz123456789

Univers 47

ABCDEFGHIJKLMNOPQRSTUVWXYZ
abcdefghijklmnopqrstuvwxyz123456789

Univers 67

ABCDEFGHIJKLMNOPQRSTUVWXYZ
abcdefghijklmnopqrstuvwxyz123456789

Wish you were here

How does design make your hometown special?

MATERIALS
- Camera (optional)
- Colored pens/pencils
- Heavy white paper (6 x 4 inches)
- Journal

When traveling you may send postcards to friends and family describing the special places you're visiting. You might pick the postcard that looks the way you feel about the place. Or you might pick one with a photograph of what the place is known for—a famous building or artwork. Or, if you're in a silly mood, you might pick one that is funny and irreverent. On the back, you write about the things you've done—trying to get all the best details in the limited space so the receiver can "see" what you've been doing. In this activity you'll become a tourist in your own hometown by designing (and writing) a postcard that captures what makes it a special place.

What makes you pick one postcard over another?

GO SIGHT-SEEING

Make a list in your journal of the things that you like most about where you live. Consider the natural environment, historic landmarks, noteworthy structures, and all the favorite activities of the "locals." Choose one that for you best sums up the character of your hometown.

Design a postcard that uses the image of what you selected and captures its spirit, which might be serious, adventurous, or fun. Do some rough sketches of the layout. Then go to the site of your chosen image and photograph or draw it as it will appear on your postcard. Select the appropriate typeface and create the final postcard. Mount it in your journal.

WRITE ABOUT IT

On a separate piece of 6 x 4–inch paper, write your postcard note to someone who hasn't been to your town. Convince them that they, too, should check out this great place. Mount this text in your journal near the image.

WISH YOU WERE HERE

87

Why are stop signs "read"?

How do colors affect each other?

MATERIALS
- Colored markers
- Glue
- Journal
- Paint brushes
- Paint in a variety of colors (including white)
- Pen/pencil
- Polaroid camera
- Roll of white butcher paper
- Ruler with metal straight edge
- Scaling ruler (optional)
- Scissors
- Sketch pad
- Tape measure

We all know that stop signs are red and white. But should they be? Since contrast helps us distinguish things and the natural environment is often green (vegetation) or blue (sky), the combination of red and white may indeed be a good choice. But maybe it's also a good choice because it is our culture's way of signaling danger. If all traffic signs were red, would we take the stop sign as seriously? This activity explores how distance and color affect our ability to read signs by having you test color combinations to see what really works best in the colorful outdoors.

RECORD BASIC MEASUREMENTS
First, measure the dimensions of an actual stop sign and the size of the type. Second, measure the space between the letters. Then measure the margins around the type on the top, bottom, and sides. Record the "stats" in your journal. Finally, measure the distance from the sign to the point where the type becomes hard for you to read. Record the measurements in your journal.

EXPERIMENT WITH COLORS
Cut several pieces of butcher paper the same height and width as a stop sign. Paint the background and the word STOP in two different colors. Make as many combinations as you can. The word STOP should be centered in the square and the letters should be the same height as on a real stop sign. Try some combinations using white as one of the colors.

TEST COLOR COMBINATIONS
Post these "signs" on a wall and stand at the hard-to-read distance you recorded earlier. Note in your journal which color combinations are easy to read and which are hard to read. Make small, 1/2-inch color samples for each combination and arrange them in order of readability.

Next, move your painted studies into different colored environments. Stand at the same distance. Note whether or not the background colors alter the readability. In your journal, compare your results with the color combinations used for road signs, billboards, and building signs. How are the colors of commercial signs similar to those of road signs? How are they different?

What color combinations are used most often in road signs? Are these effective choices?

What colors are used for: Road names? Numbers? Warnings? Tourist information? Are these effective choices?

What shapes are used for: Road names? Numbers? Warnings? Tourist information? Are these effective choices?

88

Hunit city

How can you affect an experience by changing spatial relationships?

MATERIALS
- Calculator (optional)
- Cardboard, foam core, or other stiff paper
- Photocopier
- X-acto knife

Ever watch how a group of strangers space themselves in an elevator? We can feel that our space is being "invaded" when someone stands too close, and find it awkward when they're too far away. It all depends on who you're interacting with and why.

We all have conscious and unconscious reactions to space. Designers are very concerned with issues of space and scale (the size relationship between two objects). It's their task to use these elements to help make people feel comfortable using their designs and to evoke specific feelings and behaviors. It's no accident that when you walk into a cathedral, your eye is automatically drawn upward, and you feel very small.

In this activity you'll have the chance to build models and create a variety of spatial experiences. To better perceive these spaces you will use a "hunit," a reduced version of yourself. You'll have enough models by the time you're done to have your own hunit city—a place your hunit can go no matter how it is feeling.

FIRST, KNOW YOUR SCALE
The scale you will be using is one inch equals one foot.

NEXT, MAKE YOURSELF A HUNIT
What's a hunit? You're a hunit. A hunit is a word made-up to describe a unique way to measure things—a "human unit." Your hunit will help make inches more meaningful.

So get smaller. You need to be $1/12$ of your actual size. To do this, have someone take a picture of you, or find an existing photo. It needs to be a full body shot, showing your height from head to toe.

Then calculate your height in inches and divide by 12. Enlarge (or reduce) the image on a photocopier until it is the right height. For example, if you are 5 feet 4 inches tall, your hunit would need to be $5^1/_3$ inches tall (64 inches divided by 12).

Glue your hunit to heavy paper, cardboard, or foam core, and cut it out. Add a hinge or "foot" to the back so it can stand on its own.

CHOOSE YOUR FEELING

Choose at least three of the following feelings and create spaces in which your hunit will experience each of them.

small	off balance
tall	powerful
peaceful	oppressed
anxious	lonely
narrow	cramped
wide	strange

HUNIT CITY PERFORMANCE CRITERIA

Each model space must:
- be self-standing
- have a floor plan no larger than 12 x 12 inches
- have a height approximately 12 inches
- be the same color
- be made out of only one type of paper
- be without decoration
- be viewable from above (no roof)
- have at least one door
- have at least one window
- have at least three walls

THINK AND SKETCH FIRST, BUILD LATER

Think about the places and buildings you use or know about that make you feel the emotions you've chosen. What places do you use every day that make you feel comfortable? Safe? Happy? Does scale (the space's size relative to yours) play any role?

In designing your spaces, think about what can be done to the floor(s), wall(s), window(s), door(s), or pathway(s) to communicate the feeling you've chosen. Make a series of sketches and then build them.

GET FEEDBACK

Show other people the list of feelings, your hunit, and its city. Let them try to figure out which space matches your chosen feelings.

DOCUMENT IT

Photograph your hunit inside the spaces so that the images convey the appropriate feeling. Label the pictures and arrange them in your journal.

TRY GETTING BIG

Do you think if the model were increased to full size, you would feel the same as your hunit? Find out. Using corrugated cardboard, try making the most successful models full size. You can buy sheets of 4 x 8–foot cardboard, or use cardboard boxes of all sizes (see chapter five, **Design technical skills**, for ideas on how to join the sheets). If you are working in a group and have the space, you can make a whole city. When you think you've gotten your space just right, ask other people to use your city. Did they feel what you wanted them to? Find out why or why not, and make adjustments as necessary.

On a scale of 1 to 10 . . .

How do choices of color, scale, and material affect your perception?

MATERIALS
- Designs selected from list (see below)
- Journal
- Pen/pencil
- 3 photocopies of worksheet

How often have you gone shopping with a friend, say for shoes, and couldn't stand what he or she picked out? To you, the shoes said, "Boring, boring, dull, and boring," but to your friend, the shoes said, "Hip, classy, sophisticated."

But what really makes a shoe a shoe? Basically, shoes are something to protect your feet (at least a little). But after that requirement's met, they could look like heaping bowls of fruit.

Nothing we use is neutral—we each project our own associations onto every design. These associations have to do with the people and culture we grew up in and the experiences we've had. It is the task of the designer to capitalize on these associations to make his or her design into something

more—something that somehow appeals to you so that you'll want to buy it. Or live in it. Or read it. To accomplish this designers have a kit of tools at their disposal, things like color, material, size, shape, and pattern. But before they use them, they need to think about what they're designing, and for whom. In this activity, you'll examine how color, shape, and material are used by designers. Along the way you will discover the different "shades" of meaning each of us applies to the designs we encounter every day.

LOOK FOR SOME ODD COUPLES

From the list of graphic communications, places, and products, on the next page, choose a pair of designs to analyze. It's easier and more fun if you choose examples that use color, scale, and materials differently. You'll need three photocopies of the worksheet titled "On a scale of 1 to 10 . . ." with which to analyze them. Label each sheet either color, scale, or material. You'll examine each pair three times.

The worksheet lists word pairs that describe opposite reactions you might have to a design—like funny or serious. As you analyze the design, put an "X" nearest the word you feel best describes the design. So you can compare, the top half of the line is for one design, the bottom half for the other.

Next to each word is a space to list the reason for your decision—why you think it brings out this feeling in you. This might be something like: "The red color makes it seem frightening because red reminds me of blood." Some of these will require you to really stretch your mind. Some you may not be able to figure out. But rest assured, there is a reason deep inside your brain.

COMPARE

When you're done, compare the worksheets. Decide what audience the designer whas trying to reach.

Choose any of the following to compare:

GRAPHIC COMMUNICATIONS

two cereal packages
two magazine covers
two billboards
two calendars
two advertisements
two menus

PLACES

two styles of houses
two theater facades
two restaurant interiors
two places of worship
two public restrooms
two neighborhood parks

PRODUCTS

two chairs
two telephones
two light fixtures
two cars
two dinner plates
two bicycles

NOW TRY IT WITH A GROUP

For fun (and some great debate) get a group of people together. The goal is for everyone to reach agreement. Have one person record the group's decision. It can be recorded only if everyone agrees, and once it is written down, it can't be changed.

Compare your results. Do you all "see" things the same way? Consider what else— besides color, scale, and material—may have influenced the different perceptions. Note your conclusions in your journal.

Worksheet

Name of graphic, place, or product:

Place an "X" somewhere on the scale for each opinion.

"to me, the . . . (colors, materials, or scale) make it seem:"

because:

because:

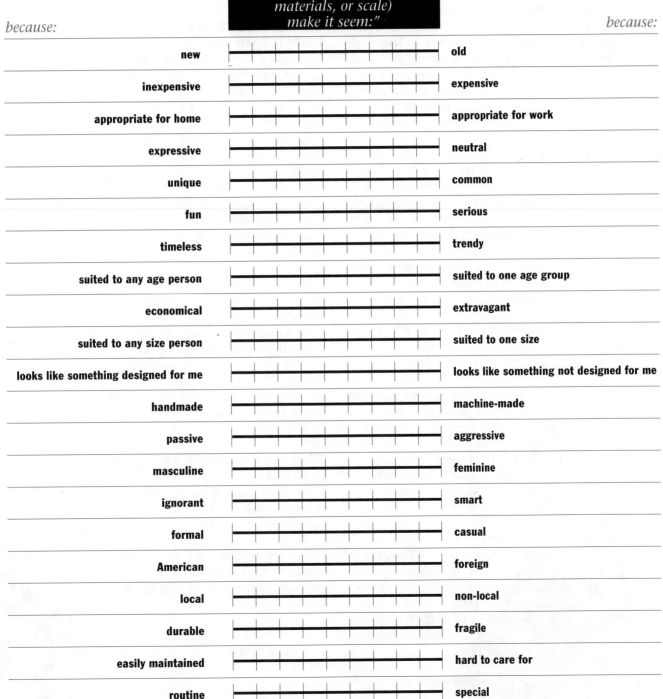

new		old
inexpensive		expensive
appropriate for home		appropriate for work
expressive		neutral
unique		common
fun		serious
timeless		trendy
suited to any age person		suited to one age group
economical		extravagant
suited to any size person		suited to one size
looks like something designed for me		looks like something not designed for me
handmade		machine-made
passive		aggressive
masculine		feminine
ignorant		smart
formal		casual
American		foreign
local		non-local
durable		fragile
easily maintained		hard to care for
routine		special

WHY DESIGN? Activities and Projects from the National Building Museum

93

"Paper or plastic?"

How do your design choices affect the earth?

MATERIALS
- Journal
- Materials appropriate for campaign, such as found images or video camera
- Pens/pencils

Frequently, before clerks bag your groceries they ask, "Paper or plastic?" The answer to this question represents more than a simple choice between two effective solutions to the problem of carrying groceries home—it also expresses our values and attitudes about the use of natural resources. Someone concerned about the state of the environment might naturally assume that paper is better. But the choice isn't as straightforward as it appears. There are environmental pros and cons to both options. In this activity you will investigate the environmental impacts of paper and plastic to discover how complicated the choice really is.

CONFUSION TO CLARITY
Imagine that an association of grocers has asked you to design an in-store campaign to inform customers about the pros and cons of paper and plastic bags—*and* to provide information about any alternatives to these choices. They plan to send the campaign you devise to all their member stores.

ANY MISCONCEPTIONS?
First, do some market research. Interview people to discover why they choose paper or plastic

bags, and what concerns or confusion they might have in making the choice.

TRACK THE TRUTH ABOUT PAPER AND PLASTIC
Now do some technical research. Investigate the life cycle of the bags—from their creation to ultimate end—and identify as many environmental impacts as you can. The steps that follow give you a place to start. Keep in mind that "environmental impacts" include not only health hazards associated with air, water, and noise pollution, but loss of things like wildlife habitat, scenic views, and access to wilderness.

To find answers, do library research or interview people associated with creating the bags. If you decide to dig *very* deeply, you may find yourself talking to bag manufacturers, miners, foresters, or even chemical engineers. Note your research in your journal.

STEP 1: ACQUIRING THE RAW MATERIAL
Is the bag made from renewable, nonrenewable, or recycled materials?

Go a step further and try to find out how and where the materials were acquired. For example, if timber was used

to create the paper bag, a forester can talk to you about responsible or "sustainable" harvesting—that is, removing trees in a way that prevents soil erosion and protects streams without radically altering the landscape.

STEP 2: CREATING THE BAG

What kinds of pollution were produced? How much energy was used?

STEP 3: USE, REUSE, AND DISPOSAL

How many times can the bag be used? Can it be recycled? How will its disposal affect the environment? What happens when the bags are buried in a landfill or burned in an incinerator?

Investigate biodegradability claims. To be truly biodegradable, the material needs to break down into basic chemical elements that can be used again by nature to make something new. Most plastics are not biodegradable, and even paper needs light and water to decompose—items in short supply in most landfills.

CONSIDER ALTERNATIVES

Brainstorm other creative options for getting groceries home, from encouraging customers to bring their own bags (the store can pass on the savings) to using other kinds of containers. Be sure to analyze these options as carefully as paper and plastic.

MAKE IT HAPPEN

How will you communicate all the information you have gathered in your research? To identify the best campaign for a busy grocery store (and not create more waste) talk to an owner and watch how customers move through the store. Your design solution might be a poster, multimedia display, or something completely different. Outline the important points you want to make, identify the images that would best illustrate your points, and decide on the language that would really grab your audience. Then convince the store owner to use your campaign. Perhaps your information solution will catch on . . .

How useful are labels in helping us make informed choices about the enivronmental impact of products? What more can be done?

What laws exist to protect all species' health by protecting air, water, and soil?

Lean on me

How do the laws of nature affect design?

MATERIALS
- Tape
- 2 boxes of similar dimensions
- 2 sheets of paper
- Weight of some kind (pebbles, a block, etc.)

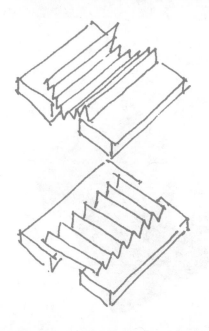

The laws of physics apply to everything. Essentially, anything you build will have to withstand a push and/or a pull. When you're sitting, gravity causes you to push on the chair. This puts the chair in compression. When you're hanging from a tree, gravity causes you to pull on the limb. Your arms are in tension.

You will find that some materials hold up well under compression (concrete, bricks, your little brother). You will find that other materials are more structurally sound in tension (rope, rubber bands, your little brother). Some materials are not suitable for anything structural (cereal, milk, your little brother).

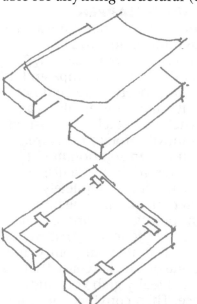

In this activity you'll get a chance to experiment with these structural principles. Working with a seemingly flimsy piece of paper, you'll discover techniques to make materials strong.

TEST SOME STRUCTURAL PRINCIPLES

Place two boxes, 6 inches apart, on a table. Lay a sheet of paper across the tops of the boxes. What happens to the paper? Any ideas for preventing this?

Now tape down the edges of the paper. What happens to the paper? Place a weight on the middle of the paper. The paper is in tension, causing it to pull against the boxes and make them move inward. This is the principle at work in a suspension bridge (but there, the "box" equivalents are secured).

Now, cut, fold, and place the paper as indicated. Note that the paper still bows—nothing is supporting the folded edges.

Now place the folded paper between the boxes as shown. What happens to the paper now? The top fold of the paper is in compression and the bottom fold is in tension. These two qualities work together to produce stability. You see this principle at work in corrugated cardboard and structural beams.

What are examples of compression in nature? In everyday objects?

What are examples of tension in nature? In everyday objects?

What are examples of triangle shapes in nature? In everyday objects?

Try standing the folded paper on edge and pressing down. Notice that the triangular structure is pretty stable? Once you start looking, you'll see that triangles form the foundation of many structures (take a look at the spokes on a bicycle for a start).

Take another sheet of paper and try to stand it on end. How well does it stand up? Can it support any weight? Fold the paper and try to stand it up. Does it stand any better? Can it support some weight? Turn the paper into a cylinder. Tape the edges. How well does it stand? Can it hold more weight? Cylinders can withstand greater degrees of compression. Columns, like those in the National Building Museum pictured above, are a good example of this.

Can't beat the system

How do natural systems affect design decisions?

WHY DESIGN? Activities and Projects from the National Building Museum

MATERIALS
- Journal
- Pen/pencil

They say you can't beat the system, and natural systems are no exception. The natural systems that create the picturesque mountains and valleys in which we nestle towns also create earthquakes; the systems that give us clear, sunny days, also cause hurricanes, tornadoes, and blizzards; and the same systems that give us drinking water also cause floods. In designing our homes and towns we can either ignore these environmental systems, or work with them. Sometimes, we do both.

Many well-known cities try to beat the system. Take Los Angeles. It's huge. With over 3.2 million people, it needs about 560 million gallons of water each day. But it's a city built in an area that's almost as dry as a desert. So how do Angelenos get their water? They have developed a lifeline. A system of pipes, channels, and tunnels brings in water from the Sierra Nevada mountains, over 200 miles away. How long can L.A. beat the system? In this activity you'll take a close look at how your home and community work with and try to beat natural systems.

DO YOU KNOW THE SYSTEM?

Nature's not the only one with systems at her disposal. Your community has developed its own set of physical, political, and social systems, called "infrastructure," to deal with many of the things nature dishes out. Infrastructure includes things like a plan to get fresh water to your faucet, and all the pipes and reservoirs needed to get it there. Or the emergency plans the government has developed to evacuate people in the event of a natural disaster. Your home also has been designed with natural systems in mind—otherwise, how would it stand up under the force of gravity? Choose one of the three systems described below to investigate.

IT'S A 6.0 AT THE EPICENTER!—GEOLOGIC SYSTEMS

Is your home or community in an area prone to landslides or earthquakes? If so, get a map from the local or regional planning office that outlines the fault system underlying the area, and locate your house. Do you want to

1994 Northridge earthquake images provided by Federal Emergency Management Agency (FEMA)

98

move? How would you find out how strong an earthquake your home can withstand? Find out when your home was built and what earthquake codes it had to meet (check the records at the local government planning office).

FLOODED STREETS AT THE TOWN CENTER!—WATER SYSTEMS

What happens in your community when it rains a little? When it rains a lot? Find out where the water goes and how it gets there. See if your local government planning office has a map of the system of pipes that handles the town's runoff. Find out how much water this system can handle and what the record rainfalls have been. This will require a little research. Next time it rains, examine what happens to water runoff in your neighborhood. What happens as it crosses asphalt, grass, and concrete? Which surface is most absorbent? Which is least?

BAD WEATHER AHEAD!—CLIMATIC SYSTEMS

What systems kick into gear when word gets out about bad weather? How do town officials find out about bad weather? How do you? What is your community's emergency evacuation plan? Talk to people at the local department of public works to find out what plans they have and how they work with other branches of government to handle weather emergencies. How is your home designed to withstand a huge snowfall or gale-force winds? How would you find out? For a start, talk to someone at the local government planning office.

TAKE A FIELD TRIP

All day long, people are taking care of your basic needs so that you don't have to think about them. If you're in a larger town or city, find out where your sewage is treated, where the fresh water is treated, and where your trash is dumped. The infrastructure we build—from dams to sewage treatment plants—is gigantic and interesting to visit. Call the plants and schedule a tour.

How effective are the structures we build to cope with nature?

How effective are the plans we make to cope with nature?

What technologies and methods are used to inform people about the plans?

What role does the federal government play in working with you and your community to handle each of these systems?

Should people be allowed to live in areas that are particularly prone to natural disasters? What are the costs and benefits to our society? Who pays?

Still can't beat the system

How do natural disasters affect community design?

MATERIALS
- Journal
- Pen/pencil
- Photocopy of the activity

1993 Midwest flood images provided by Federal Emergency Management Agency (FEMA)

That we are a part of nature and not separate from it is inescapable. Like all other species, people must adapt as the earth changes. However, humans have the most highly developed ability to gain and use knowledge. We use that knowledge to create and use tools, and organize ourselves to use resources. But no matter what our abilities, when natural systems and humans collide, the impact is not only physical, but emotional. To be suddenly left without a home or any of your belongings is devastating. In this activity, you will discover the impact of a natural disaster on one small community in Illinois, and how the residents coped.

READ ALL ABOUT IT!
The article from the *The New York Times* that follows describes the affect of the floods of 1993 on Valmeyer, Illinois. As you read, use the "Questions for coping" listed to the right as a tool to analyze what you read from a design perspective. Write your answers in your journal.

WRITE ALL ABOUT IT!
Has your town had to deal with a natural disaster? If so, how well did the human systems developed to cope do? Do some research. Then use the "Questions for coping" as the basis of your own newspaper editorial about the crisis. See if your local newspaper will publish it. Or, if you can, go on-line via computer so that others can find out what you know.

MAKE IT 3-D
If your research inspired some design solutions (like moving *your* town), make a map or model of your ideas.

QUESTIONS FOR COPING:

How did past generations work with the natural system of flooding?

What structures did later generations design to try to beat the natural system of flooding?

What was the effect of the flood on the buildings and other structures in the town? On the people of the town?

What connections exist (emotional or physical) between the people and the old town?

What are the objections some people have to moving the town?

Are the people who are staying planning to work with or beat the natural flooding system?

What are the residents' concerns in creating the new town? What improvements are planned?

What emotional needs must be met at the new site?

What natural flood system concerns exist at the new site?

How are the residents in the new town going to work with the natural flooding system?

How can the residents afford to create a new town?

What role do local, state, and federal government agencies play in dealing with the consequences of the flood?

350 feet above flood ruins, a river town plots rebirth

BY ISABEL WILKERSON, THE NEW YORK TIMES

Valmeyer, Illinois, Oct. 26, 1993—The Mississippi had its way with this old railroad town, settling in for as long as it pleased and leaving the place dust-caked and barren, an American Pompeii. Now the people of Valmeyer say they got the river's message.

They voted to move a mile and a half east to the bluffs where they used to shoot deer and rabbits, up by the hickory and maple forest they used to drive past to get to their valley, on the hill where they planted a wooden star at Christmas that could be seen clear across the river in Missouri. Until the river drove them away, most of Valmeyer's 900 residents had never imagined living anywhere but in the flat, rich bottom lands where one could watch the sun rise and set and cornfields stretched to the horizon.

A BLUEPRINT FOR THE BATTERED

But on a brisk night in a tavern outside town, a janitor, a bank teller, a retired shoe factory worker, a couple of secretaries, a government worker, a teacher, and a print shop machinist debated passionately about sidewalks, as if the future of the town hung in the balance. Finally, the janitors and the teacher got up from the Formica topped table and stood side by side to see if 4 feet was indeed wide enough for two pedestrians to walk comfortably abreast.

These are matters of great significance to battered and heartsick Valmeyer. Many people have lost the homes their great-grandfathers built. They can no longer visit with the neighbors as they used to, or catch up on the day's gossip now that Schneider's grocery store is gone. "You're lost," said Donna Tucker, a Valmeyer refugee. "You have no meaning to your life anymore. You don't get up and do the things you used to do. You miss the familiar. It's like someone died. And something did die. The town died."

Nearly every town within walking distance of the river has been flooded sometime this century. People used to glue their furniture back together, clean up, and move back, taking their chances with nature. Not this time. With government help, about 50 towns in the Midwestern flood region from Rockford, Minnesota, to Festus, Missouri, are considering moving parts of themselves to higher grounds. Valmeyer is the only one planning to move the whole town away from the river. Town officials expect to begin selling lots of up to an acre each by December 15, adding the sales revenues to a bond issue and government grants to raise the $25 million the move is expected to cost.

For three months, townspeople have been scattered in government trailers and relatives' spare bedrooms in cities like St. Louis and Chicago and Waterloo, Illinois—places they say no Valmeyer native belongs. Once a week they meet in groups of 10 or 12, with country music in the background and urgency in the air, arguing over street lamps and curb heights with the devotion of a mother planning her firstborn's nursery.

That nursery is now 500 acres of cornfields and forest rising 350 feet above the old town. Walter Stemier, the dairy farmer who owns the land, has agreed to sell it for about $3 million. "He's our salvation," said Charlotte Gartzke, a secretary on the design committee.

REAL PROBLEMS, MANY FEARS

Breathtaking as it is, on the edge of that hollow that leads to the valley, the site has it problems. The owners of an old quarry nearby have mineral rights to land. There is a sinkhole the new owner must build around.

And there are the kinds of concerns that spread fast in a small town. "It's mines up there" said Yvonne Early, a resident who plans to stay in the old town. She was recalling fears raised at a town meeting that openings in the sides of the quarry were old mine shafts that might extend

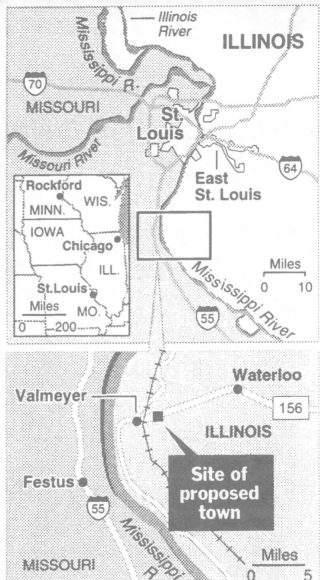

under the new site. Besides, she said: "It's across from a dairy farm with all that manure. You go up there, it stinks to high heaven."

So far, 425 of the 600 flooded households around Valmeyer have applied to the Federal Emergency Management Agency to help them relocate on the new site. The committees planning the move are doubling up on the meetings to complete their work in time for the hearing in mid-November. Ultimately, the plans need to be approved by town, trustees, and state and federal officials who are to help pay for the move.

"Everybody's so anxious to get it going and move back," said Allan Guttmann, president of the Valmeyer school board and a member of one of the relocation committees. "If we don't get moving, people will get disgusted waiting and move somewhere else. You can't put your life on hold forever."

It was homesickness as much as anything that pushed townspeople to vote by a 2-to-1 margin last month to move the town so they could all be together again and things could return to what they were. "I want to be able to go into the post office and grocery store and know everybody," said Bobby Klinkhardt, the print shop machinist who is a member of the town design committee.

Half the people are related. Many are descended from the first farm settlers, the Meyers, who inspired the name Valmeyer, short for Valley of the Meyers. There had been floods before, but they had never taken everything. This time, the river ransacked people's honeymoon homes, toppled baptismal fonts that had christened generations, washed out streets named after people's great-uncles. The water sat in some homes for three months. Valmeyer flooded twice—first when levees broke upstream on August 2, and again on September 10, before residents could finish cleaning the muck from the first flood. That was when people said they could not fight anymore.

"As soon as I saw it, I knew it was no hope for that town," Mrs. Tucker said. "I would never trust that river again." Townspeople are learning what their ancestors knew all along: the river that blessed them with bumper crops one year could crawl out of its banks to punish them the next.

In the days before levees and flood walls, when people were even more vulnerable to the Mississippi, farmers lived in the bluffs and came down to what is now Valmeyer to farm the rich bottom land. "They would bring down their mules and horses, sow their wheat, then go back home," said Floyd Meyer, an 80-year-old descendant of the original settlers. "They brought enough food to stay for weeks at a time. They didn't live in the bottoms because of the floods, I'm afraid that's what it's going to go back to."

A NEW KIND OF TOWN
Now, almost as therapy, ordinary people are remaking a town from scratch. "It's scary,"

Mrs. Gartzke said. "It's like a kid with building blocks." This is the chance to have the kind of town they never had before. Town leaders say they do not want any "pole sheds" downtown or "mobile homes on wheels." They want sidewalks on both sides of the street, four feet wide at least; and grass parkways, too. They want those wrought-iron-type lamp posts with the tops that look like gaslights, not the wooden poles that old Valmeyer had.

They have been driving around looking at other towns, and they want what other towns have—hiking and bike trails, a civic center, a movie theater, a real restaurant instead of a couple of tables in the tavern, and a doctor if they can get one. Some residents say this is getting pretty fancy for a town that has never even had a traffic light. Some worry that if the plans get too elaborate, nobody will be able to afford to move up on the bluff. The most stubborn critics—about 10 to 20 families, who are vowing never to leave the bottom lands—say the new site will not be the same town, that nothing else could ever be Valmeyer.

SOME CLING TO THE OLD
So while maps are being unveiled for the new town and tours are being given of the cornfields where the new school and city hall will stand, people like Ed Kempen are down in the bottom lands, putting up new wallboard in gutted houses, replacing windows that caved in and kitchen cabinets that were torn from the walls. Mr. Kempen says he cannot bear to leave the vegetable garden he knows will come back again some day. "The soil is richer than what you can buy," he said.

Next door, a furnace repairman pulled up to the home of Susan Schillinger, who was putting in new tile and hanging wallpaper, as if oblivious of the fact that the rest of the town looked like it had been bombed. She said she could not leave: "I've got two dogs buried in the backyard."

Such people stay at their own risk. They know that the levees are not yet repaired and that the river could rage again next spring. They know that the houses left by people moving up the hill will be razed, the properties turned into park land. The village says it cannot afford to provide the few people left in old Valmeyer with running water or working sewers while building the new town, although Mayor Dennis Knobloch said eventually the old town would share utilities.

But the bottom dwellers, saying it would be too expensive to start over again, are drilling wells, installing septic tanks, and bracing for a long winter. "We're either stupid or brave," said Keith Cooper, one of the last people on his block. Those awaiting the new Valmeyer are making do for now. Most moved to the nearest town, Waterloo—a relative metropolis, about 10 miles northeast of Valmeyer, with 5,072 people and four-way stop signs—and are having a hard time getting used to the big city. Some have trouble sleeping without the train passing at 2 A.M. as it did back home. And people who never had keys in Valmeyer have to remember to lock their doors.

"Some people are sleeping with a loaded gun now," said Peggy Frank, president of the Valmeyer Parent-Teacher Organization. Waterloo had one homicide last year, it's the first in two decades. Valmeyer keeps calling its people home. Every morning, Donna Tucker's husband, Tom, a retired railroad worker, gets into his truck as if he's going somewhere. With no lawn to mow or wood shop to tinker in, he drives around all day. "Just killing time," Mrs. Tucker said. "He rides over to Valmeyer just to look at it."

I remember it well

How do emotion and memory affect your attitude toward design?

MATERIALS
- Colored pens/pencils/markers
- Paper (8½ x 11 inches)
- Pen/pencil

People have a strong emotional relationship with the things we use. Because places are created to hold human activity, they also hold our memories—with all their attendant emotions. Without the meaning we bring, our house would not become a home; a cathedral would be nothing more than a pile of stones; and a skyscraper would not be a symbol of corporate strength. In this activity you will use your memory to explore a meaningful place from your past. As you do so, you'll exercise a part of your brain critical to designing—the ability to create and manipulate images in your mind.

REFLECT ON IT
Think back to your childhood and remember a place that you either liked very much or disliked—even hated or feared. Close your eyes and imagine yourself back there. Why did this place make such a strong impression on you?

DESCRIBE IT
Take 15 minutes to communicate this special place on paper. Describe it as precisely as you can using words and images. What can you remember about it? What can't you remember about it? What do you see, hear, smell, taste, touch, and feel?

TALK ABOUT IT
If you are in a group, have each person talk about her or his place. Compare the kinds of places and experiences being remembered. Look for patterns: Are the places similar or very different? What emotions are associated with them? Why? Do most of the memories involve other people or social experiences? Which senses provide the strongest memories? Why? How is culture reflected in the places?

How does the passing of time affect your memory?

How successful are words and images in describing memories?

What memories do you associate with objects, like jewelry, or graphic communications, like posters?

Who says it's ugly?

What influences your attitudes toward design?

MATERIALS
- Journal
- Pen/pencil
- Worksheet

"Well, there's no accounting for taste!" "I just like it." Obviously, we all have different tastes. If everyone had the same taste in cars, for example, there wouldn't be so many different models and so many different colors.

What is "taste" anyway? Since objects are just a combination of materials, shapes, colors, and patterns, how can there be such a thing as "good taste"? Taste is an evaluation we make of an object. It is a set of hidden rules made up of associations we have with things. These might be based on childhood memories, on listening to what our family and friends think, or on what "experts" tell us. So it makes perfect sense that tastes differ. In this activity you'll examine the connections between what you value and what you find aesthetically pleasing.

CLARIFYING YOUR TASTES
Use the worksheet titled "Who says it's ugly?" to rate your opinion—from really ugly to really beautiful—of the objects and places listed. Some are illustrated on this and the following page. The second column asks you to list your associations with the object/place (see worksheet example for tooled western belt). Your associations may be with individuals, groups, places, memories, dreams, etc. The third column asks you to examine the object/place for physical clues as to why you've made your associations. The next column asks you to think about who

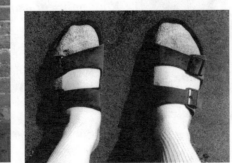

influenced you to form your opinion. The final column asks you to think about who might have an opposite opinion.

HOW DO THESE OPINIONS AFFECT YOUR LIFE?
Now that you've examined your opinions, look for patterns. Do you like the appearance of some objects but dislike what they represent? Why? Are you attracted to the functions of some objects but unattracted to their form? Why?

Do you act differently toward people who like the things you don't? Do all your friends have the same taste? Have you discovered some of your hidden or not so hidden stereotypes? Check with others to see if their conclusions are similar or dissimilar to yours—you may be surprised at what you find. Determine who or what has been most influential in affecting your aesthetic opinions. Note your conclusions in your journal.

Do the following people share your opinion?
Your parents?
Your brothers and sisters?
Your friends?
Your teachers?
Your neighbors?
Local politicians?
Members of your religion?
People in your clubs or organizations?

Do any of these factors influence your opinion?
Television shows?
Magazines?
Movies?
Books?
Radio?
Advertising?
Your age?
Your physical condition?
Your career?
Your gender?
Your race?
Your income?
Your political leaning?
Where you live?
Your national origin?

Are there any objects you would like to outlaw? Why?

Does considering how others feel about the items affect your opinions?

What would life be like if we all shared the same tastes?

Worksheet

What's your opinion?	Really ugly	Ugly	Okay	Beautiful	Really Beautiful	What do you associate with this item?	What qualities of the item make you think this?	Who/what helped you form your opinion?	Who might have the opposite opinion?
Tooled western belt		X				Texas, cowboys Mexico, westerns	leather tooling plant decoration	friends, TV, photos parents	Texan, my uncle
Painting on black velvet									
Graffiti									
African neck rings									
Poodle									
Lincoln Continental									
Cigar store Indian									
La-z-Boy recliner									
Birkenstocks									
Diamond ring									
Female body builder									
New York City street									
Hoover Dam									
Las Vegas strip									
Stealth Bomber									
Desert landscape									
Flowered postage stamp									
Opera									
Fur coat									
Tattoo									
Denim jeans									
Modern office building									

They don't build 'em like they used to

How has the environment shaped American houses?

MATERIALS
- Journal
- Pen/pencil

People who came to America during the 1600s and 1700s settled over a wide area, encountering vastly different climates and a variety of natural resources to use for building materials. Although the settlers may have wanted to build houses that looked like those in their home countries, they often had no choice but to adapt old building methods to fit new local conditions.

You'll begin this activity by trying to match four early-American houses with the regions in which they were built. Then, you'll examine your home and visit a building supply store to find out why it's no longer easy to assign housing styles to specific regions.

STUDY YOUR GEOGRAPHY
Begin by looking at the map below of the continental United States. In your journal, list what you know about the topography, climate, and natural resources available in the regions of the country where each of the four boxes is located. If you don't know about a region, do some research to find out before you go on.

MATCH THE HOUSE TO ITS REGION
The worksheet on the next page contains photographs of four types of houses that were built in these regions during the 1600s and 1700s. See if you can match each house to its region. To do this, use the climate and natural resource information you just listed and the information you get by closely examining the design of each house. Write what you discover on the worksheet. Pay careful attention to the architectural elements like the roof, chimney, porch, windows, etc. How many are there? Where are they placed? How are they designed to make the structure particularly well suited to its environment? Also think about the building materials. For example, how can wood or brick help control the climate inside a house? To find out if you made the right match, look at the bottom of page 110.

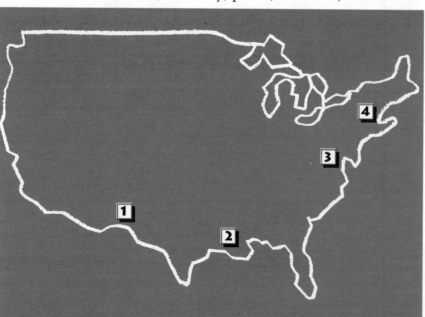

Architectural elements suited to the climate:

_____

_____

Natural resources used as building materials:

_____

_____

Region for which this house is best suited: ☐

_____

Architectural elements suited to the climate:

_____

_____

Natural resources used as building materials:

_____

_____

Region for which this house is best suited: ☐

_____

Architectural elements suited to the climate:

_____

_____

Natural resources used as building materials:

_____

_____

Region for which this house is best suited: ☐

_____

Architectural elements suited to the climate:

_____

_____

Natural resources used as building materials:

_____

_____

Region for which this house is best suited: ☐

_____

HOW IS YOUR HOUSE SUITED TO YOUR CLIMATE?

The homes that most of us live in were built in the 1900s. In your journal, make two lists: one for the architectural elements of the house, like the roof and windows, that control climate and make living more comfortable in the summer and winter, and when it rains and snows; the other for the mechanical systems (like fans and air-conditioning). Then put a check mark by the techniques that were available in the 1600s and 1700s. How many are the same? How many are different?

WHERE DO BUILDING MATERIALS COME FROM TODAY?

Now look at the materials from which your house is built. Choose two or three of the architectural elements listed above, like the roof, exterior walls, windows, or doors, and list the raw materials they are made from. Go to your local building supply or hardware store, find these building elements, and find out who manufactured them. Call (if there is a toll-free phone number) or write the manufacturer to find out where the raw materials came from and where the architectural elements were assembled.

Then draw an outline of the United States in your journal. For each building element, put a dot where the raw material came from, where the part was assembled, and the location of your town—then connect the dots. Were the raw materials obtained locally? Were they assembled in your region? How far were the raw materials transported from their point of origin to your town? Why might a builder choose to use some materials that were locally produced and some that came from other parts of the country?

UNDERSTAND WHAT HAPPENED

From the 1600s through the early 1800s, dwellings were built to be suitable to regional climates and were built with locally available materials. During the mid to late 1800s, mass-produced building materials were distributed throughout the country by rail and other transportation networks. In addition, architectural magazines and books began to be widely circulated. Together, these factors enabled people to build almost any type of house anywhere. Beginning in the late 1800s and early 1900s, the availability of electricity and natural gas allowed people to build houses with central heating, and later with air-conditioning. With electric lights and other mechanical systems, builders and homeowners could pay less attention to climate. So if you see a wide range of building styles in your neighborhood, you know part of the reason why.

What do you think might be some of the long-term effects of modern climate-control systems on the environment? On fossil fuels?

What reasons other than climate might cause a builder to select one building material over another? One architectural element over another?

Top left: Louisiana (2); right: New Mexico (1)
Bottom left: Virginia (3); right: New England (4)

Getting there from here

What influences our transportation choices?

MATERIALS
- **Clipboard**
- **Journal**
- **Pen/pencil**
- **Worksheet**

Would you use a car to go two blocks? Most of us would think that's a waste of gas. But what if you're carrying five large, heavy boxes? Then a car might be just the right choice. Many things influence our transportation choices: distance, time available, number of people traveling, our physical condition, cost, weather, topography, and safety. But without a doubt, the look of our neighborhoods, cities, and countryside has been shaped to a large degree by the transportation methods our culture prefers. In this activity you'll record the transportation choices people in your area are making, interview them to determine their reasons for their choices, and consider the consequences of them.

KEEP YOUR EYES ON THE ROAD

- grocery store
- office building
- place of worship
- public library
- restaurant
- school
- shopping mall
- stadium/arena
- theater

First, select a site, or sites, to observe. It should be a place where you can comfortably count people on the go. Some ideas are listed at left. Then select two different times of day to repeat your study. These should be times when the use is heaviest.

ON YOUR MARK, GET SET, COUNT!

In your journal keep a tally of the transportation choices people are making. First tally how they got there. Make a column for pedestrians, cyclists, motorists, and bus/mass transit riders. Give yourself a good hour to gather your data. Then interview as many people as possible at each site to find out what influenced their choices. The questions at the right give you a place to start. Write their responses in your journal.

ANALYZE THE DATA

Understanding that this isn't scientific research and that your "margin of error" may be greater than what is acceptable by CNN or Gallop pollsters, rank the modes of transportation from most to least used. List and rank the factors behind what makes some choices more popular. Then consider the short- and long-term environmental impact of these choices. Note these in your journal.

IMAGINE THE OPPOSITE

Go back to the site(s) and imagine what it would be like if the order of choices were completely reversed. For example, what would the shopping mall be like if most people used bikes to get there? Would the shopper's needs be as well served? In your journal use words and images to describe how different each area would look. Make a second drawing to describe how things will be in the future if we made these different choices. Finally, make a third drawing to describe how things will be in the future if we continue to make the same choices.

"Dare to dream,
and when you get through dreaming,
wake up and do."
—*Frederick D. Van Amburgh*

Designing

PART TWO

*The next two chapters
describe the process for solving
design problems and provide
technical skill-building activities.*

Every design problem has its own special character, and each problem solver has her or his own preferred method. The 10 steps outlined in this chapter offer you one way to solve a problem.

Keep in mind that although we've outlined a series of steps, solving design problems doesn't happen in a straight line. The steps listed, however, are basic to the design process and several will probably come around more than once as you clarify your problem and solution. You'll find a checklist at the end of each step to assist you.

Also included are references to specific activities from the **Design awareness** part of the book. These may help you better understand a concept or learn or practice a skill, like negotiating a solution to a design-based conflict taking place in your community, or building your group's teamwork skills.

CHAPTER

The design process

4

STEP 1:	**Identify the need for change:** *Does someone have a problem?*
STEP 2:	**Investigate the need:** *Are you solving the right problem?*
STEP 3:	**Establish performance criteria:** *What defines a successful solution?*
STEP 4:	**Write the design brief:** *How can stating the problem make it easier to solve?*
STEP 5:	**Generate ideas:** *How can you expand your thinking?*
STEP 6:	**Edit and develop ideas:** *Which ideas have the most potential?*
STEP 7:	**Test ideas:** *How can feedback improve your solutions?*
STEP 8:	**Communicate proposed solution(s):** *It's show time! How can you "sell" your ideas?*
STEP 9:	**Evaluate your process:** *Did you do what you needed to do?*
STEP 10:	**Implement the solution(s):** *How can your ideas become reality?*

Identify the need for change

Does someone have a problem?

Design is one of the things we do to meet our needs and satisfy our desires. So to begin designing you have to identify what the need is (meaning, what isn't working or isn't happening) and who has the need. You can identify a basic need in one of the following ways.

YOU ALREADY KNOW OF A NEED

This is the easiest situation. You want something changed because it's been bugging you or someone else in your home or community for some time. Perhaps your neighbors want to create a playground for local children. Perhaps a disabled relative lives with you, so you want to improve accessibility in your home. Perhaps you are tired of always misplacing your keys. If so, you're ready to advance to Step 2.

YOU DON'T YET KNOW OF A NEED

Maybe you're so excited about design that you want to go out and find a challenging problem to solve. To help you recognize an unidentified need—your own or someone else's—try one of the following activities from the Design awareness part of the book:

"Can't get no satisfaction"
Wanted: The Design Gang
Checking out the neighborhood
Making the grade
Disabled by your environment
The Goldilocks Syndrome
Utopia
Routine or special

YOU'RE FEELING CREATIVE AND WANT TO INVENT A NEED

Most designers work when someone else comes to them with a need. For fun and a challenge, you be the designer and invent a client with a need. Just use your imagination and fill in the blanks under "Client(s)" and "Need" on the next page.

For example, your client could be a female chef who uses a wheelchair, lives in New York City, and needs accessible storage in her home. She has a project budget of $50,000. Or your clients could be parents of two- to six-year-old children (boys and girls) in your neighborhood, who need a safe place for their children to play. Their project budget is $500.

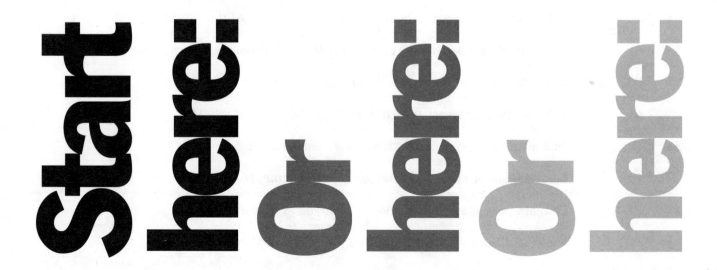

Start here: or here: or here:

CLIENT(S):

age(s): _____

gender(s): _____

physical limitation(s): _____

location: _____

profession(s): _____

project budget: _____

NEED:
(use these or invent your own)
a way to transport something perishable
a space in which to sleep
storage space
a place in which to study
a place to sit
an ecological solution to trash
a place in which to relax
a place in which to wait for medical appointments
a place in which to play
a way to communicate the time
a place in which to discuss business
a shelter from rain or snow
a park that feels safe
a place in which to enjoy music
signage
an urban place in which to enjoy wildlife

Pretty simple?
Wait until you get to the next step . . .

NEED IDENTIFICATION CHECKLIST

☐ **Identify the need and who has it**

☐ **Identify what isn't working or happening**

BiZarro by Dan Piraro

I KNOW THOSE SIGNS AREN'T MEANT FOR US, BUT I STILL FIND THEM INCREDIBLY PROVOCATIVE!

NO DUMPING

PET POOP IN THE PARK

FOR EXAMPLE . . .
Park users in the imaginary community of Hilldale (population 100,000) want a solution to the problem of pet poop in their five parks. They no longer want to step in, sit in, or smell pet poop.

The city council has commissioned a design team to investigate and propose a solution to the problem.

Excerpts from the team's notes (in red) are used throughout this chapter to illustrate the evolution of their solutions.

Step 2

Investigate the need

Are you solving the right problem?

OK. You've identified that someone has a need, and a change must be made to satisfy it. The problem may seem pretty straightforward. But if you look at the need closely and from different angles, you will almost always find that it's more complicated than you first thought. Needs don't exist in a vacuum. They are affected by many things and many things affect them. Another word for "things" is context. You'll need to be concerned about at least three major contexts as you investigate your problem: time, culture, and the environment.

So before you run to the drawing table or start making prototypes, do some investigating to make sure you are solving the right problem. For each context, identify:

• the issues you need to investigate
• the questions you need to ask—Who? What? When? Where? Why?
• the research you need to do to get the answers

CONSIDER TIME

Your problem doesn't exist only in the present; it also had a past, and it will have a future. Find out how this problem came to be. How long has it been a problem? When is it a problem? What attempts have been made in the past to solve it? How might the problem change in the future?

CONSIDER CULTURE

Culture determines our laws, customs, values, attitudes, behaviors, and ways of organizing ourselves into groups—among many other things. In thinking about your problem, ask yourself: Who are all the people and groups connected to the problem, and what is their connection? What are people's attitudes toward the problem? What behaviors are they practicing that affect the problem? What laws affect the problem?

CONSIDER THE NATURAL ENVIRONMENT

How does climate or geographic location affect the problem? What about something as simple as the season, or the amount of light? What animals and plants are affected by this problem, and how do they affect the problem?

If you want to learn more about how context affects design, try the following activities from the Design awareness part of the book:

Back to the future . . . again
Need another trash can?
Wanted: The Design Gang
Zeitgeist objects
Learning how you learn
Lean on me
Can't beat the system
Still can't beat the system
I remember it well
Who says it's ugly?
They don't build 'em like they used to

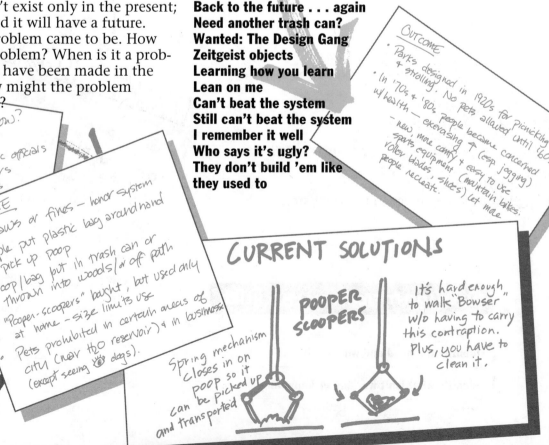

Why is pet poop (PP) a problem now?
• Who/what were the parks originally planned for?
• Were they designed for pet use?
RESEARCH TO DO
• Talk to dept. of Parks & Rec.
• Talk to local planning office

How is problem dealt w/now?
RESEARCH TO DO
• Interview Parks & Rec officials & sanitation workers
• Interview pet owners

PLASTIC SHOPPING BAG GROSS!
Plastic bag is convenient until you need it and you actually can feel the soft, warm poop. Then what? To the landfill!

OUTCOME
• No laws or fines—honor system
• People put plastic bag around hand + pick up poop
• Poop/bag put in trash can or thrown into woods/or off path
• "Pooper-scoopers" bought, but used only at home—size limits use
• Pets prohibited in certain areas of city (near H2O reservoir) & in businesses (except seeing eye dogs).

OUTCOME
• Parks designed in 1920s for picnicking & strolling. No pets allowed until '60s.
• In '70s & '80s people became concerned w/ health—exercising ↑ (esp jogging)
—new, more comfy & easy to use sports equipment (mountain bikes, roller blades, shoes) let more people recreate.

CURRENT SOLUTIONS

POOPER SCOOPERS

Spring mechanism closes in on poop so it can be picked up and transported

It's hard enough to walk "Bowser" w/o having to carry this contraption. Plus, you have to clean it.

How do other cities deal w/PP?

RESEARCH
• Library – find similar size cities ⇒ call their Parks dept.

OUTCOME
• Fines, signs, hona system
• France (Paris) – machine developed to clean sidewalks of poop (looks like small street sweeper)

RESEARCH—HOW TO FIND OUT ABOUT THESE CONTEXTS

It's too bad that the word *research* has such a dry, technical sound, because research is the thrill of the chase in solving design problems. It's the excitement of discovering the information that's the key to your solution. It should be called something like "Ah ha!" or "Really?!"

Because you don't want to spend a lot of time gathering great but useless information, planning your research is essential. Identify the most effective approach to getting the information. Ask yourself: Will this get me the answers I need? Once you've investigated all the parts of the problem, and gathered and recorded information along the way, you're ready to do some serious (and fun) problem solving.

SOURCES OF INFORMATION
FIELD STUDY

Field study means using the space or object yourself, and watching how other people do or don't use it. Document your observations— map them, count them, or film them. To learn more about techniques for field study, see the Design technical skills chapter of this book.

YOURSELF

What life experiences have you had that relate to this problem?

OTHER PEOPLE

Search out and talk to experts on the subject and people connected to or affected by the problem. You'll find that many people love to share what they are interested in or working on. For tips on interviewing, see the Design technical skills chapter of this book.

LIBRARIES

Have other people examined this problem? Consult the literature.

ATTITUDES/BEHAVIORS
Why is PP a problem for people?

RESEARCH TO DO
• Survey pet owners/users (i.d. best sites –times of day/week)

Poop on shoes

OUTCOMES
• 85% think poop is unsanitary ⇒ disease
  How bad is it? ⇒ more research (VERIFY)
• Odor bothers 40%
• Non-pet owners annoyed by "irresponsible" pet owners.
• 60% of pet owners think they should clean up after pets
• People say grooved soles of newer shoes → retain poop longer – much harder to clean (but don't slip as easily w/old flat bottom shoes)
• Poop tracked into homes (+ cleanup), businesses. Hard to clean off clothes (when sat in). People slip on it

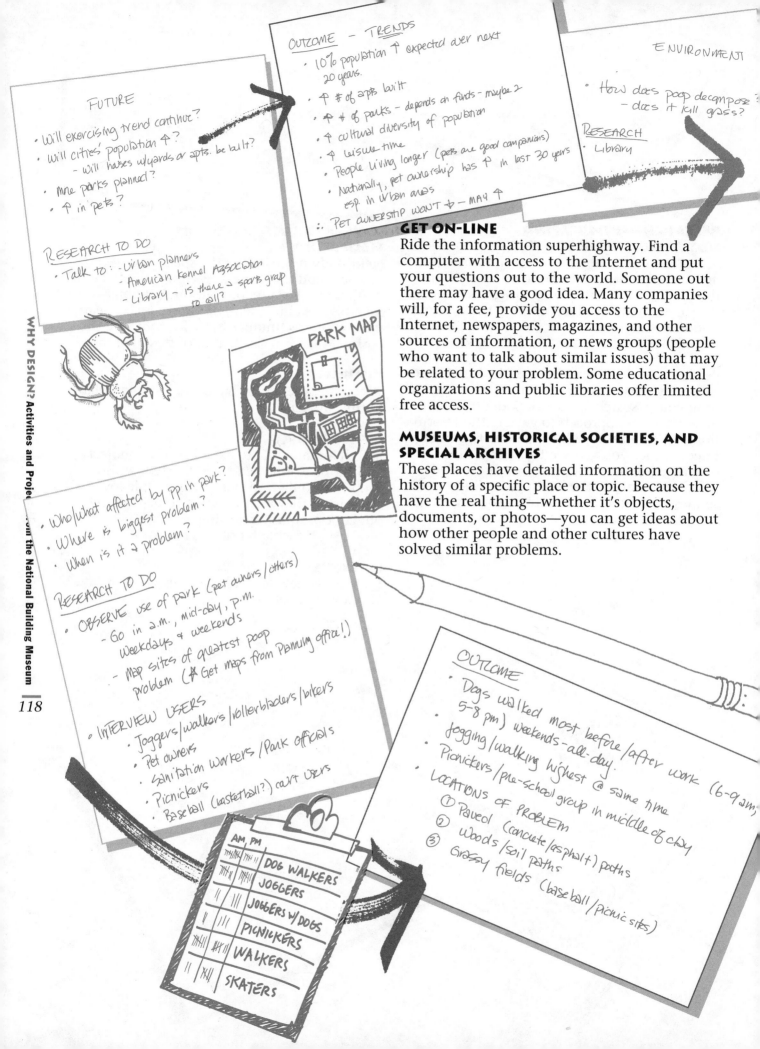

FUTURE
- Will exercising trend continue?
- Will cities' population ↑?
  - Will houses w/yards or apts. be built?
- More parks planned?
- ↑ in pets?

RESEARCH TO DO
- Talk to: - Urban planners
  - American Kennel Association
  - Library - is there a sports group to call?

OUTCOME - TRENDS
- 10% population ↑ expected over next 20 years.
- ↑ # of apts built
- ↑ # of parks - depends on funds - maybe 2
- ↑ cultural diversity of population
- ↑ leisure time
- People living longer (pets are good companions)
- Nationally, pet ownership has ↑ in last 30 years esp. in urban areas
- ∴ PET OWNERSHIP WON'T ↓ — MAY ↑

ENVIRONMENT
- How does poop decompose - does it kill grass?

RESEARCH
- Library

PARK MAP

- Who/what affected by PP in park?
- Where is biggest problem?
- When is it a problem?

RESEARCH TO DO
- OBSERVE use of park (pet owners / others)
  - Go in a.m., mid-day, p.m. weekdays & weekends
  - Map sites of greatest poop problem (☆ Get maps from Planning office!)
- INTERVIEW USERS
  - Joggers / walkers / rollerbladers / bikers
  - Pet owners
  - Sanitation workers / Park officials
  - Picnickers
  - Baseball (basketball?) court users

AM	PM	
丨丨丨丨 丨丨丨丨	丨丨丨 丨丨	DOG WALKERS
丨丨	丨丨丨	JOGGERS
丨丨	丨丨丨	JOGGERS w/DOGS
丨丨	丨丨丨	PICNICKERS
丨丨丨丨 丨丨	丨丨丨丨 丨丨	WALKERS
丨丨	丨丨丨丨 丨丨	SKATERS

OUTCOME
- Dogs walked most before/after work (6-9 am, 5-8 pm) weekends-all-day.
- Jogging/walking highest @ same time
- Picnickers/pre-school group in middle of city

LOCATIONS OF PROBLEM
① Paved (concrete/asphalt) paths
② Woods /soil paths
③ Grassy fields (baseball/picnic sites)

GET ON-LINE
Ride the information superhighway. Find a computer with access to the Internet and put your questions out to the world. Someone out there may have a good idea. Many companies will, for a fee, provide you access to the Internet, newspapers, magazines, and other sources of information, or news groups (people who want to talk about similar issues) that may be related to your problem. Some educational organizations and public libraries offer limited free access.

MUSEUMS, HISTORICAL SOCIETIES, AND SPECIAL ARCHIVES
These places have detailed information on the history of a specific place or topic. Because they have the real thing—whether it's objects, documents, or photos—you can get ideas about how other people and other cultures have solved similar problems.

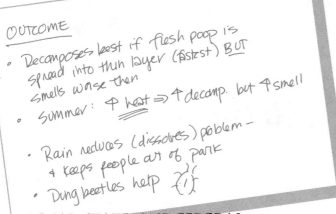

OUTCOME
- Decomposes best if fresh poop is spread into thin layer (fastest) BUT smells worse then
- Summer: ↑ heat ⇒ ↑ decomp. but ↑ smell
  - Rain reduces (dissolves) problem — + keeps people out of park
  - Dung beetles help {?}

SEASONAL EFFECTS:

Poop breaks down faster in warmer climates and in frequent rains.

ATTITUDES/BEHAVIORS

- Why do people own pets?

RESEARCH
- library (any psychological studies?)

OUTCOME
- Companionship
- Instill responsibility in kids
- Fun
- W/fewer people having kids (or when partner dies) is replacement.

- How do pet owners use park?
- Other behaviors.

RESEARCH
- Observe pet owners / other users

OUTCOME
- 50% clean-up after pet
- 60% walk on paved paths
  40% in wooded areas (fields are crossovers)
- 80% of dogs on leash
- People walk dogs all year-round — use by others is highest in summer; lowest in winter; moderate in fall/sp
- People like to go barefoot on grass
- when poop is stepped in (+ noticed) people try to wipe off or get stick + get out of soles.

LOCAL, STATE, AND FEDERAL GOVERNMENT

Government agencies are the places to go for questions or information about things that directly affect the public. These include issues related to law, health, and safety. Find the special department that deals with your topic. For example, the county planning department is the place to go for information on land use and for a variety of detailed maps. Local governments usually have departments of parks and recreation, public works, and building inspection. The federal government handles things like census information. To find out which subjects the federal government addresses, look in the *Federal Statistical Directory*.

MANUFACTURERS

Companies have a lot of information about the materials and products they produce. Call 1-800-555-1212 to see if the company you are interested in has a toll-free phone number.

NATURE

Sometimes we humans are so busy trying to develop our own solutions that we don't see all the ideas provided by other animals and plants. An ant may already have solved your problem. Think creatively and look for obvious comparisons. Then try to make connections to the less obvious ones.

NEED INVESTIGATION CHECKLIST

- [ ] **Consider the history of the problem**

- [ ] **Consider who is affected by the problem and how they are affected**

- [ ] **Consider cultural factors, including people's attitudes and behaviors, laws, and customs**

- [ ] **Consider the natural environment**

Step 3

Establish performance criteria

What defines a successful solution?

You've done all this research, talked to all these people, and have stacks of notes and visual documentation to prove it. You are pretty sure you've clearly identified what the problem is and who is affected by it. Before proceeding you need to ask yourself whether this is a problem design can help solve. In your investigation you may have discovered there are bigger social and political issues that must be addressed. Perhaps design can help address them.

If you determine that design is a good tool for tackling the problem, the next step is to decide what a solution must do to be considered successful. This is called the "performance criteria." Performance criteria are unique to each problem. If you are concerned with creating a "sustainable design"—one that takes into account the long-term effects of the solution on people and the environment—some general performance criteria

include: the solution must be safe, durable, efficient, satisfy aesthetic needs and desires, and have minimum impact on the environment. List the performance criteria for your problem, and then prioritize them. Decide the absolute minimum your solution would have to do to solve the problem.

From this point on, you'll use the performance criteria to keep you on track, constantly referring to them to make sure you're heading in the right direction. In Step 4, you'll reflect on everything you've done so far and then record your conclusions on something called a design brief.

To learn more about sustainable design, try the activity **What a piece of junk!** in the Design awareness part of the book.

120

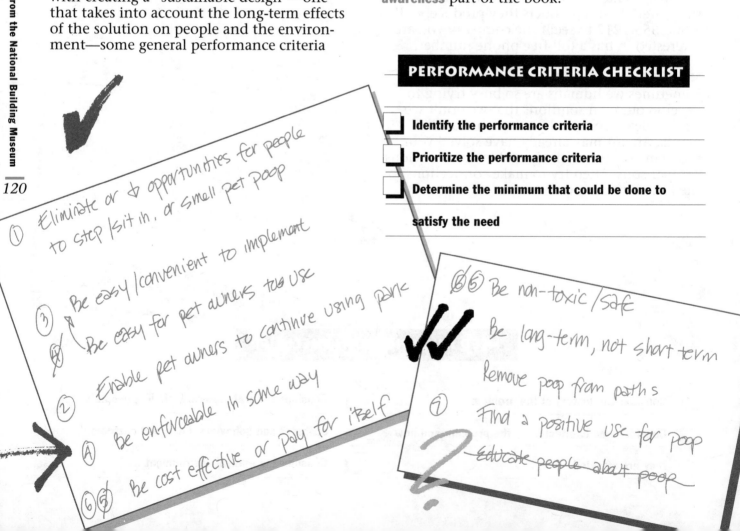

PERFORMANCE CRITERIA CHECKLIST

☐ Identify the performance criteria

☐ Prioritize the performance criteria

☐ Determine the minimum that could be done to

satisfy the need

① Eliminate or ↓ opportunities for people to step /sit in, or smell pet poop

③ Be easy /convenient to implement

④ Be easy for pet owners to use

② Enable pet owners to continue using park

④ Be enforceable in some way

⑥⑤ Be cost effective or pay for itself

⑥⑤ Be non-toxic /safe

Be long-term, not short term

Remove poop from paths

⑦ Find a positive use for poop

~~Educate people about poop~~

Step 4

Write the design brief

How can stating the problem make it easier to solve?

STOP! Do not proceed until you complete the form on the following two pages. It's called a "design brief" but it probably won't be brief. It's a written summary of your journey so far, and it requires you to stop and think about where you're going.

Dr. Edwin Land, inventor of instant photography and the Polaroid camera, said it very simply, "If you are able to state a problem, any problem, it can be solved." The design brief is your opportunity to clearly state the problem. It includes the problem's parts (the need, who has it, what isn't working or happening), and the factors that affect the problem.

Think of the design brief form as a tool to help you organize the information you've collected and outline the steps you must take to solve the problem.

Photocopy the brief and use it for every problem you want to tackle. Think of it as a contract between you and your client—a promise of "satisfaction guaranteed."

The design brief

Need/problem:

_____

_____

Client:
_____

People affected:
_____

Past, present, and future of the problem:

_____

_____

_____

_____

_____

_____

Attitudes that may need to be changed:
_____

_____

Behaviors that may need to be changed:
_____

_____

Laws and customs affecting situation:
_____

_____

Physical site issues:
_____

_____

Climatic/seasonal conditions affecting situation:

_____

_____

_____

Other animals and plants connected to situation:

_____

_____

_____

Energy (fossil, geothermal, solar, etc.) concerns:

_____

_____

Performance criteria—A successful solution must do the following: (Rank in order of most to least important.)

_____

_____

_____

_____

_____

_____

_____

_____

_____

_____

_____

_____

Minimum acceptable performance criteria:

_____

_____

_____

PET POOP IN THE PARK DESIGN BRIEF

Need/problem: People who use the five city parks want a solution to the problem of pet poop. They do not want to step in it, sit in it, or smell it.

Client: City Council

People affected: Pet owners; other park users (exercisers, recreational); Park workers; city sanitation workers; home-owners; businesses—all ages

Past, present, and future of the problem: The parks were designed in the 1920s and 40s. No pets were allowed until '60s. Increase in recreational use since 1970s has led to increased pet poop + increased conflict with other needs (jogging, picnicking) There are no laws about pet owners picking up poop — relies on honor system. 50% of pet owners pick up poop + throw it in a trash can. Projections indicate an increase in city population + more apartment will be built. Increase also expected in cultural diversity of population. Pet ownership likely to increase.

Attitudes that may need to be changed: • Pet owners who feel poop is not a problem (for them)
• Some people feel it's the city's responsibility   • negative feelings by non-pet owners toward pet owners on this problem.

Behaviors that may need to be changed: • encourage people to pick up poop / take responsibility

Laws and customs affecting situation: No laws except leash law; no fines.

Physical site issues: Parks are diverse — most include wooded areas, paved paths, courts (tennis, basketball), + fields. Poop is greatest on ① paved paths ② wooded/soil paths ③ fields + baseball diamonds.

Climatic/seasonal conditions affecting situation: Pet use constant all year round; highest use by others in summer / lowest in winter.

Other animals and plants connected to situation: Insects (dung beetles) decompose poop; flies attracted to it.

Energy (fossil, geothermal, solar, etc.) concerns: Solar (at the moment) ⇒ heat decomposes poop/ increases odor. No fossil fuel issues

Performance criteria—A successful solution must do the following: (Rank in order of most to least important.)

① Decrease or eliminate opportunities for people to step/sit in/smell poop

② Enable pet owners to continue using park

③ Be easy to maintain, implement, use; be long-term

④ Be enforceable

⑤ Be environmentally sensitive

⑥ Be cost effective

⑦ Find a positive use for poop

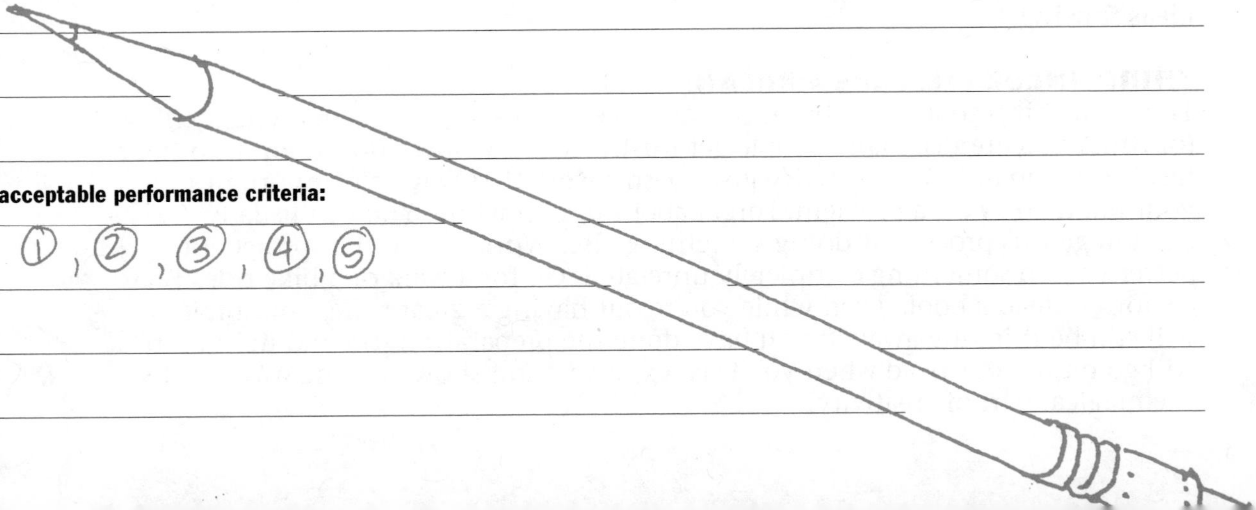

Minimum acceptable performance criteria:

①, ②, ③, ④, ⑤

Step 5

Generate ideas

How can you expand your thinking?

Poop is like ... litter
– recycle cans ⇒
cleaner environment
AND generates income

How can smell be eliminated/masked?
– wind (machines?)
– fragrant plants

BUT FIRST, A FEW THOUGHTS ABOUT CREATIVE THINKING
Now that you've clearly outlined the problem and what a successful solution must do, it's time to start thinking about the solution itself. The ability to imagine creative solutions to problems is one of the qualities that make us human. It's what helped us design the ladder needed to climb out of the evolutionary pool. Good design solutions also have to evolve. They grow from generations of different, constantly changing ideas. Simply stated, the more ideas you have to choose from, the greater the odds for success.

BECOMING A DESIGNSTEIN
A lot of us think only a select few individuals are creative—geniuses like Einstein, da Vinci, Spielberg, or maybe your crazy artist friend. We think of them as creative because they "see" things differently, and what they see often changes the way *we* see things. But everyone has creative potential. You can actually learn how to be more creative. Many of us also think that being creative means thinking of something that has never been done before. But that rarely happens. Most creative ideas result from making new connections between things that already exist.

TRY THREE THINGS TO INCREASE YOUR CREATIVITY:
FIRST, PREPARE YOUR BRAIN.
This means understanding the real problem and learning everything there is to know about it. Ask questions. Research everything connected to the problem, and then examine things that don't seem to have any connection (yet). Talk to as many people as possible. Look at similar problems. Look at nature. When you're done, keep looking. Examine the problem from different perspectives. Use all your senses.

SECOND, GENERATE LOTS OF IDEAS.
In developing solutions, quantity is important. The philosopher Emile Chartier summed it up: "Nothing is more dangerous than an idea when it is the only one you have." There are a lot of good ideas out there, and you need to choose from many to choose the best. We all get stuck trying to come up with new or different ideas. On the pages that follow are some tried-and-true things you can do if, and when, this happens. You can also do the activities, **Mother Nature knows best** and **Thank you, Mr. Gecko** in the Design awareness part of the book to get your ideas flowing.

THIRD, INCUBATE. TAKE A BREAK.
The great thing about your brain is that it keeps working even when you aren't (or think you aren't). Many people get frustrated when ideas don't pop into their heads on demand. But creativity just doesn't work that way. It's important to let your brain chew on a problem. Forget about it for a while. You can usually encourage this process by doing something else. Work on another project or, better yet, do something completely unrelated. Go for a walk or a bike ride. Take a shower. Read a book. Even while you're out having a great time, your brain will still be thinking away. If you have done the preparation, the old light bulb will go on in your head when you least expect it, and show you the way. That's the magical part of creativity.

Do you think you're creative?

What do you consider your most creative activities?

When are you most creative? Least creative?

Where are you most creative? Least creative?

Do deadlines make you more creative? Less creative?

What are catalysts to your creativity? Obstacles?

Can you be creative when someone else is telling you what to do? Why? Or why not?

Does self-confidence enhance creativity?

How is human waste disposed of?
- *toilet (receptacle) ⇒ sewage*
- *Pipes → sewage treatment plants ⇒ landfill or ocean.*
- *food can be composted (w/o meat)*

investigate "Clivus Multrum" (composting toilet)

Poop is like...fertilizer
- *people sell fertilizer*
- *good for gardens*

How do other cities deal w/ pet poop?
- *restrict pet access --→ user fees!*
- *fines for not picking up poop*
- *some states have shoe clean-off stations— H₂O basins or fountains*
- *Bird guano (& bat) is harvested in other countries for fertilizer + is very profitable*

METHODS FOR GENERATING IDEAS
Try these if you get stuck. Most can be done alone or in a group.

BRAINSTORMING
Why would you want a storm in your brain? Isn't everything too cloudy as it is? More reason for a storm! Things always clear up after a good storm.

Brainstorming is the process of generating as many ideas as you can as quickly as you can. There are a few rules: Every idea is brilliant—at least initially. No idea can be defeated before it has a chance to see the light and really shine. Quantity is everything. You can look at the quality of the ideas later. Now you need more ideas. Brainstorming can be done alone, but it works better with more brains. Someone else's ideas may inspire a few more from you.

To brainstorm, you need a big piece of paper. All participants should have their favorite writing and drawing tools. Start by reviewing the performance criteria. Everyone should write and draw, getting every idea down on paper. Go somewhere with each idea. Then go somewhere else with it. Make connections. Break things up. Put things back together differently. Get up and move around. And never take too much time. Brainstorming works best when it's fast and dirty.

GET OUT OF YOUR SKIN
Be someone or something else. Be your Uncle Harry, an imaginary creature, a little kid, a roller skate, or a visitor from another planet. Better yet, be someone directly involved with your problem. You could even take turns being each of the personalities. How would they solve the problem? Any new ideas?

WRITE ON
To get some ideas going, try writing a letter to someone who lives in another part of the country. Explain the situation in detail. Or write a story that takes place at the location of your problem. Include all the real characters, some conflict, and, of course, a happy ending. Any new ideas?

TALK TO YOURSELF
Here's a fun way to get thinking about your problem and its potential solutions. Have a debate with yourself. Close the door (if you embarrass easily) and, as passionately as possible, argue both the pros and cons of the situation. Any new ideas?

DO A MATRIX
A matrix is a structured way to force two ideas together. Often, the combination or connection suggests a new idea. The easiest matrix to make begins with a list of all the words you associate with the problem. Put the list along the left side of the matrix and across the top. Every intersection (other than where the same two words meet) is a potential new idea. How many are there?

solutions:
scarabs
rain/wind
fragrant flowers
plastic bags
composters
scoops
fines

(columns: scarabs, rain/wind, fragrant flowers, plastic bags, composters, scoops, fines)

"Bag of Beetles" you could get a bag of beetles when you enter park and use them as needed!!

"scoop squirt gun": could a scooper spray water on poop and clean itself off?

"Flower Fines" You could "pay-off" your dues by donating fragrant flowers.

"Bag of Rain" Why not carry a bag of water (water balloon?) to "rain" the poop away?

"Peat Moss Scooper" Why not make the cones out of something easily composted?

How does nature solve problem?
• weather ⇒ decomposition ⇒ nitrogen (fertilizer ...)
• insects (dung beetles)

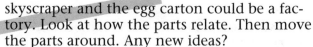

EGYPTIAN SCARAB
(DUNGBEETLE OR JUNEBUG)
Communities of scarabs can easily break down large piles of dog poop in a relatively short time.

SKETCH THE PROBLEM

Use a pencil and tracing paper and sketch the problem as you see it. After a few minutes put another piece on top and start again, this time changing one part of the problem. It doesn't matter what. Continue putting more papers on top so that the sketch evolves into something different. Try not to stop and think. Let your thinking happen through the pencil. Any new ideas?

SHOOT SOME IDEAS

Take a still or video camera to the scene of the problem. Alter your perspective (get down to knee level or climb a ladder) and document what you see. Looking through a lens helps you frame your thoughts. Taking the pictures helps you see your thoughts. Any new ideas?

DIAGRAM THE PROBLEM

Take the problem apart and place each part in a circle (or bubble). Keep redrawing the placement of the bubbles and creating new connections between the items. Any new ideas spring to mind?

COLLAGE THE PROBLEM

Find images from magazines and newspapers that represent all the parts of the problem. Look for scraps of packaging, junk mail, and anything else you can cut up or stick on (popsicle sticks, fabric, leaves). Create a collage that visually presents the problem. Use differences in size and shade of color to communicate what's most important. Any new ideas?

TAKE IT TO THE THIRD DIMENSION

Use the objects around you to model your problem. Try to pick objects that symbolize the parts that make up the problem. For example, how could what's in your refrigerator represent scale relationships between buildings in your neighborhood? The milk carton could be a skyscraper and the egg carton could be a factory. Look at how the parts relate. Then move the parts around. Any new ideas?

MAKE ANALOGIES AND STRANGE COMPARISONS

Think about how your problem is similar to other problems that have been faced in the past. How is it similar to those found in nature? Or make a strange comparison. Say you're trying to find a better way to sharpen pencils. Pick something (anything) that's very different—like a squirrel or a banana—and compare it to your problem. Go with any associations that spring into your head. For example, you might imagine the squirrel holding the pencil in its paws and chewing all around it. Or you might think about peeling the pencil like you'd peel a banana. Any new ideas?

IDEA GENERATION CHECKLIST

- [ ] Brainstorm
- [ ] Become someone else
- [ ] Write
- [ ] Debate the pros and cons
- [ ] Do a matrix
- [ ] Sketch the problem
- [ ] Photograph or videotape
- [ ] Diagram the problem
- [ ] Collage the problem
- [ ] Model the problem
- [ ] Make analogies and strange comparisons
- [ ] Talk to others

Master Idea List

- Poop septic tank - "Poop Pot"
- Beetle for eating poop (scarb)
- "Poop-away" decomposition spray
- Dog-free zones
- Fines
- Dog-run areas
- Eliminate dogs from parks
- User fees
- Volunteer maintenance / community service
- Gardens w/ poop fertilizer
- "Poop-shoot" – recyling / compost containers
- Shoe clean off areas (fountains or basins)
- Poop sticks for digging poop out of shoe soles
- Poop scoops
- Education program – signs, pamphlets
- Recycle poop ⇒ fertilizer
- Poop smell-away spray
- Hose down paths or people carry pressurized H₂O bottles for spraying poop

PET POOP SEPTIC TANKS?

TICKET
$
$ $
$ $ $

Fines for people who fail to obey new ordinances. Frequent abusers would pay more.

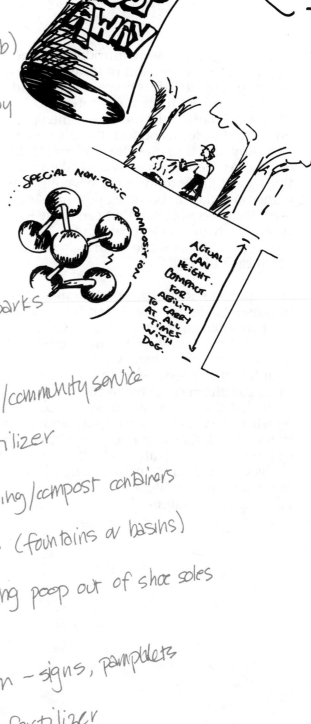

THE AMAZING POOP AWAY

SPECIAL NON-TOXIC COMPOSITION

ACTUAL CAN HEIGHT. COMPACT FOR ABILITY TO CARRY AT ALL TIMES WITH DOG.

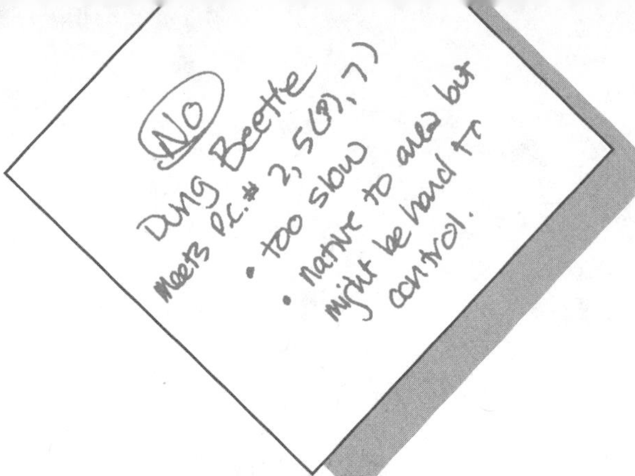

Edit and develop ideas

Which ideas have the most potential?

In the handwritten note (top right):

> NO
> Dung Beetle
> Meets P.C. # 2, 5(9, 7)
> • too slow
> • native to area but
>   might be hard to
>   control.

In the last step you were introduced to techniques for generating lots of ideas. The goal of this step is to edit ideas down to a few and develop those with the most potential. At this point you may think you have come up with one idea that seems perfect. But it's best not to limit yourself to one idea yet. Pursue three or four. As these ideas grow and take shape, those most likely to meet the overall performance criteria will become apparent. And you may find pieces of each that can come together to create an even better idea. The techniques in this section will help you develop each idea further.

How do you know which of your many ideas to pursue? Refer to your design brief and use the performance criteria you established. Choose those that show the most promise in meeting your objectives. As you look over your list, think about how the contexts of time, culture, and the environment affect each choice. Ask yourself about the costs and benefits of each alternative idea—and not just in terms of dollars. For example, which groups or individuals will gain or lose if you solve the problem in various ways? What do those affected by the problem see as potentially good and bad solutions?

The answers to these questions will lead you to more questions and more data to collect. For example, if your solution ideas involve making something, talk to the people who are doing the construction. See if they think the materials you have in mind are wise choices. Get recommendations for other materials to try. Learn from their experience so you don't have to "reinvent the wheel." Start playing with and comparing the materials.

You may need to develop a new set of performance criteria for each selected idea. For example, if you've decided a poster is part of your solution, what will make the poster communicate well?

If you want to learn more about the effect design solutions have on people, animals, and the environment, try the following activities in the **Design awareness** part of this book:

Design detective
What if?
Satisfied customer
"Can't get no satisfaction"
Town meeting—Where to put the park
Eye of the beholder
What a piece of junk!
Hey bikers, take a hike!
Wish you were here
"Paper or plastic?"
Can't beat the system
Still can't beat the system

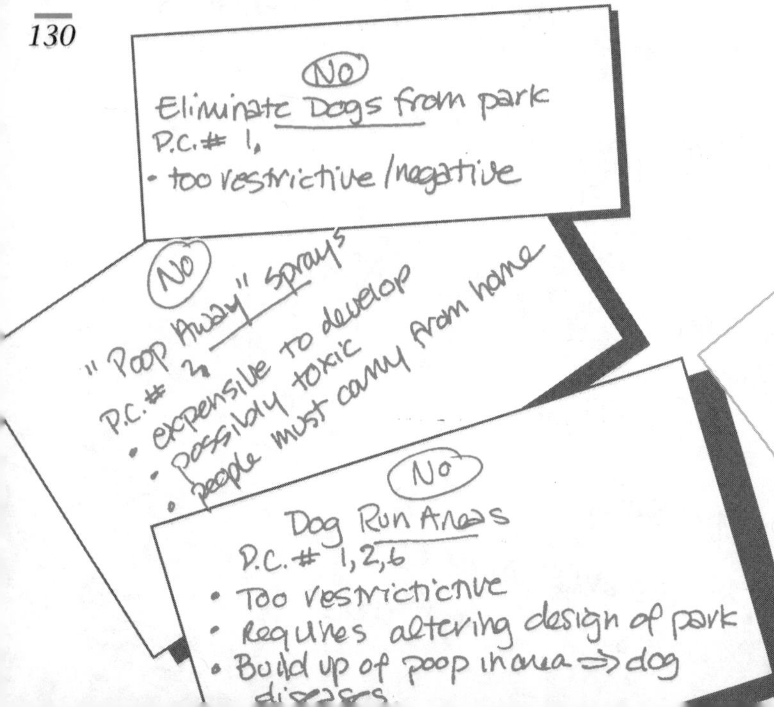

Handwritten notes (bottom of page):

> NO
> Eliminate Dogs from park
> P.C.# 1,
> • too restrictive/negative

> NO
> "Poop Away" sprays
> P.C. # 2,
> • expensive to develop
> • possibly toxic
> • people must carry from home

> NO
> Dog Run Areas
> P.C.# 1, 2, 6
> • Too restrictive
> • Requires altering design of park
> • Build up of poop in area ⇒ dog
>   diseases

> NO
> Poop Septic Tanks
> P.C. # 1, 2, 3,
> • smells
> • waste of poop

> NO
> Hose down paths
> P.C. # • slippery sidewalks
> • Doesn't work for grass
> • requires constant attention

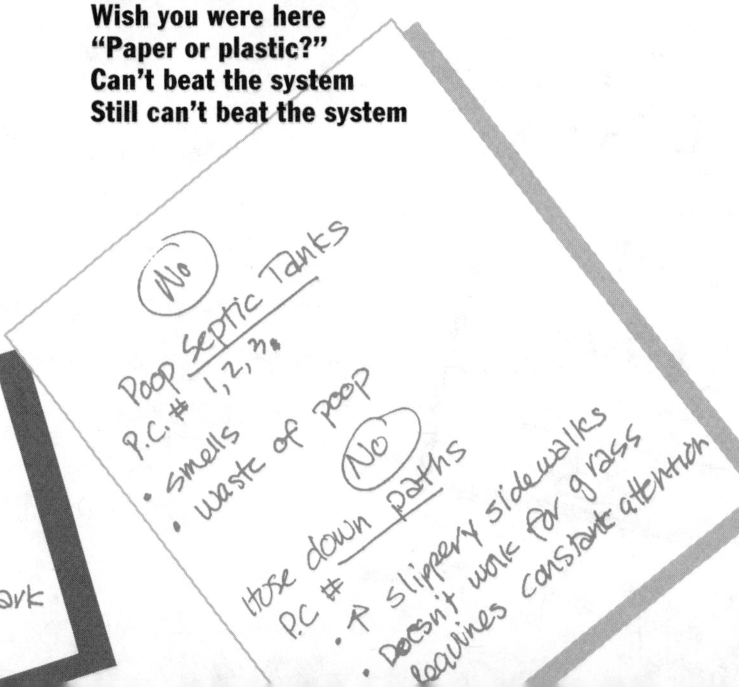

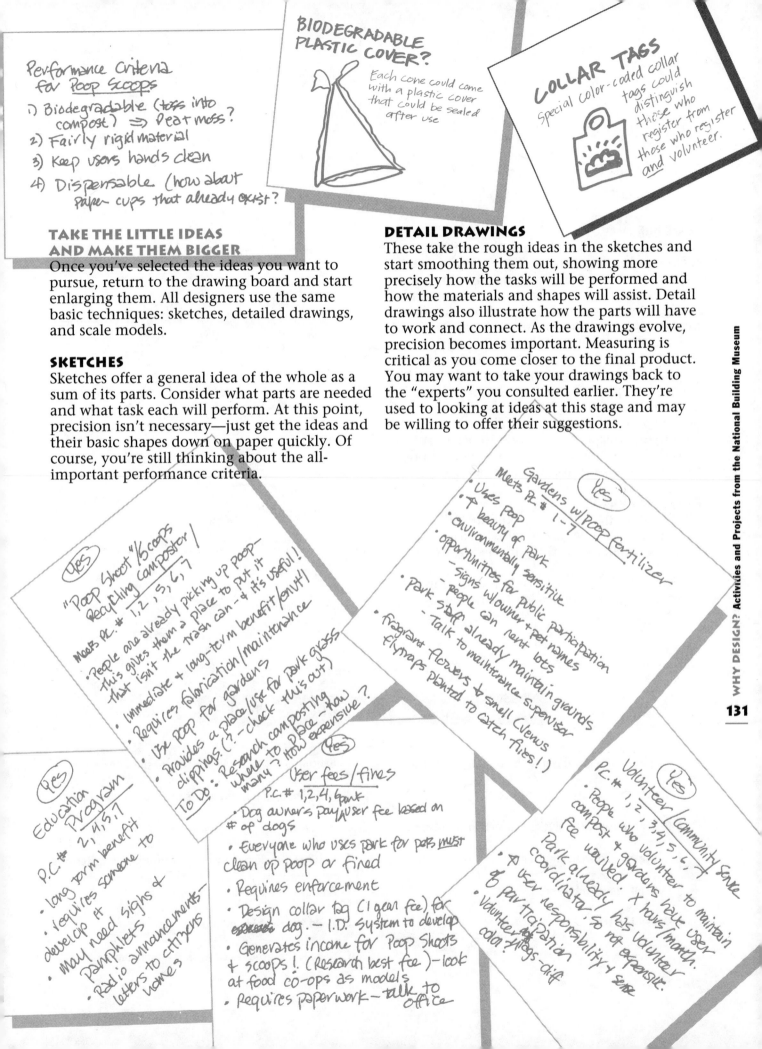

Performance criteria
for Poop Scoops

1) Biodegradable (toss into
   compost) ⇒ Peat moss?
2) Fairly rigid material
3) Keep users hands clean
4) Dispensable (how about
   paper cups that already exist?

BIODEGRADABLE PLASTIC COVER?
Each cone could come with a plastic cover that could be sealed after use

COLLAR TAGS
Special color-coded collar tags could distinguish those who register from those who register and volunteer.

TAKE THE LITTLE IDEAS AND MAKE THEM BIGGER

Once you've selected the ideas you want to pursue, return to the drawing board and start enlarging them. All designers use the same basic techniques: sketches, detailed drawings, and scale models.

SKETCHES

Sketches offer a general idea of the whole as a sum of its parts. Consider what parts are needed and what task each will perform. At this point, precision isn't necessary—just get the ideas and their basic shapes down on paper quickly. Of course, you're still thinking about the all-important performance criteria.

DETAIL DRAWINGS

These take the rough ideas in the sketches and start smoothing them out, showing more precisely how the tasks will be performed and how the materials and shapes will assist. Detail drawings also illustrate how the parts will have to work and connect. As the drawings evolve, precision becomes important. Measuring is critical as you come closer to the final product. You may want to take your drawings back to the "experts" you consulted earlier. They're used to looking at ideas at this stage and may be willing to offer their suggestions.

Yes
"Poop Shoot"/Scoops
Recycling composter/
Meets P.C. # 1,2,5,6,7
• People are already picking up poop—
  this gives them a place to put it
  that isn't the trash can—& it's useful!/
• Immediate + long-term benefit/benefit/
• Requires fabrication/maintenance
• Use poop for gardens
• Provides a place/use for park grass
  clippings (? — check this out)
To Do: Research composting — how
  many? where to place? how expensive?

Yes
Gardens w/poop fertilizer
Meets P.C. # 1-7
• Uses poop
• ↑ beauty of park
• environmentally sensitive
• opportunities for public participation
  — signs w/owner + pet names
  — people can rent lots
• Park staff already maintain grounds
  — Talk to maintenance supervisor
• Fragrant flowers + smell (views
  flytraps planted to catch flies!)

Yes
Education Program
P.C. # 2,4,5,7
• long term benefit
• requires someone to
  develop it
• may need signs &
  pamphlets
• Radio announcements—
  letters to citizens
  homes

User fees/fines
P.C. # 1,2,4,6
• Dog owners pay user fee based on
  # of dogs
• Everyone who uses park for pets must
  clean up poop or fined
• Requires enforcement
• Design collar tag (1 year fee) for
  dog — I.D. system to develop
• Generates income for poop shoots
  + scoops! (Research best fee) — look
  at food co-ops as models
• Requires paperwork—talk to office

Yes
Volunteer/Community Service
P.C. # 1,2,3,4,5,6,7
• People who volunteer to maintain
  compost + gardens have user
  fee waived. X hours/month
• Park already has volunteer
  coordinator, so not expensive.
• ↑ user participation + responsibility
• Volunteer collar flags - diff.

P.C. for Poop Shoot Composter
1) Easy to put poop in w/out contaminating hands
2) Easy to maintain
3) Easy to identify
4) Materials: Durable, non-corrodable, H₂O proof
   (check recycled plastic (!)
5) Place for scoop dispenser

TOP ↑

inexpensive alternative to movable receptacles
would be compost "mounds" with a door on one
side or a gridded cover with door-like hinges.

SECTION

↑ ↑ ↑

POTENTIAL OPENING FOR POOP SHOOT

stops!

Add chambers for grass clippings

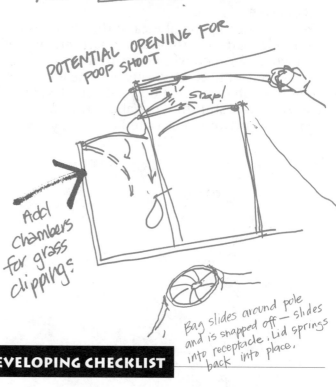

Bag slides around pole and is snapped off— slides into receptacle. Lid springs back into place.

MODELS

Models, usually in scale, take the evolving ideas one big step further. They allow you to explore both the whole and its parts in three dimensions. Now you can walk around each potential solution and study it from different perspectives. By adding correctly proportioned, self-standing cutouts of people (try using photographs from magazines), you can begin to understand how the solutions will "fit" their users. It's typical at this stage for unexpected problems to arise. Go back to the drawing board to work these out. Mistakes are much easier and cheaper to fix when they can still be erased. Again, don't be shy. Show your models to the experts and listen to their advice.

PROTOTYPES

These are models that approximate a finished solution. Prototypes are invaluable for testing ideas, especially with the intended users.

For information on how to do any of these "idea developers," take a look at the **Design technical skills** chapter.

IDEA EDITING AND DEVELOPING CHECKLIST

☐ Edit a lot of ideas down to the few most likely to satisfy the performance criteria

☐ Research existing solutions to similar problems

☐ Research materials and suppliers

☐ Consult manufacturers

☐ Consult users

☐ Sketch ideas to study the sum of their parts

☐ Make many detail drawings to better understand the parts

☐ Refer to the design brief for performance criteria

☐ Add precision to the drawings

☐ Build the best ideas into models

☐ Repeat the process to work the bugs out

Test ideas

How can feedback improve your solutions?

Part of the search for good solutions involves examining your ideas critically. Designers constantly question their objectives, values, methods, and solutions. They ask questions about whether they've considered everything they should have, and whether their solution will really do the job. This process of asking questions about your work is called *critiquing*. You can critique your own work and have others critique your work.

Giving a critique doesn't mean being negative. Anyone who puts ideas on the line and attempts to make things better is taking a risk and deserves nothing but applause. Critiquing means identifying what is working and what isn't. It means anticipating potential mistakes and suggesting corrections. It means foreseeing potential successes and building on them. It is more than simply saying, "I like it" or "I don't like it." What is more relevant, and more helpful, is a comment like, "I think it's working well because . . ." or "I don't think it's working yet because . . ." Most of all, a critique should keep the designer moving toward meeting the performance criteria.

Knowing whom to show your work and when will ensure that you get the best feedback. When ideas are in the early, rough stages, go to people who will not squash them. As you get further along, you'll need to talk to people who are going to be affected by your solution. Although it is really hard, put your ego (and sense of ownership) aside and focus on the needs of the audience. When having your work critiqued, listen to what each person says and jot down notes about the things that are useful. It is up to you to decide which comments seem helpful and valid, and which don't. Remember that everyone has a different opinion and a different point of view.

When you critique someone else's work, think about the words you are using. You have the power to crush someone's spirit by thoughtless comments. Remember that all ideas are good, and they can usually be made better by incorporating insightful criticism.

Use the critique questions on this page as a guide and generate more as you go.

CRITIQUE QUESTIONS:

What is the basic problem this design must solve?

How does this design meet the performance criteria?

What needs to be improved?

How are the contexts (factors) that shape the problem addressed? What might cause the context to change?

How is this solution similar to existing solutions or similar problems?

Does this design take into account the failures and successes of existing solutions?

Does the selected form make the design easier to use? Is it pleasing to the eye of the user?

How will the solution work? How will it be made? Does the technology exist to make it?

How much will it cost? Is it worth it?

What resources are needed? What resources are available?

What are the social and environmental consequences of this design? Will it cause trouble?

Do we really need it? Does the planet really need it?

COMMUNITY SERVICE
Volunteers could help pick up poop not taken care of by pet owners

POOP COLLECTION

AUDIENCE TESTING

If possible, let the people who will use your final solutions try the proposed solutions. Audience testing gives you immediate and practical feedback. For the most part, people are glad to know their opinions may influence the results. It works best when you test more than one prototype because the comparison helps people see what they like and what they don't. The secret of audience testing is to become as invisible as possible. You want to give the audience the minimum information necessary and then let them have a go at your prototype(s). Your job is to step back and observe. After they're done, you can ask all the questions you like. For hints on creating "bias-free" questions take a look at "Surveying & interviewing" in the Design technical skills chapter of this book.

CONE & PEAT MOSS GUIDE
Peat moss chip helps pet owner guide poop into cone w/o getting hands dirty. Chip can be then put in cone to be composted.

IDEA TESTING CHECKLIST

☐ **Receive critical feedback**

☐ **Test more than one solution**

☐ **Do not bias audience before or during testing**

Step 8

Communicate proposed solution(s)

It's show time! How can you "sell" your ideas?

Well, you have worked endless hours on your design problem and have come up with what you believe are incredible solutions. Now the task is to let other people know about them—to communicate them. This section is divided into two parts: preparing for your presentation and giving your presentation.

DON'T YOU SEE WHAT I MEAN?

Fortunately, good communication and presentation have been topics of discussion for centuries. Over 2,500 years ago the Greek philosopher Aristotle came up with three simple (but not easy) guidelines for a good presentation: offer a logical, well-structured argument; prove your credibility; and appeal to the emotions of your audience. Over the years, people have expanded on these and developed other models of communication.

Basically, communication requires four things:
a message to send
a sender (that's you)
a means of sending the message
a receiver (listener, reader, audience)

Sounds straightforward. But for effective communication you need to consider one last, extremely important thing: interference, or noise. It occurs between the time a message is sent and the time it is received. It's anything that gets in the way. Noise can take many forms—from language differences to age differences to the physical distance between you and your audience.

If you think about all these things in advance, chances are good that your communication will be effective.

PREPARING FOR YOUR PRESENTATION
WHO'S LISTENING?
(OR, KNOW YOUR AUDIENCE)

To whom are you communicating and why? Is it to people who are affected by the problem? To someone who has the power to make your solution a reality? To an audience of mixed ages, a group of teenagers, or a group of adults? Think about the physical, emotional, and social needs of different people in your audience. Are people upset about the problem you're tackling? Do they want to listen to you? Consider the wide range of the people's physical and mental abilities.

A presentation usually goes hand-in-hand with a critique. Once you've presented your ideas, it's the audience's turn to express opinions. Think about what their main concerns will be, what they may ask you, and have your answers ready.

THINK ABOUT THE NOISE

What are the circumstances under which you will be presenting? Where will it take place—in a big auditorium or a small office? How far away will the audience be? How much time will you have—as much as you need, or five quick minutes? What time of day—are people going to be tired after a day at work?

✓ Place: High school auditorium
✓ Who'll be there: City council, pet owners, other park users
✓ Time: 7:30pm
✓ Amount of time: 20 minutes
✓ Equip. needed: Slide projector, microphone, overhead projector, easels, pointer

SELECT THE BEST VEHICLE

Consider the best verbal and visual ways to present the information. Use language—written, spoken, and visual—to its best advantage. What is the best technique to illustrate your problem? What is the best method for describing the solution? Consider the physical noise—the size of the group and how far away they'll be. Consider what would make the presentation lively and engaging—what will attract the audience's attention? Listed below are some presentation options and an explanation of what each can offer.

WRITING

Reports and summary statements are good for situations when the audience is dispersed or when you want them to take something away to reflect on. Remember that some people don't like to read information, and most people don't have a lot of time. Think about how you can include images like photos, sketches, diagrams, charts, and graphs to help convey what might otherwise be only text.

LABELS/TYPE

This is important in reports or displays. Consider the basics of size and color: Is the text large enough? Does the color make the text stand out so people can see it? Also consider how the typeface can assist in creating a feeling or mood. If you want to convey elegance or a sense of fun, how does your choice of type help?

DRAMATIC PRESENTATION AND ROLE-PLAY/SIMULATION

These are good for engaging the audience's emotions. Drama can not only help people relate to a problem they don't know much about, but help them better understand different points of view. While these techniques can be risky with certain audiences, the results are often worth the risk.

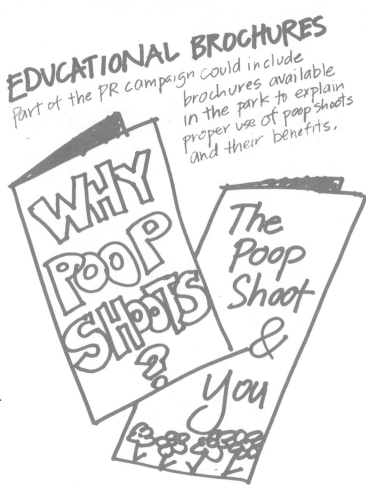

IMAGES

Drawings, photographs, maps, plans, diagrams, cartoons, and collages help the audience see what the physical solution will actually look like. They don't say "seeing is believing" for nothing—images help make things real for people. Images are great in reports or displays that will stay up for a while, but they don't work well across a large room. Always make sure the size you select is appropriate for the situation.

AUDIO/VISUAL

Slides and video can work well for any size audience. When projected on a large screen they are especially effective for large audiences. Slides and video can be used to capture or express a specific mood, or activity, such as people having fun. Video is great for capturing and describing a spatial problem. It's a way to take people who haven't experienced the problem and move them through it. However, in order for it to be effective, you need to use a room that can be darkened. Audio can create wonderful sound pictures, capturing a mood or emotion.

MODELS

These are very important to help people visualize such three-dimensional solutions as environments or products. It's best to use materials that will simulate the real thing as closely as possible.

GIVING A PRESENTATION
FIRST THINGS FIRST: ORGANIZE YOUR MESSAGE SO THAT IT MAKES SENSE

Now that you know who's listening and under what conditions you'll be presenting, it's time to think about the message—the substance— and edit and organize it. What does your audience need to know? *Really* need to know? After you've worked so hard, it's natural to want to tell them everything. It all seems essential. And it was—to you—when you were developing your ideas. But how are you going to use the precious moments of your audience's attention?

Ask yourself what information is essential to explain your problem and solution in a way that will be understood and persuasive. Put yourself in your audience's shoes. Then prioritize the information.

ORGANIZE YOUR MATERIALS
Make sure you have everything you need arranged in the order that you'll need it. If you are handing things out, make sure you have extras.

INTRODUCE YOURSELF
If anyone in the room doesn't know you, introduce yourself by name and by title. Explain why you're involved with the problem.

EXPLAIN THE PROBLEM
Tell the audience why it is a problem, for whom it is a problem, and how you know it's a problem (here's your chance to use all that research).

STATE THE PERFORMANCE CRITERIA
Before you show your solution, tell the audience all the things a successful solution must do, and why.

EXPLAIN YOUR SOLUTION
Tell them why it satisfies the needs of the people who are affected by the problem. Don't assume people understand or even remember the specifics of your problem, but tell them what they need to know. Don't get caught up in minute detail. Explain difficult concepts and don't use jargon. For example, naming a specific typeface may be irrelevant, but explaining why you made the type larger (you wanted to meet the needs of an older audience) is certainly worth mentioning.

SHOW THE WORK
Display the work so that the audience sees what you want them to see *when* you want them to see it. If you show them everything at once, they will look at everything and you'll lose their attention. Have a logical reason for the order you choose.

THIS BEAUTIFUL GARDEN MADE POSSIBLE BY THE GENEROUS DONATIONS OF TED, TROOPER, SPARKY PINK, CHARLIE, MUFFIN, MOLLIE, ED, BOSCO, BEAR, CLOVIS, BERTHA & ERNIE WILBUR, MIKE, FIFI, ROVER JOEY, SPIKE, ALI, SIMON, BRUNA, CARL, STING, RONA, LISL, ARTHUR, ZOE, TIPPER, ROSIE, ZAK, ELLIOT, OTIS, AND MANY OTHERS WHO WISH TO REMAIN ANONYMOUS

LOOK GOOD, ACT THE PART

Part of making an audience feel good about your work is making them feel good about you. Demonstrate that you respect their time and attention by being on time, well dressed, and ready to go. Be friendly and professional. Enjoy being there. You've done a lot of work—be proud of it. When you're feeling good, people pick up on it and they are more likely to respond favorably. Think about your body language, and make eye contact with all the people who have come to hear you.

LISTEN AND ENCOURAGE FEEDBACK

Ask and answer questions. Don't be defensive. Be willing to compromise and make changes. Take notes. Credit any comments to the people who made them.

THINK BACKWARD AND THEN FORWARD

When you're done, think about how well you (and your solution) performed. What didn't go as well as it should have? How will your next presentation be improved?

PRACTICE, PRACTICE, PRACTICE

To get comfortable, practice giving the presentation or visualize yourself giving it. Have someone act as your audience while you practice. Or have someone videotape you and watch your body language. Look for unconscious fidgeting and concentrate on eye contact. Practice referring to your notes and materials without ruining the continuity of the presentation.

PRESENTATION CHECKLIST

- [ ] Consider audience
- [ ] Consider noise
- [ ] Consider vehicle
- [ ] Organize message
- [ ] Organize materials
- [ ] Get prepared
- [ ] Take notes

POOP SHOOT (FRONT)

unique opening discourages trash deposits

peat moss guides stored at top of cone dispenser

Stone pavers direct pet owners to cones and to depository. Flowers planted close to PoopShoot benefit from compost and fragrance masks any unpleasant smells.

POOP SHOOT (BACK)

Vents on sides allow air to pass through to speed up Composting process

Rear door slides up allowing easy removal of new compost.

Evaluate your process

Did you do what you needed to do?

Now that it's all over, what did you learn from this experience that will make you a better designer—in all aspects of your life? The most important part of the whole process is learning from your experience, so that you can change and improve your next design endeavor. The following questions can help you evaluate your effort.

IDENTIFYING THE NEED FOR CHANGE

How did you identify the problem, need, or opportunity for change?
How did you identify the specific audiences/users affected?
How did you determine what specific needs were to be met and/or what behaviors or attitudes were to be encouraged?

INVESTIGATING THE NEED/PROBLEM

What investigations did you carry out to find out more about it?
What contexts did you examine?
Where did you look for information and advice?
What information did you collect?
How much information did you collect?
How did you record it?
What background reading did you do?
How did you evaluate your material?
What social, environmental, safety, and economic factors did you consider?

ESTABLISHING THE PERFORMANCE CRITERIA AND COMPLETING THE DESIGN BRIEF

Did you identify all the smaller problems within the original problem?
How did you determine what would make a successful solution?
How did you determine what needed to be done in order to make the solution work?
On what basis did you prioritize the criteria?
How did you determine the minimum you could do to satisfy the need?
Did you write a complete design brief?

GENERATING AND DEVELOPING IDEAS

How many ideas did you generate as a starting point?
What innovative ideas/solutions did you consider?
How did you choose which to follow up?
What ideas or experiences influenced your thinking?
How did you use your research materials?
What connections did you make?
What constraints did you consider?
What problems did you encounter?
How did you get around the problems and constraints?
What imaginative elements are evident in your work?
What techniques/processes did you use to develop the design?

EVALUATING AND TESTING IDEAS

How did you determine the best methods for finding out whether possible solutions would satisfy the user's need?
How well does each idea address the performance criteria?
Did you consider what other things might be affected by changing the current situation?
How did you test your ideas?
How effectively did you use your materials?
How efficiently did you use your materials?

COMMUNICATE PROPOSED SOLUTIONS

Did the audience understand your solution?
How did you explain the need and whose need it is?
How much information/data did you use to support your view?
Why did you select your chosen vehicles for presenting your solution?
How will you incorporate the feedback you received?

Implement the solution(s)

How can your ideas become reality?

The problem you just solved may have been serious or lighthearted. You may have tackled a real problem or just wanted to stretch your mind with an intellectual challenge. It may have resulted in a three-dimensional product or remained on paper.

You may find you've become so energized by your ideas and the whole process that you want to make your solution(s) a reality. Identify what it's going to take. Does a law need to be changed? Get political—fight city hall. Do your neighbors need to work together? Use your design skills to help get them involved. Need to raise money? Find an appropriate foundation and write a grant proposal, or talk to the people who benefit from your solution and see if they'll help out—local businesses are great for that. Find out about issues you care about, who is addressing them, and who has the power to do something about them. Gather some like-minded souls and go out there and just do it!

The stories that follow are examples of people across the country who have done just that—identified and tackled real design problems in their own communities.

NEW LENOX, ILLINOIS

To avoid boring building and landscaping in the suburban Illinois town where he resides, New Lenox Village Board President John Nowakowski persuaded his town council to enact an "anti-monotony" ordinance. The thrust of Nowakowski's initiative is to encourage the flourishing of varied design solutions in his community's built environment. Some projects include varying rooflines, window treatments, and other touches on the fronts of buildings. Also, neighbors are urged to experiment with different landscape designs, not just the standard trees and rosebushes. Other communities outside Chicago have joined the "anti-monotony" movement begun in New Lenox, in hopes of keeping the suburban sprawl of identical buildings from dumping their hometowns into the "design doldrums."

SPENCERPORT, NEW YORK

Designing to comfort others, eight students who have disabilities worked hard to create colorful, hand-decorated, and comfy pillows for young patients at Strong Memorial Hospital's Adolescent Unit in nearby Rochester. The pillow design project was initiated to celebrate "Make a Difference Day," a national day of doing good, sponsored by *USA Today Weekend*. The designers, ages 12 to 21, made colorful patterns on pillows using a variety of materials; one student with cerebral palsy, for example, used a paint-soaked sponge to make a lively pattern.

BAINBRIDGE ISLAND, WASHINGTON

Portable shelter was a design problem that James Davis, a boatbuilder, chose as a challenge. The designer now prides himself on creating a structure that bridges the gap between tents and permanent buildings. In developing his design solution, Davis had to consider factors such as weight and durability. The result is a tight fabric cover over a lightweight, but strong, aluminum frame. Presto—portability! The frame features arched rafters and carefully designed, thin interior buttresses; the bays between the buttresses can be customized to accommodate bunk beds, shelves, desks, or other equipment. Unlike most tents or other portable structures, Davis's design provides wall space and lots of room for stuff. A prototype of his design will be used by scientists studying in the Antarctic during the summer season.

NEW YORK, NEW YORK

In building for what he calls "a survival situation," Thomas Davis's design decisions were affected by both childhood memories and the world around him. Davis, who is homeless, lives under a New York City expressway along the East River in a refuge that is his own very personal design creation. Davis's shelter took two months to create: a plywood frame with a tarp covering, angled so that the rain runs off. The bottom of his home is lined with formica panels he found that keep out moisture and rats. Davis put wheels on his home so he can move it around. A fish-shaped wind gauge on the top, both decorative and useful, was inspired by the blimps Davis saw floating above the East River and by whirligigs in gardens he saw as a child.

TULSA, OKLAHOMA

Public transportation is a necessity for many residents of Tulsa, and the need for a shelter at the bus stop outside the building that houses the Margaret Hudson Program posed a problem for the community. A shelter to protect commuters in inclement weather was particularly vital for the Hudson Program stop since that program helps to support and educate teenage mothers. These young women and their babies use public transportation to get to school. The design solution was a basic one. The prefabricated kit of plywood and nails seemed straightforward to the 17 volunteers who offered to set it up. As work progressed, however, the prefab turned problematic and the volunteers got discouraged. An extra volunteer, with construction experience and some additional tools, helped save the day, and the shelter became a basic but effective design reality.

HOPE, NEW MEXICO

The community came together and fulfilled a need by transforming an abandoned school building into a new community center. Rather than demolish the existing schoolhouse in favor of a modern structure, the citizens of Hope opted for "adaptive reuse"—which basically means recycling a building. Thanks to lots of volunteer time and effort, Hope now boasts a terrific community center featuring a place for adults to gather, the Hope Police Department, and the town library. The next community project is to fix up the old school's gym and design weight-room facilities for community use.

RICHMOND HILL, NEW YORK

Two high-school art classes undertook a mural project to spruce up their aging neighborhood. The students began their design process by surveying the areas they felt needed help and designating the structures that were most in need of beautification. The young designers then began measuring the sites, drawing elevations, and finding historic photos to get an idea of what Richmond Hill's built environment looked like when the neighborhood was new. The students decided that the most effective design plan would be to cover today's deteriorating buildings with murals that evoke the way the neighborhood originally looked. Once they finalized their design concepts, the classes presented their ideas to local planning boards and asked for financial support. After all their planning, the students pulled together to bring the design to life and painted six scenes of local landmarks onto the walls of older buildings.

NEWARK, CALIFORNIA

Designing with the earth in mind and keeping a lid on dumping is the design problem a group of sixth-grade Girl Scouts tackled. In an effort to help the environment, specifically the aquatic ecosystem in nearby San Francisco Bay, the girls created eye-catching stencils that were applied to manhole covers in their neighborhoods. The stencils—which read, "No dumping; drains into the bay,"—have helped to heighten the community's awareness of the damage dumping does to the delicate balance of life in the bay.

FARGO, NORTH DAKOTA

More than 200 student volunteers from the Air Force Junior Reserve program visit their local Veterans Administration Hospital monthly, bringing good cheer and good designs with them. The cadets design and make greeting cards for every patient and hand deliver them during their visits. These Junior Reservists brighten the lives of some special people at the hospital and are the only visitors some patients ever get. The cards, designed and crafted by hand, are cheery reminders of the visits and they also help to enliven the patients' hospital rooms.

NEW CANAAN, CONNECTICUT

A group of eighth graders, designing ways to serve their community, have focused their efforts on a preschooler's daycare center close to their school. Not only do the students devise activities—ranging from songs to skits—for the tots on Wednesdays, they have also pitched in to help rehabilitate the dilapidated daycare facility itself. Students repainted the inside of the center, planned and painted a mural to cover graffiti on the exterior, and spruced up the landscaping around the building. Also thanks to the eighth graders, part of the center's parking lot is now a kid-designed playground for the little ones.

WASHINGTON, D.C.

Residents with fond memories of Meridian Hill Park, now called Malcolm X Park, are fighting to revitalize their favorite green space. Many recall the design features of the once-well-kept park, such as the goldfish in the fountain pond, the archways, and the statues. Located in the heart of downtown, this park had fallen prey to drug dealers and neglect; trash and graffiti were everywhere. Today, concerned residents, the Friends of Meridian Hill, have added plantings to the site and cleaned off the graffiti as part of their campaign to enhance the park and make it safe for community enjoyment. "The government can't do it alone," one resident stated. Now the park has 42 new trees, planted by caring neighbors, that will help bring the space back to life for the community.

SANTA FE, NEW MEXICO

Struggling to save the physical expression of their communities' spiritual heritage, the New Mexico Community Foundation enacted a statewide plan to promote preservation and save decaying adobe churches. The Foundation's concept was to encourage civic pride and empower individual communities to preserve their own landmark churches. The Foundation successfully embarked upon this ongoing project, conducting dozens of workshops on adobe preservation, developing preservation plans for 34 churches, and working to get the word out about these distinctive indigenous structures.

SOMERVILLE, MASSACHUSETTS

A community development program explored ways of expressing cultural identity through design. The program found that in urban areas characterized by dense immigrant populations, a unique community identity can be fostered through the use of culturally inspired signs, architecture, and planning. Also, a community's own ethnic pride in its heritage, when expressed through design, can help to rejuvenate it economically. The Somerville development program produced a book, a plan, and a 22-minute film documenting its study of ethnic populations and community design.

PHOENIX, ARIZONA

Working in conjunction with *America the Beautiful Fund*, students at the Metro Tech High School carpentry class designed a gazebo and wheelchair garden at the Westward Ho Hotel for Senior Citizens. Due to their efforts, the hotel residents can now enjoy a block-long garden all year long.

HOMESTEAD, FLORIDA

Working in conjunction with *America the Beautiful Fund,* elementary school students at the Palmetto School created their own raised-bed garden with a Native American structure called a "chickee," a mural of their own design, and folk sculptures. When it was destroyed by Hurricane Andrew, they rebuilt it bigger and better than ever and started their own farmers market at the garden to help hurricane victims.

UPPER ARLINGTON, OHIO

Thoughtful landscaping can be a good way to establish the identity of your neighborhood, according to the Council of the City of Upper Arlington. They began a public awareness campaign to promote the information generated by a study that explored ways that vegetation planning and landscape design can help individual communities form and express their own unique identities. Materials were produced—an informational brochure, a slide presentation, and how-to materials—to help communities assess the structural and aesthetic needs of their neighborhoods and devise plantings to suit those needs.

144

Design technical skills

The seven techniques presented in this chapter introduce you to important design skills that will help you tackle the activities in this book and most design problems you attempt to solve. Of course, you're going to need to practice the techniques to get really good at them.

Observing
Surveying & interviewing
Drawing
Model making
Creating collages
Photographing & videotaping
Organizing visual information

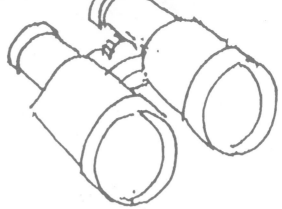

Observing

They say that actions speak louder than words. Well, observation is one way to find out if this is true. Observation is watching people's behavior—with no questions asked. It can tell you who uses a design (a graphic, place, product, or system), how many people use it, and how they use it.

THINGS TO KEEP IN MIND

Although it can be time-consuming and somewhat hard to quantify, being an eyewitness has its advantages. You are able to see things other people might not consider worth mentioning, wouldn't want to discuss, or don't remember.

However, observation can be tricky. It is affected by personal opinion, so people can misinterpret what they see. The quality of data collected through observation depends on the accuracy of the observers, so it's helpful to involve more than one person in the process. It's always best to supplement observation with other information-gathering techniques, like interviews and statistics.

THE BASICS

Because you can't be everywhere and see everything at all times, it will be necessary to select a representative sample of people to observe (see "Surveying & interviewing" for information about selecting a sample). Be careful in selecting the time of day and location of your observation, and decide whether you want to hide yourself or let people see you as you observe. You may decide to set up a special place where you can invite people to use a specific design, or you might find yourself standing on a street corner with a clipboard. You can gather your data by counting or writing notes about what you see. Or you can take photos or videos and analyze what you see. Photographs have the advantage of enabling you to count things accurately, whereas video lets you examine interactions between people and between people and designs.

USING THE DATA

The data you collect will become valuable information only after you have analyzed it, interpreted it, and drawn some conclusions. Several graphic techniques (including maps, pie charts, and bar graphs described here) can help you analyze your data and communicate it so that others will understand and use it. After you've plotted the data, look for patterns, trends, and cycles.

Keep in mind that, in creating these visual aids, it's your responsibility to be sure your information is accurate. You can influence how someone interprets a chart by the scale and proportions you use. Be sure to account for extreme high and/or low points, or for any events that might exaggerate the information and affect your conclusions. Take a look at a variety of newspapers and magazines to see how these tools can be used.

MAPS

These are good for analyzing and communicating information that has spatial or geographic dimensions. For example, you might want to see (and show) where things are placed or located at a site, or see how land use in a specific area has changed over time. In this case you could map what exists there during a specific year, and then what exists 10 years later. If you create a base map (a plain outline of the area) on clear acetate, you can make the change visible by overlaying the maps you create for each time period (also on acetate, or tracing paper).

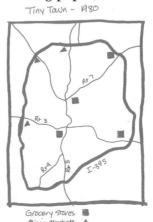

Tiny Town - 1980

Grocery Stores ■
Mini-markets ▲

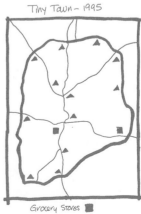

Tiny Town - 1995

Grocery Stores ■
Mini-markets ▲

Surveying & interviewing

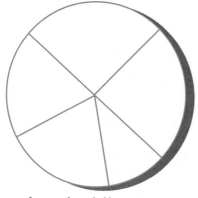

PIE CHARTS
These are good for showing percentages, parts, or proportions of the topic you are investigating. For example, you might want to show the different age groups using a specific site or design.

BAR GRAPHS
These are good for showing magnitude and numbers of items. They provide information about quantities as well as about relative proportions.

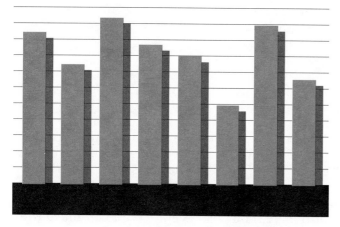

Surveying and interviewing are important techniques for getting the information you need to solve a design problem. This information can be in the form of facts learned from people who are well informed about your problem. It can also take the form of opinions, feelings, and observations of people affected by the problem. Identifying the right people to interview can help ensure that you identify a problem accurately and that you develop a design solution that meets a variety of needs. Also, comparing your perceptions with those of others helps you determine whether you are on target or way off base in your thinking.

TYPES OF SURVEYS
Sometimes you need to find out what a lot of people think about a subject. In this case you'd use a *survey* (a poll of a sample of people). A survey requires no special knowledge on the part of the respondents. Since you can't talk to everyone, the main thing is to pick a random sample (the "who" and "how many") that is representative of the audience affected by the problem. If you shoot for 10 percent of the total group you're dealing with, you'll be in good shape. Otherwise, you can't make generalizations about what the whole group thinks. There are lots of books on how to pick a random sample, so if you decide to do this, check them out.

Survey questions are usually "close ended"— meaning that people choose an answer from a list you provide. Survey techniques vary. Be sure to choose one that will capture the kind of information you want. A few of these are listed below:

The simplest type of close-ended questioning is called *dichotomous response,* which is a fancy way of saying that people either answer "yes" or "no" (or "agree" or "disagree"). The advantage of this is that it is easy to tabulate. The disadvantage is you won't get in-depth information.

Multiple choice is another type. Depending on what you want to know, you can word the question to let people choose more than one answer, or just one. It's important that you list all the possible choices. For example, "How often do you use this object—one to five times a week, six to ten times a week, eleven to fifteen times a week, more than fifteen times a week?"

Rating scales are used to discover people's preferences or attitudes toward things. One type lists several statements about a topic. People can strongly agree, agree, be neutral, disagree, or strongly disagree. For example, "Only students should be able to use this playground." Another type, called a semantic differential, uses a scale with opposite descriptors (often adjectives) on each end. For example, "This building makes me feel: calm/nervous, tired/energized." A scale is used between the words to indicate how close the person's opinion lies to one descriptor. So that you don't forget a potentially important response, be sure to include an "other" category.

Checklists give you a sense of what people want—or think they want. For example, "What things do you look for in a new television set? Check as many as apply."

INTERVIEWS

Sometimes you need to get detailed information. In this case you select specific people—experts or people connected to the problem in some way—and talk to them one-on-one. This type of *in-depth* interview is customized to the individual and can be time-consuming. Its advantage is that you spend time with a person, so you not only hear what he or she says, but can also watch for body language.

USE INTERVIEWING, TO DISCOVER:

What a user does at/with this object, site, graphic?

Why a user uses it?

What the user's perceptions are of it?

What the user thinks it should do?

How successful or unsuccessful the user thinks it is?

What the user likes or dislikes about it? Why?

How it meets or fails to meet the user's needs?

What could be done to make the user want to use it more?

What problems the user has identified?

What the user thinks can be done to solve the problems?

GENERAL GUIDELINES FOR DEVELOPING QUESTIONS

Make questions short, clear, simple, and not potentially embarrassing (keep age and income questions broad). Make questions bias-free. This means the person describes exactly what he or she means—your question doesn't sway him or her to one point of view. Bias can show up in qualifying words, like "just" or "a little." For example, "In using this park, would you rather play sports or just sit?" The word "just" implies a pro-sports bias.

Be careful not to phrase questions in a way that makes people feel "abnormal." For example, "Like most visitors to this park, do you . . ." They may hesitate to answer honestly because they don't want to appear different from others.

Try not to suggest answers if the person seems to be struggling. Allow time for thinking and responding. Watch your own body language—especially your facial expressions. Continually smiling and nodding, offering words of agreement, or saying "good" or "right" can make people feel that there is a right or wrong answer—they may want to tell you what they perceive you think is right.

INTERVIEW POINTERS

Be prepared with a written list of questions. Use a clipboard if you will be conducting interviews outside or standing up. You may want to take a tape recorder (watch out for volume and dead batteries).

Look official if you are representing an institution. Wear an identifying badge and bring information or brochures to pass out to people who might express interest in what you are doing.

Smile and look confident as you approach people. Introduce yourself, your organization, and your purpose.

Tell the respondent how long the interview will take and ask if he or she has time to participate. Don't take it personally if someone doesn't want to be interviewed. If the person declines, don't press it. Be polite and move on.

Note the general characteristics of the individual—age, sex, race, and where he or she is from.

Be assertive, considerate, and articulate. Listen carefully. It's very easy to be thinking ahead to your next question and miss what is really being said.

Be prepared with follow-up questions if that is appropriate.

When the interview is complete, don't forget to say "thank you."

Drawing

As kids we started out drawing until we learned to write like grown-ups. And, unfortunately, a lot of us stopped drawing. Those who were really good were encouraged to continue while the rest of us looked on (and continue to look on) with envy. Can you imagine the first cave dwellers holding back their need to communicate because they were afraid someone would grunt if their drawing was ugly?

Because so many people have a fear of drawing, the activities in this section are designed not to intimidate you but to illustrate how easy image making can be. You will relearn how to draw. You will learn new ways to draw. And you will learn how to make images without drawing.

If you follow these exercises and practice in your journal, your drawing will improve. You may even feel like a kid again (better get out the refrigerator magnets).

MATERIALS
- **Graph paper (at ⅛ inch)**
- **Journal or paper**
- **Marker or pen**
- **Pencil (soft lead or #2)**
- **Tape measure**

Drawing in design has two primary goals: to communicate what you see and to visualize what you don't see. Designers use drawings to stimulate their thinking (their communication with themselves) and to improve their communication with others.

THE TYPES OF DRAWINGS DESIGNERS USE MOST OFTEN:
doodles
bubble diagrams
sketches
plans
elevations
sections
axonometrics

Doodles, sketches, and bubble diagrams are easy ways to get your mind moving, get your ideas on paper, represent objects, and illustrate connections.

Plans, elevations, sections, and axonometrics are more precise methods for communicating specific details from a particular point of view—as if you were standing and looking up, down, or directly at the real object. You can measure these to provide an accurate picture of the object with no distortion.

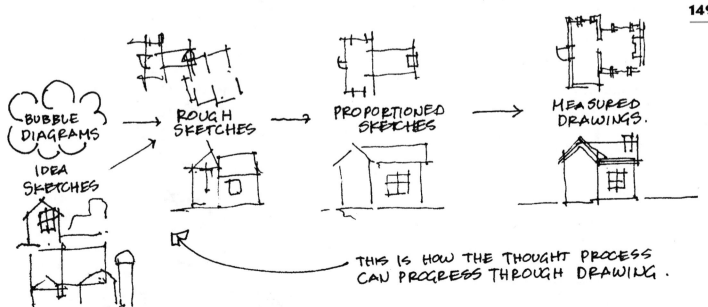

BUBBLE DIAGRAMS
IDEA SKETCHES → ROUGH SKETCHES → PROPORTIONED SKETCHES → MEASURED DRAWINGS.

THIS IS HOW THE THOUGHT PROCESS CAN PROGRESS THROUGH DRAWING.

DOODLES

Use these to get going.

It makes sense to start drawing by doing the kind of drawing you already do—when you're on the phone, listening to a boring lecture, or playing with a steamy bathroom mirror. This kind of easy-thinking drawing is actually very productive, because when you're drawing, you're thinking visually.

TRY DOODLING

Doodle a square. Draw more squares adding extra detail as you go. Repeat elements if you like. Doodle a square that is different from the others. Keep going until you've completed a sequence of 12 variations. Neatness doesn't matter, and no one cares how real your doodles look. Just watch your mind work.

Doodle something that isn't a square, something nongeometric.

Go find some doodling you've already done. Look for patterns. If you tend to doodle in certain ways, try some new ways.

BUBBLE DIAGRAMS

Use these to organize your ideas, design elements, and make visible logical connections between parts.

A bubble diagram is a set of simple blobs, each representing a part of the design. Blobs are quick and easy to draw, and easy to change and move around. The goal of a bubble diagram is to examine and test relationships between elements.

TRY BUBBLING

Add the following elements to the bubble diagram below:

| front entry | bathroom | bedroom | back entry |
| garage | garden | family room | |

The sizes and shapes of the bubbles can be used to communicate relationships and levels of importance. What are the advantages and disadvantages of the locations you've chosen?

Next, create a bubble diagram for some things that already exist. Analyze the parts of a magazine page or an automobile dashboard and bubble them in your journal.

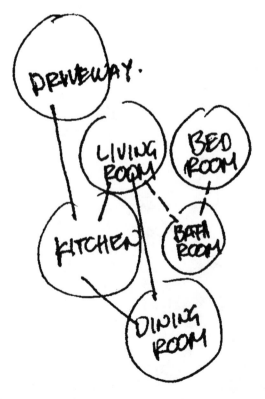

BUBBLE DIAGRAM.

SKETCHES

Use these to refine your ideas.

Of all the kinds of drawing designers do, sketches are the most common. You'll be glad to know that sketching is also the easiest to learn.

Sketching freezes ideas so you can inspect them more closely. It requires no tools other than a pen or pencil and some paper. No one cares if your lines are straight. In fact, they shouldn't be. If they are, you're being overly cautious.

Sketches should depict real things without looking exactly like them. They should have just enough detail to communicate the essence of the object you're drawing and nothing more.

TRY SKETCHING

As a warm-up—and just to prove how unimportant beauty is in sketching—sketch the following objects in your journal with the hand you don't use for writing. Spend no more than 30 seconds per object. Draw with or without looking at the actual objects.

coffee cup
pencil
bicycle
American flag
fly
tennis shoes

Now sketch each of these with your preferred hand. Notice a difference? You may find they both do an adequate job of communicating, so don't worry! Stretch yourself further to illustrate what you don't see by sketching the insides of some of these objects.

DRAWING FROM GEOMETRIC SHAPES

Almost all objects can be drawn from a combination of these shapes or parts of them.

DRAW THE FOLLOWING TWO-DIMENSIONAL SHAPES:

curve
circle
triangle
rectangle
square

Using only these shapes, draw a cup, book, sailboat, and watch.

DRAW THE FOLLOWING THREE-DIMENSIONAL SHAPES

sphere
cone
cylinder
cube

Using only these shapes, again draw a cup, book, sailboat, and watch.

ANNOTATE THE SKETCHES

To "annotate" is to add words to your sketches in order to explain or describe things that the image can't convey. For the sailboat, you might use words to explain the type of sail or how the boat moves.

LOOK AROUND YOU

See the basic geometry in the designed and natural world. From where you are sitting, sketch what you see using only the shapes you just practiced. Sketch simple objects and complicated ones. Try people. Try indoor and outdoor places. If you can understand what you've drawn, you can talk visually to yourself. If someone else "gets it," you can consider yourself a successful visual communicator.

PLANS

Use these to see what your object looks like from above.

A plan is a horizontal view from above. It can be of the exterior of your object or of a sliced section through it. A plan brings ideas closer to reality by introducing precision and scale. The best way to get precision and scale is to look at the object from a 90 degree angle. This eliminates distortion. The plan view of an apple would look like this:

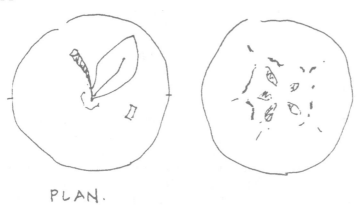

PLAN.

Now, try drawing a plan view of a pencil. Try an exterior plan view and a plan section. As with many plan views, you may have to imagine what the interior looks like.

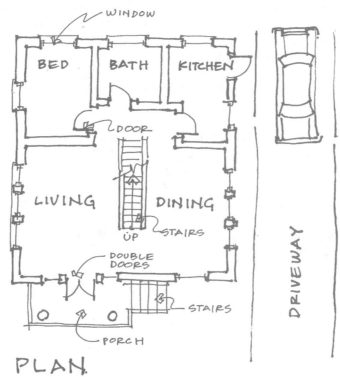

PLAN.

TRY A FLOOR PLAN

Some objects, like buildings, are too big to be drawn full size. Some, like the inner workings of a pen, are too small to be drawn full size. Functional drawings need to be scaled.

Practice making a big object small. This requires using a smaller increment. Try 1/8 inch = 1 foot to represent a larger unit of measure.

Using a piece of graph paper (at 1/8 inch), measure the walls of your bedroom and an adjacent room. Carefully translate each foot of measurement into a correlating interval on the grid. This drawing is known as a "floor plan." If your measurements do not fall exactly at 1 foot, adjust your drawing accordingly. For example, if they fall at 6 inches, just draw the line representing the wall halfway to the next grid line.

The annotated floor plan to the left illustrates how you can show windows, doors, and stairs.

ELEVATIONS

Use these to see the many faces (interior and exterior) of your object.

Your plans show the view from above. We humans tend to be more grounded in viewpoint. We like to look at things at eye level. To best see vertical surfaces, we use elevations. The elevation of the apple would look like the drawing to the left.

Draw an elevation of the exterior of your pencil.

TRY A SCALED ELEVATION

Draw an elevation of one of the walls of your room. This drawing is known as an "interior elevation." Again, use the graph paper to draw the wall at $1/8$ inch = 1 foot.

Hint: You already have the horizontal measurements drawn on your floor plan. If you can't actually measure vertical height, estimate it by comparing it with dimensions that you know, like the width and height of your window.

ELEVATION

ELEVATION

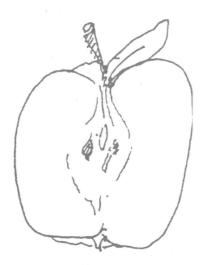

SECTION.

SECTIONS

Use these to see what a slice through the inside of your object looks like.

Designers commonly refer to the vertical slices as "sections," while the horizontal ones are simply called "plans." So, a section view of the apple would look like the image to the left.

Slice your pencil in half vertically. You can do this mentally or physically. Draw the exposed section.

TRY A SCALED SECTION

Draw a section of the inside of your room, an adjacent room, and the spaces above and below your room. If you don't know what these spaces are, "guesstimate"—make a knowledgeable guess. Use the graph paper, scaling your drawing as accurately as you can without actually measuring adjacent spaces.

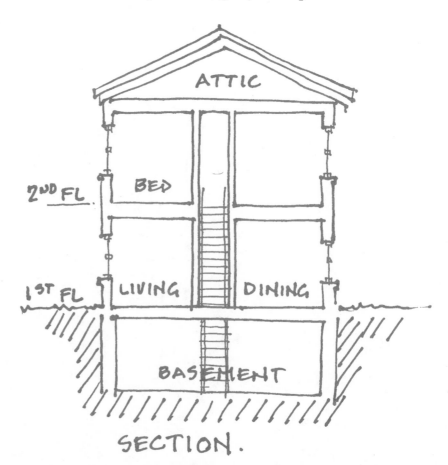

SECTION.

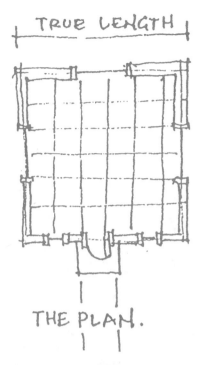

TRUE LENGTH

THE PLAN.

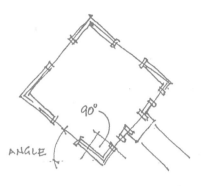

ANGLE 90°

TWISTING THE PLAN.

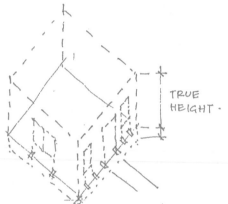

TRUE HEIGHT.

PROJECTING LINES UP /AND DOWN.

AXONOMETRICS

Use these to see more than one side of an object at the same time—that is, three dimensionally.

These drawings are created on a flat surface and imply three dimensions. They represent objects close to the way we are used to seeing them in the real world.

Axonometric drawing is an example of this type of drawing. It is a quick method, can be done relatively accurately freehand, and allows key outlines to remain at true dimension.

SOLIDIFYING DEFINITION.

TRY AN AXONOMETRIC DRAWING

This process is a lot like connect-the-dots. Draw an axonometric of your room using the floor plan you created. Follow the steps and illustrations on this page,

1. Rotate your floor plan at an angle. The typical angles used are 30/60 or 45/45 degrees.

2. Draw lines straight up from the four wall corners (at their true dimension). Some lines may be taller than others.

3. Draw the top plan of the room.

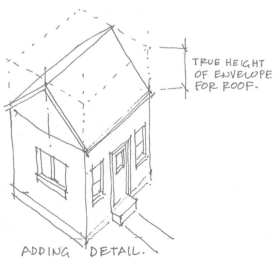

TRUE HEIGHT OF ENVELOPE FOR ROOF.

ADDING DETAIL.

DRAWING TOOLS

Technical drawings help people envision things precisely. Drafting tools make it easier to draw precisely. The activities throughout this book have been designed to be performed without these tools to simplify and demystify the drawing process. But you may find the following helpful in achieving a higher level of precision and understanding.

Straightedges and T-squares

These tools allow you to draw a consistent, horizontal line. With these instruments, your lines can be parallel.

Triangles

These tools (30/60, 45 and adjustable), used with a straightedge, allow you to draw perpendicular or diagonal lines.

Scales

These tools are like rulers with several sides. Each side has a different scale ($^1/_8$ inch = 1 foot, $^1/_4$ inch = 1 foot, etc.) that enables you to quickly and easily draw an object proportionally smaller.

PENCILS ARE NICE FOR SKETCHING. THE RANGE OF LINES IS GREAT.

PENS ARE GOOD FOR SKETCHING ALSO. THE LINES ARE CRISPER.

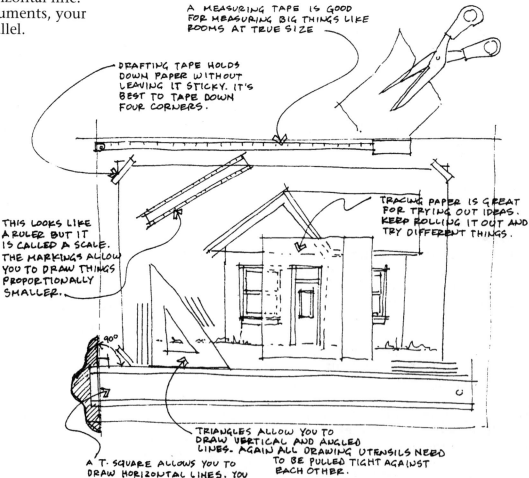

A MEASURING TAPE IS GOOD FOR MEASURING BIG THINGS LIKE ROOMS AT TRUE SIZE

DRAFTING TAPE HOLDS DOWN PAPER WITHOUT LEAVING IT STICKY. IT'S BEST TO TAPE DOWN FOUR CORNERS.

THIS LOOKS LIKE A RULER BUT IT IS CALLED A SCALE. THE MARKINGS ALLOW YOU TO DRAW THINGS PROPORTIONALLY SMALLER.

TRACING PAPER IS GREAT FOR TRYING OUT IDEAS. KEEP ROLLING IT OUT AND TRY DIFFERENT THINGS.

90°

TRIANGLES ALLOW YOU TO DRAW VERTICAL AND ANGLED LINES. AGAIN ALL DRAWING UTENSILS NEED TO BE PULLED TIGHT AGAINST EACH OTHER.

A T-SQUARE ALLOWS YOU TO DRAW HORIZONTAL LINES. YOU HAVE TO PULL IT TIGHT AGAINST YOUR BOARD

Model making

Models take concepts a step closer to reality. Models are used to make small and full-scale prototypes of objects you design. Some people like to draw their ideas and then make a model to check assumptions developed in their drawings. Some people prefer to create models straight from their heads in order to play with different ideas. In this book's activities you will have the chance to make a variety of models. The two basic kinds are study and presentation.

STUDY MODELS

These can be rough constructions, put together quickly. They are meant to be torn apart and added to, helping you to visualize objects and test them. You can think of these as three-dimensional sketches. They can also be made to exact structural tolerances to check how well the structure withstands forces. Airplanes, for instance, are often built with the final materials and shape in miniature model form to test aerodynamic quality in wind tunnels.

If you're making the model to study its exterior, try using clay. Clay models allow you to change form and components quickly.

PRESENTATION MODELS

Presentation models or presentation mock-ups, although often not full-size, are built to look like the final project. They include enough detail to suggest what the structure will look like.

Like the objects they are representing, models need to stand up to certain conditions. How well they are put together usually determines how long they last.

SELECTING MODEL-MAKING MATERIALS

In certain situations some materials work better than others: *heavy paper* (like poster board) is good for small models; *foam core*, which is expensive, is good for medium-size models; and *corrugated cardboard*, which is inexpensive, is good for making things full-size. It is also used for the bases of models, and structural elements on small models.

HOW TO FOLD STIFF MATERIALS

The best way to get crisp folds or create cylinders out of rigid things like cardboard and foam core is to "score" them. All you need is a

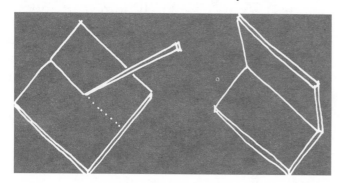

blunt, pointed object, like a dead ballpoint pen, a butter knife, or the dull side of a scissors, and a straight edge or ruler.

Simply line up the ruler where you want the fold and gently but firmly drag the point along the edge. Be careful not to rip the material. Your goal is to dent the material about halfway through. Then you can fold it. To create a cylinder you'll need to make multiple, parallel scores, and bend each until you get the right shape.

HOW TO JOIN THINGS TOGETHER

The principles for joining models are similar to those for larger objects. The paper and other materials you select need to be rigid enough to stand on their own and have enough surface area to allow for adequate adhesion. Always consider how visible the joints will be, especially in presentation models.

ADHESION

To glue materials together, you need to provide enough surface for the glue to hold onto. Then you can tape the model with easily removable masking tape until it sets—usually in about two minutes. There is an art to adhesion. Think about which of the techniques below best fits your task.

Edge gluing: Use when you want a very clean joint on paper. This requires the most care. Run a thin bead of glue along one edge of the piece to be joined.

GLUE AT EDGE

Tab gluing: Use for gluing a large surface area when you don't require as much precision. Think ahead to determine which pieces will need tabs.

APPLY GLUE AT FOLDED TAB AND PRESS TOGETHER.

Flap gluing: This is the easiest method, but it isn't very neat. It's easy because you don't have to plan the location of flaps ahead of time, and you don't have to be very precise.

APPLY GLUE TO INSIDE OF FLAP AND PRESS SIDES INTO CORNER OF FLAP

PINNING AND TAPING

Pinning and taping are good when you need something quick and temporary. In fact, you may need to tape a model while the glue sets. It is not the best method if you are going to be moving the model often. Use pins only with thick, easily pierced materials like foam core.

MODELS OF SURFACES AND ENVIRONMENTS

You can buy ready-made materials for models, like printed paper or contact paper. Scale buildings and other features can be purchased from model railroad stores or toy and craft stores. Or you can use the ideas below.

WATER

Use mirrors or ripple glass to indicate water. Glossy paint varnish works well on a surface because it shines. Paint it over a blue surface to look like water. Snow can be made using spackling compound found in hardware stores. It can be built up in layers to represent big drifts.

PLANTS, BUSHES, AND TREES

For trees, start with thin but sturdy twigs. Leave them bare (for winter) or take some steel wool—the kind used for cleaning pots and pans—and form it around the twig to represent leaves. Use glue or wire to attach it to the twig. For bushes, simply pull a piece of the steel wool into the shape you want. Spray paint it to appropriate seasonal colors.

ROCKS AND HILLS

Clay or putty works well to indicate small rocks. Pinch off small pieces and roll them into balls in the palms of your

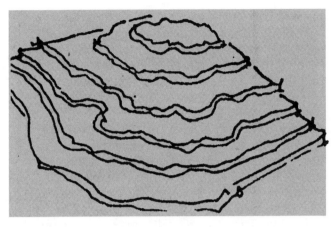

hands. Then shape them into irregular forms, as you see in nature. Larger rocks can be cut from Styrofoam and painted. Hills can be formed by adding layers of cardboard or foam core in gradually decreasing sizes. A quick-drying plaster can even the sloping surfaces and then be painted.

ROADS

Use paint to indicate asphalt or brick paths. To suggest texture, apply paint over very fine sandpaper and then mount on a board. To simulate concrete, sprinkle fine sand over white glue painted on the road.

Creating collages

You can often communicate an idea visually without doing any drawing. Using images found in other drawings, photographs, magazine clippings, or scraps of packaging, and combining them in new ways can be both fun and visually intriguing.

Illustrations on pages 8 and 25 in this book were made in the collage style. Collage combines images from many different sources into one cohesive visual idea. Unlike most forms of drawing, collage often has strange but acceptable relationships between the parts. We accept these odd mixtures because we're not expecting realism.

Look through this book and in magazines for more examples of this alternative form of drawing. Notice how not all of the parts are the same size and that usually one or two look more important. The others seem to support these main images. Notice also the variety of colors, shapes, and textures. Do they blend or do they contrast with each other? Paying attention to these techniques helps distinguish the parts and gives the illustrations their unique character.

START A COLLECTION

One of the frustrating things about collaging is that sometimes you have all the parts but the one you really need. You then spend too much time tracking it down. To avoid this (it's still going to happen sometimes), start collecting images now, even before you need them. Every time you see something that's interesting, cut it out, take a picture of it, or photocopy it. Then file it someplace where you can find it when you need it. Many designers have file cabinets filled with stuff they haven't used but know they're going to. This collecting, by the way, is a great visual exercise—it builds brain muscles that you probably didn't know you had.

NOW TRY COLLAGING

Choose one or all of the following themes:
How you feel about drawing
How television influences culture
How a cyclist feels getting around in city traffic
How nature exists in the built environment

MATERIALS
- Glue
- Images found in drawings, photographs, magazine clippings, or scraps of packaging
- Journal

Cut out as many sample parts for each theme as you can find. Choose your collage parts carefully. Look to see how the pieces you are using carry the meaning from their original message. This can either distract from or enhance your basic idea.

Build the illustrations in your journal by starting with the most significant elements. Use differences in size to indicate what is most important. You may need to reduce or enlarge your originals on a photocopier.

Resist the temptation to load the compositions with too many parts. When you're done, compare them to the collages in this book and in magazines.

YAkiTty
YakITty
Yak

Photographing & videotaping

PHOTOGRAPHS

One key ingredient found in all photographs is light. You can find it many places, but one of the best sources is overhead: the sun. Without light you can't make photos. Without an understanding or appreciation of the qualities of light you can't make "good" photos.

Before you take any photograph, always ask yourself how the light is going to affect the photo. Is it the right time of day? Would a time closer to sunrise or sunset give you better, more dramatic light and shadow? Is there enough light? Is there too much light? Is the light in the eyes of your subjects? Will a glare cover up important details?

Another technical concern, one you may be able to manipulate depending on your camera, is something called "depth of field" or the amount of information that's in focus. Sometimes you want everything in focus. Sometimes you don't. Having everything but your subject slightly out of focus helps the viewer focus on your subject.

VIDEOS

The same principles that apply to photography also work in video. But there are three new issues to think about—sound, movement, and sequencing.

SAY WHAT?

Home video cameras, which you most likely will use, can not produce the same quality audio recording you find on music videos. If you understand what they can do and what they can't, you're less likely to be disappointed with the results. One thing these cameras do well is to record talking up close, which makes them useful for narration.

SLOW DOWN, PLEASE

Videos are excellent ways for showing movement through space. They work well for documenting how people negotiate their way through buildings and for showing the entirety of an environment. Consider how you use the camera to get your viewers where you want them. Moving the camera too slowly may put your audience to sleep. Moving the camera too fast will blur important details and possibly make viewers sick.

HOW DID YOU GET THERE SO QUICKLY?

Without the use of an expensive editing machine it will be difficult to make fluid shifts from one "scene" to the next. So plan ahead of time and storyboard your parts so they fit together logically. A storyboard is a visual outline of your story. It is a sequence of small, TV monitor-shaped images representing each significant visual point you plan to make. It includes important camera angles and changes (like wide shot or close-up).

NOW PRACTICE COMPOSING PHOTOS

Open up most family photo albums, and you'll see the same thing. It's called a "snapshot." The subject of the picture is right smack in the center. Most of us take pictures this way without even thinking. But if you look closely at

DAK 5046 LPP   9   KO

8A

9

the work of photojournalists and famous portrait photographers, you'll notice more attention to the arrangement of their subjects.

A good photo can make you feel a certain way simply by how it is organized. We call this organization "composition." As in English essays or songs, structure can greatly affect the ability to communicate in a photograph. In this activity you'll practice composing photographs so that next time you'll think before you snap.

MATERIALS
- **Full body image of a person from a magazine**
- **Paper (8½ x 11 inches)**
- **Photocopier**
- **X-acto knife or scissors**

CUT OUT THE PARTS
Create at least three different-sized versions of your magazine image. Cut each out carefully so that no paper remains around the edges. Then take a blank sheet of white paper and cut out a 3 x 5–inch rectangle from its center.

COMPOSE AN IDEA
Communicate each of the feelings listed below by placing one of your images inside the frame. Consider carefully the relationship of the image to the frame. Try a few layouts for each.

funny	scared	wild
sad	tall	bored
confident	short	

EVALUATE
Trace or photocopy your best composition for each. Give them to other people, along with the list of feelings, to see if they can match all eight.

KEEP YOUR EYES PEELED
Continue looking at the work of professional photographers to see how composition can be used to evoke an emotional response. Feature stories in newspapers and magazines are good places to look. Sketch or include samples of the most successful photographs in your journal. Next to the images, write why you think they communicate so well.

Organizing visual information

When you talk to someone, you think about what you want to say and why, and you organize your words appropriately. If you're asking for a raise, you don't begin by saying "Give me more money." You know that you have to ease into that kind of request. If you're ordering fast food at a drive-through restaurant and there's a line of cars behind you, you probably wouldn't choose that moment to ask the manager all the ingredients in the secret sauce.

You know that you can add emphasis by talking louder. To get someone's attention you can scream if you have to. Or you can lower your voice to let your listeners know that the message is just for them. You can use a special word that, by its unique sound, makes people notice. Or to get your audience to listen and feel comfortable, you can tell a joke. The same is true for visual communication. You have to decide the appropriate time and place to deliver your message. By treating the parts of your message differently, you can control how the message is perceived. Look at the example below. Would you have chosen to emphasize the same words?

NOW PRACTICE ORGANIZING A MESSAGE
Creating a poster for a lost pet, is a need we hope you'll never have—but, if you do, wouldn't you want the poster to be effective?

MATERIALS
- Colored pens/markers
- Image of pet
- Paper (8½ x 11 inches)
- Type from newspapers or magazines
- Typewriter or computer

"HERE KITTY, KITTY, KITTY (PAUSE) HERE KITTY, KITTY, KITTY"
You're actually going to design two posters—one that you think will work well and one that you think won't. Each poster will say the same thing but not in the same way. Use different typefaces, scale, and placement, but don't add or delete any words. Each poster needs to include the name of pet (answers to the name of . . .), image of pet, owner's name, owner's phone number, reason pet is so special, physical description, and where pet was last seen.

THE RIGHT WAY, THE WRONG WAY
Now design an effective poster. Look back at the language examples at the beginning of this page. What could you do visually that would be similar?

Make the ineffective poster *really* ineffective. Consider what would be the least important information and design the poster so that the audience reads that first. (That doesn't necessarily mean that the first thing read is at the top of the page.)

NOW TRY THIS
Study several pages in this book. How was hierarchy (relative importance) communicated? Consider typeface choices, scale, color, and placement? Can you see the underlying framework (grid) of each page?

GLOSSARY

AMERICANS WITH DISABILITIES ACT

ORGANIZATIONS TO CONTACT

Resources

BIBLIOGRAPHY

ESPECIALLY (BUT NOT ONLY) FOR EDUCATORS

EDUCATORS' INDEX

Glossary

AESTHETIC—relating to the qualities of people, places, ideas, or things considered beautiful.

ANTHROPOMETRICS—the study of the size of the human body in relation to the objects it uses.

ARCHITECT—one trained in the art and science of conceptualizing, planning, communicating, and coordinating the building of structures.

ARCHITECTURE—the buildings and enclosed spaces in which people live, work, and play.

ASYMMETRICAL—not equally balanced; off center.

AXONOMETRIC—a three-dimensional drawing of objects.

BIODIVERSITY—the large variety and number of life forms, environmental systems, and habitats that coexist.

BUBBLE DIAGRAM—a visual means of showing and testing relationships among elements in a design.

BUILT ENVIRONMENT—the designed and assembled structures, graphics, and products that together create the places in which people live, work, and play.

COLLAGE—a combination of images taken from many sources to form one visual idea.

COMPRESSION—the state of being pressed down under a weight.

CRITIQUE—a form of careful questioning and judicious evaluation of something (a design) in order to improve it.

CULTURE—a tool humans use for coping with the natural environment and with people from their own and other groups; a system of beliefs, attitudes, habits, and customs; a system of social organizations, language and speech patterns, material possessions, tools, and industrial skills.

DESIGN—the area of human experience, skill, and knowledge that reflects concern with changing and appreciating surroundings in light of specific material and spiritual needs (adapted from definition by Bruce Archer). A simpler definition is: getting from the existing to the preferred.

DESIGN BRIEF—a written record of the parts of a design problem, including the need, the person or group in need (the client), and the situations affecting the need.

DESIGN PROCESS—the steps in imagining, planning, and communicating a solution to a problem. This can also include the act of producing or implementing the solution.

DETAILED DRAWINGS—drawings that show the specific physical characteristics of a design.

DIMENSIONS—the length, width, and height of rooms or objects.

ELEVATION—a drawing of a single vertical surface of an object or building.

ERGONOMIC—designs that take into account both the functioning of the human body and the newest engineering techniques in order to create a product suited to human use.

FABRICATION—construction or manufacture of a design.

GRAPHIC DESIGNER—one who specializes in conceptualizing, planning, and creating visual communications using images and type. These include posters, magazines, packaging, and signs.

HABITAT—an environment suited to the survival needs of an animal or plant.

HIERARCHY—a ranked series based on relative importance.

PATTERN—a series of repeated elements.

PLAN VIEW—a straight-down view of an object or structure. This view can also be of a horizontal slice through the middle.

PERCEPTION—awareness of the elements of the environment through physical senses.

PERFORMANCE CRITERIA—a list of the things a design solution must do to be considered successful.

PRODUCT DESIGNER (also known as an industrial designer)— one who specializes in conceptualizing, planning, and communicating the creation of objects such as products, instruments, equipment, furniture, transportation, and packaging.

PROPORTIONS—the relationship of size, width, length, height, and volume in a design.

PROTOTYPE—an exact model of a designed object.

SCALE—the relationship between the sizes of two items.

SECTION—a view of a slice through an object or structure. Usually refers to vertical slice.

SKETCH—a quick, simple drawing of a real object which offers just enough detail to communicate its essence.

SOCIETY—people who identify themselves as a group and share a distinct culture.

STRUCTURAL MEMBER—one of the supporting pieces of a structure.

STRUCTURE—anything built or constructed.

STYLE—the grouping or classification of similar designs.

SURVEY—to gather data in order to analyze an aspect of a given item.

SUSTAINABLE DESIGN—a design that, in its conception, planning, and production takes into account its long-term impact on society, the environment, and the economy; and addresses such issues as energy conservation, human health and safety, waste production, and alternative uses.

SYMBOL—anything used to represent or stand for something else.

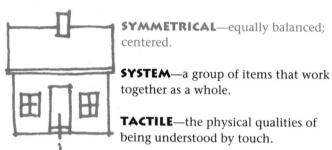

SYMMETRICAL—equally balanced; centered.

SYSTEM—a group of items that work together as a whole.

TACTILE—the physical qualities of being understood by touch.

TECHNOLOGY—the knowledge, processes, and tools with which people manipulate their environment. This can range from a ballpoint pen, to agriculture, to brick laying.

TENSION—the stretching or straining of a building component when a load is applied.

URBAN PLANNER—one trained in the art and science of conceptualizing, planning, communicating, and coordinating the creation of plans and policies for land use in such geographic areas as towns or cities.

VALUE—the worth or importance of one thing relative to another.

ZONING—a classification system used to divide a community's land into different uses, like residential or industrial.

Americans with Disabilities Act

The ADA, a law passed in 1990, makes it illegal to discriminate against anyone who has a mental or physical impairment that substantially limits one or more major life activities. It applies to areas of employment, public services, transportation, public accommodations, and telecommunications.

WHAT IMPACT DOES THE ADA HAVE ON DESIGN?

The ADA has an impact upon design in many ways. For example, in order to comply with the law, a business or institution must ". . . remove architectural barriers and communication barriers that are structural in nature, in existing facilities, where such removal is readily achievable." Meeting this requirement may mean providing a ramp instead of stairs and making curb cuts on sidewalk corners for people who use crutches, braces, walkers, or wheelchairs; or providing large-print publications for persons with visual impairments.

The effect of this law has been to generate designs that work for people with special needs, as well as for everyone else. For example, the ramps and curb cuts on sidewalks accommodate the person using a wheelchair, as well as a mother pushing a stroller, a person riding a bicycle, a shopper with a cart of groceries, and many other users. Similarly, large print makes reading easier for everyone, not just people with visual impairments. Design that benefits everyone is called *universal design*.

Organizations to contact

Design

AMERICAN CENTER FOR DESIGN
233 E. Ontario Street, Suite 500
Chicago, IL 60611
Phone
312-787-2018
FAX
312-649-9518

This membership-based organization is made up of design professionals, educators, and students. In addition to promoting excellence in design education and practice, it serves as a national center for the accumulation and dissemination of information regarding design and its role in our culture and economy. The American Center for Design is a primary link between professionals in all design disciplines and the research, ideas, and technologies that are reshaping design practice. It provides information services related to emerging trends, education, professional practice, methodology, tools, strategic design, history, criticism, and theory.

AMERICAN DESIGN COUNCIL
107 South Street, Suite 502
Boston, MA 02111
Phone
617-338-7210
FAX
617-338-6570

As a coalition of the nation's leading design organizations, the ADC promotes cooperation among the executive leadership of the design disciplines to encourage public discussion of design issues; to strengthen the relationship between design and improved quality of life; and to foster design excellence as an effective instrument of social, environmental, and economic policy. The following groups belong to ADC: American Architectural Foundation, American Center for Design, American Institute of Architects, American Institute of Graphic Arts, American Society of Interior Designers, American Society of Landscape Architects, Association of Professional Design Firms, Design Management Institute, Industrial Designers Society of America, Institute of Business Designers, International Interior Design Association, National Endowment for the Arts, Organization of Black Designers, Package Design Council, and Society of Environmental Graphic Designers.

AMERICAN INSTITUTE OF ARCHITECTS
1735 New York Avenue, N.W.
Washington, DC 20006-5292
Phone
202-626-7300
FAX
202-626-7587

The goal of this professional society for architects is to enhance the profession's ability to create quality architecture and to satisfy client and public needs. AIA committees monitor issues that affect architectural practice and advise Congress on land use, environmental safeguards, affordable housing, urban development, and other built and natural environment topics. AIA's programs include the Regional/Urban Design Assistance Teams, which work with communities to help them address issues of change in decaying urban areas, and the Search for Shelter program, which assists local groups to address the needs of the homeless in their communities. AIA underwrites public television programs about design and publishes both technical and popular books through its own publishing house, AIA Press. It also offers educational programs for young people through the nation's schools. The research and reference collections in the AIA's library, along with the Rare Books and Archives collection, form the largest compilation of material on the profession of architecture in America. AIA Online offers an array of services including information on marketing and construction, the AIA membership roster, and job referral.

AIGA

AMERICAN INSTITUTE OF GRAPHIC ARTS
164 Fifth Avenue
New York, NY
10010
Phone
212-807-1990
FAX
212-807-1799

AIGA advances the graphic design profession through competitions, exhibitions, publications, professional seminars, educational activities, and projects in the public interest. AIGA chapters enable designers to represent their profession collectively on the local level. The AIGA national conference covers topics including professional practice, education, technology, the creative process, and design history.

AMERICAN PLANNING ASSOCIATION
1776
Massachusetts
Avenue, N.W.
Washington, DC
20036
Phone
202-872-0611
FAX
202-872-0643

This national organization is comprised of professional planners and private citizens working together for better planned communities. APA offers current information on planning issues, practice, and techniques, and is an advocate of planning in national, state, and local forums. Through its chapters and divisions, APA gives members systematic ways to work on problems they have in common and to affect national planning policies. Of particular concern is the translation of responsible environmental policy into practical land-use regulations or other local and regional planning tools. The American Institute of Certified Planners, the professional institute of APA, provides the only national certification of planners. APA members become AICP members through combined qualifications of experience, and training, and by passing a written examination. The AICP's Planners' Training Service gives in-depth training on specific topics through a variety of nationwide workshops. APA also provides educational materials for secondary school educators.

AMERICAN SOCIETY OF INTERIOR DESIGNERS
608
Massachusetts
Avenue, N.E.
Washington, DC
20002-6006
Phone
202-546-3480
FAX
202-546-3240

The society is membership-based and the official source of information on all matters regarding the interior design profession and its practice. ASID encourages excellence in the practice of interior design by assisting its members to professionally serve the public. ASID publishes brochures about the latest developments in interior design that demonstrate to the public the value of the profession. Their Student Charter Membership program allows students to meet professionals in the field, compete in professional design award programs, and participate in career development conferences. As a constituent of the National Council for Interior Design Qualification, every interior designer applying for professional membership in the ASID must first pass the NCIDQ licensing examination.

AMERICAN SOCIETY OF LANDSCAPE ARCHITECTS
4401 Connecticut
Avenue, N.W.,
5th Floor
Washington, DC
20008-2302
Phone
202-686-ASLA
FAX
202-686-1001

This national professional society represents private, public, and academic practitioners of the landscape architecture field in 46 chapters across the United States. The organization provides educational opportunities, information regarding legislation, and professional citizenship to its members, as well as continued commitment to professional standards. The ASLA Information Resource Center provides a central source of information to its members and includes books, journals, and statistical data. DESIGNETWORK is a 24-hour, on-line service that provides members with advanced information for the design professions, including electronic mail, seminars, and publications.

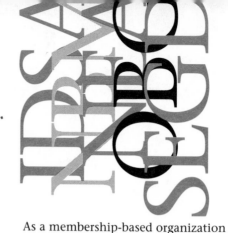

BARRIER FREE ENVIRONMENTS, INC.
P.O. Box 30634
Raleigh, NC 27622
Phone
919-782-7823
FAX
919-787-1984

BFE is a design firm that specializes in design issues that confront the disabled and older people. BFE's work includes architectural and product consultation and design. It embodies the concept of universal design in which all elements and features are usable by all people to the greatest extent possible. Over the years, BFE has developed several design manuals in an attempt to share their more successful work. These manuals illustrate and provide details of the many features that improve access for people with disabilities.

COOPER-HEWITT, NATIONAL DESIGN MUSEUM
Smithsonian Institution
2 E. 91st Street
New York, NY 10028-9990
Phone
212-860-6871
FAX
212-860-6909

Cooper-Hewitt is the only museum in the United States devoted exclusively to historical and contemporary graphic, architectural, and industrial design. It preserves, documents, and expands an international collection approaching 250,000 works in such fields as drawings and prints, rare books, textiles, wall coverings, furniture, ceramics, glass, metalwork, and jewelry. The museum's library contains more than 50,000 volumes, a picture library of over 1,000,000 images, and a growing archive of twentieth-century designers' work. The museum also provides professional development and museum training, through a graduate program with Parsons School of Design, offering research fellowships and internships in the history of decorative arts. The museum provides educational programs for children and adults, including lectures, seminars, workshops, tours, family events, and gallery talks, and creates interpretive materials and activities for schools, teachers, and museum visitors.

GRAPHIC ARTISTS GUILD FOUNDATION
11 W. 20th Street, 8th Floor
New York, NY 10011
Phone
212-463-7730
FAX
212-463-8779

As a membership-based organization the guild works to assure that all graphic artists are treated fairly and rewarded appropriately in business. The guild lobbies in Washington, D.C., on behalf of graphic artists and serves as a watchdog over copyright infringement. It also serves as counsel and protector in negotiation and payment disputes. The guild distributes to its members news on industry issues that directly affect their taxes and income. To affirm the value of artists working together to improve standards of pay and working conditions, the guild advocates the highest standards of ethical conduct in the marketplace.

INDUSTRIAL DESIGNERS SOCIETY OF AMERICA
1142 E. Walker Road
Great Falls, VA 22066
Phone
703-759-0100
FAX
703-759-7679

The society is a national nonprofit organization for professionals who design products, instruments, equipment, furniture, transportation, toys, exhibits, packaging, and environments. IDSA's major goals are to promote the development of innovative and responsible products and systems, to create and make available a body of professional literature, to recognize outstanding industrial design achievement, to foster high standards of professional integrity, and to assist in the development of quality educational programs in industrial design.

The Great Hall of
the National
Building Museum

NATIONAL BUILDING MUSEUM
401 F Street, N.W.
Washington, DC
20001
Phone
(202) 272-2448
FAX
(202) 272-2564

The National Building Museum is a private, nonprofit institution created by Congress in 1980. Its mission is to examine and interpret the many aspects of building in America so that people, by learning about the past and present, can make informed and enlightened choices in determining the built environment of the future. The museum provides educational programs for children and adults, including lectures, seminars, workshops, tours, family events, and gallery talks, as well as programs and materials for teachers and students. Among the museum's publications are *Blueprints* (a quarterly journal featuring articles about all aspects of the built environment), *Washington: Symbol and City* (an educator's guide used to prepare students for a visit to the nation's capital, or to compare Washington planning and design issues with those in their home towns), and this book, *Why Design?* The museum also collects artifacts, records, drawings, photographs, and documents relating to all aspects of building.

NATIONAL ENDOWMENT FOR THE ARTS DESIGN PROGRAM
1100 Pennsylvania Avenue, N.W., Room 627
Washington, DC 20506
Phone
202-682-5437
FAX
202-682-2564

This federal agency, by funding a variety of design-related projects, supports work of exceptional merit that will advance the design arts and benefit the public. The program also attempts to strengthen the institutional fabric of the design field by forging active partnerships with existing programs and organizations to advance the quality of design. It promotes excellence in the disciplines of architecture, landscape architecture, urban design and planning, historic preservation, interior design, industrial and product design, graphic design, and costume and fashion design.

ORGANIZATION OF BLACK DESIGNERS
717 D Street, N.W., Suite 500
Washington, DC 20004
Phone
202-659-3918
FAX
202-347-5829

OBD promotes a greater awareness of the presence or the lack of presence of African Americans within the design professions. It also seeks to motivate more blacks to pursue careers in design, to draw attention to the achievements of black designers, to provide information about opportunities and markets for black designers, and to serve as a forum regarding those opportunities. The organization includes architects, interior, graphic, automotive, industrial, and fashion designers.

WHY DESIGN? Activities and Projects from the National Building Museum

171

Disability

SOCIETY OF ENVIRON-MENTAL GRAPHIC DESIGNERS
One Story Street
Cambridge, MA 02138
Phone
617-868-3381
FAX
617-868-3591

A professional organization, the society seeks to increase public awareness of the discipline of design and promote high standards of professional conduct within the field. Projects range from signs, exhibit design, and large scale sign systems, to public art programs. Members are drawn from the fields of graphic design, architecture, interior design, industrial design, landscape architecture, research, education, and manufacturing. The Education Foundation, established in 1987, addresses the lack of formalized training in environmental graphic design through an Annual Student Grant Program and is developing an environmental graphics education program for design schools and universities. It has created nationally recognized safety and recreation symbols.

U.S. ARCHITECT-URAL AND TRANSPOR-TATIONAL BARRIERS COMPLIANCE BOARD (ACCESS BOARD)
1331 F Street, N.W., Suite 100
Washington, DC 20004-1111
Phone
800-USA-ABLE [872-2253] for technical assistance
Phone
202-272-5434
FAX
202-272-5447
TTD
202-272-5449

An independent federal agency, the Access Board was created in 1973 to enforce requirements for access to federally funded buildings and facilities under the Architectural Barriers Act of 1968. The agency also sets guidelines under the Americans with Disabilities Act of 1990 and provides technical assistance and information on removal of architectural, transportation, communication, and attitudinal barriers affecting persons with disabilities. The Access Board also conducts research in a variety of areas including ramp slope and landings, space and reach range requirements for persons using power wheelchairs and three-wheeled scooters, interior circulation in transportation vehicles, and public information for persons with cognitive disabilities.

AMERICAN FOUNDATION FOR THE BLIND
11 Penn Plaza, Suite 300
New York, NY 10001
Phone
212-502-7661
FAX
212-502-7771

A nonprofit organization founded in 1921 and recognized as Helen Keller's cause in the United States, the American Foundation for the Blind (AFB) is a national resource for people who are blind or visually impaired, the organizations that serve them, and the general public. AFB's mission is to enable people who are blind or visually impaired to achieve equality of access and opportunity that will ensure freedom of choice for the rest of their lives.

THE ARC (A NATIONAL ASSOCIATION ON MENTAL RETARDA-TION)
500 E. Border Street, Suite 300
Arlington, TX 76010
Phone
817-261-6003
FAX
817-277-3491
TDD
817-277-0553

"The Arc" is the new name of a 44-year-old organization known for many years as the Association for Retarded Citizens of the United States. It is the nation's largest volunteer organization solely devoted to improving the lives of children and adults with mental retardation, and of their families. The Arc is committed to securing people with mental retardation the opportunity to choose and realize their goals of where and how they learn, live, work, and play. The association also fosters research and education regarding the prevention of mental retardation in infants and young children.

NATIONAL EASTER SEAL SOCIETY
230 W. Monroe Street
Chicago, IL 60606
Phone
312-726-6200
TDD
312-243-8880

This national, nonprofit organization was established in 1919 to provide rehabilitative service to children affected by physical disabilities. The national organization and a network of 135 affiliates across the United States provide services and support to over a million adults and children who have physical and cognitive impairments. The national organization is a leader in advocating for the inclusion of people of all abilities in all aspects of our society, including the built and natural environment, the work place, and the family home.

Historic Preservation

NATIONAL INFORMATION CENTER ON DEAFNESS
Gallaudet University
800 Florida Avenue, N.E.
Washington, DC 20002-3695
Phone 202-651-5051
FAX 202-651-5054
TDD 202-651-5052

The National Information Center on Deafness (NICD) is a centralized resource of accurate and up-to-date information on all aspects of hearing loss and deafness. Located at Gallaudet University, the world's only liberal arts university for deaf students, NICD has access to experts knowledgeable in the field of deafness and to other resources not available anywhere else in the world.

NATIONAL REHABIL-ITATION INFORMATION CENTER (NARIC)
8455 Colesville Road, Suite 935
Silver Spring, MD 20910-319
Phone 800-346-2742
301-588-9284
FAX 310-587-1967

The NARIC is a clearinghouse for numerous publications, available on two databases, pertaining to all aspects of disabilities.

Engineering

AMERICAN ASSOCIATION OF ENGINEERING SOCIETIES
1111 19th Street, N.W., Suite 608
Washington, DC 20036-3690
Phone 202-296-2237
FAX 202-296-1151

The American Association of Engineering Societies' mission is to advance the knowledge and practice of engineering in the public interest; and to act as an advisory, communication, and information exchange agency for member activities, especially regarding public policy issues.

HISTORIC AMERICAN BUILDING SURVEY/ HISTORIC AMERICAN ENGINEERING RECORD
National Parks Service/ Department of the Interior
P.O. Box 37127
Washington, DC 20013-7127
Phone 202-343-9618
FAX 202-343-9624

These two organizations were established to survey and document America's historically and architecturally significant buildings, industrial, engineering, and transportation resources, and the working and living conditions of the people associated with them. Recognizing that many significant technological resources cannot be saved, structures and objects are documented through measured and interpretive drawings, large-format photographs, and written data. The staff of engineers, architects, historians, illustrators, and photographers, conduct a nationwide program of documentation in cooperation with state and local governments, private industry, professional societies, universities, and preservation groups, as well as other federal agencies.

NATIONAL TRUST FOR HISTORIC PRESERVATION
1785 Massachusetts Avenue, N.W.
Washington, DC 20036
Phone 202-673-4000
FAX 202-673-4038

This nonprofit organization is responsible for encouraging public participation in the preservation of sites, buildings and objects significant in American history and culture. Regional offices act as the point of contact for preservation organizations in their regions. The National Trust identifies and acts on important related issues by initiating demonstration projects and model programs and by advocating preservation policies. Programs include the National Main Street Center, which assists towns in retaining the character of their main street while revitalizing it for changing times, and the protection of historic properties nationwide.

Environment

CONCERN, INC.
1794 Columbia Road, N.W., Washington, DC 20009
Phone 202-328-8160
FAX 202-387-3378

This nonprofit organization provides environmental information to community groups, public officials, educational institutions, private individuals, and others involved in public education and policy development. Its goal is to help communities find solutions to environmental problems that threaten public health.

KEEP AMERICA BEAUTIFUL
Mill River Plaza 9 W. Broad Street Stamford, CT 06902
Phone 203-323-8987
FAX 202-325-9199

KAB is a national, nonprofit, public education organization dedicated to improving waste-handling practices in American communities. The KAB system works to change individual attitudes and behaviors and relies on communities' support in achieving its goal—sustaining a reduction in litter as a first step towards improving local environments.

NATIONAL WILDLIFE FEDERATION
1400 16th Street, N.W. Washington, DC 20036
Phone 202-797-6800
FAX 202-797-6646

This educational organization's goal is to promote responsible and effective conservation, the wise use of natural resources, and the protection of the global environment.

NATURE CONSERVANCY
International Headquarters 1815 N. Lynn Street Arlington, VA 22209
Phone 703-842-8745
FAX 703-841-9692

The Nature Conservancy preserves plants, animals, and natural communities that represent the diversity of life on Earth by protecting the lands and waters they need to survive. The operator of the largest private system of nature sanctuaries in the world, the Conservancy owns and manages more than 1,500 preserves throughout the United States and millions of acres worldwide. The Conservancy uses nonconfrontational, market-based economic solutions to protect habitats—a "win–win" approach to conservation.

RESOURCES FOR THE FUTURE
1616 P Street, N.W. Washington, DC 20036
Phone 202-328-5000
FAX 202-939-3460

The mission of this nonprofit organization is to create and disseminate knowledge that helps people make better decisions about the conservation and use of their natural resources and the environment. They conduct research and public education on natural resources and environmental issues.

ROCKY MOUNTAIN INSTITUTE
1739 Snowmass Creek Road Old Snowmass, CO 81654
Phone 303-9273851
FAX 303-927-4178

The goal of this nonprofit research and education foundation is to foster the efficient and sustainable use of resources as a path to global security. Program areas include energy, water, agriculture, economic renewal, energy security, transportation, and green development services.

Community Service

SIERRA CLUB
730 Polk Street
San Francisco, CA 94109
Phone
415-776-2211
FAX
415-854-9405

This nonprofit organization promotes conservation of the natural environment by influencing public policy decisions. Its mission is to explore, enjoy, and protect the wild places of the earth; to promote responsible use of the earth's ecosystems and resources; and to educate and enlist humanity to protect and restore the quality of the natural and human environment.

UNION OF CONCERNED SCIENTISTS
26 Church Street
Cambridge, MA 02238
Phone
617-547-5552
FAX
617-864-9405

This organization is dedicated to advancing responsible public policies in areas where technology plays a critical role. It is a partnership between scientists and committed citizens. UCS is working to encourage responsible stewardship of the global environment and life-sustaining resources; to promote energy technologies that are renewable, safe, and cost-effective; and to reform transportation policy and curtail weapons proliferation.

AMERICA THE BEAUTIFUL FUND
219 Shoreham Building, N.W.
Washington, DC 20005
Phone
202-638-1649
HOTLINE
800-522-3557

The ABF was started in 1965 as a national, nonprofit organization and has developed more than 50,000 citizen-initiated volunteer projects to save the natural and designed environment. ABF provides support to volunteer community projects in all 50 states, operating as a clearinghouse of ideas for existing community projects and as a catalyst for new ones. Projects help preserve and revitalize local heritage, cultural and historical sites, seashores, streams, and wetlands across the country, and provide donations of surplus seeds to community gardens and hunger relief programs.

POINTS OF LIGHT FOUNDATION
1737 H Street, N.W.
Washington, DC 20006
Phone
202-223-9186
FAX
202-223-9256
TDD
202-659-9229

The Points of Light Foundation is a nonprofit, nonpartisan organization whose mission is to engage more people more effectively in volunteer community service to help solve serious social problems. The foundation develops and promotes strategies and methods to recruit and engage more volunteers in direct and consequential community service. The foundation works with a nationwide network of more than 500 Volunteer Centers to help them become key community resources.

THE STUDENT CONSERVATION ASSOCIATION, INC.
P. O. Box 550
Charlestown, NH 03603-0550
Phone
603-543-1700
FAX
603-543-1828

The Student Conservation Association uses student volunteers to accomplish critical conservation work in national parks. SCA volunteers refurbish trails, construct barrier-free trails, restore wetlands, prune trees, and use problem-solving skills in a variety of other conservation projects. The SCA features a resource assistant program, a high-school program, a conservation career development program, and a wilderness work-skills program. All programs offer hands-on opportunities to learn conservation skills.

Bibliography

The materials listed here cover the range of subjects touched on in this book. Some provide background information, some provide technical information or theory, and some provide a cultural context.

• denotes material targeted to high-school age and younger.
∞ denotes material especially for educators.

CONFLICT RESOLUTION/COMMUNICATION

Bolton, Robert. *People Skills: How to Assert Yourself, Listen to Others, and Resolve Conflicts.* New York: Simon and Schuster, 1986.

Fisher, Roger, and William L. Ury. *Getting to Yes.* Boston: Houghton Mifflin Co.,1992.

Rusk, Tom, and D. Patrick Miller. *The Power of Ethical Persuasion: Winning Through Understanding at Work and at Home.* New York: Penguin Books, 1994.

CREATIVE AND VISUAL THINKING

Adams, James L. *Conceptual Blockbusting: A Guide to Better Ideas.* 3rd ed. Reading, MA: Addison-Wesley Publishing Co., 1986.

De Bono, Edward. *Lateral Thinking: Creativity Step by Step.* New York: Harper Collins Publishers, 1973.

McKim, Robert. *Experiences in Visual Thinking.* Boston: P.W.S. Publishers, 1980.

•Von Oech, Roger. *Creative Whack Pack.* Stamford, CT: U.S. Games Systems, 1989.

DESIGN EDUCATION/ACTIVITY BOOKS

∞Adams, Eileen. *Art and the Built Environment.* London: Longman, 1982.

∞Botrill, Pauline. *Designing and Learning in the Elementary School.* Reston, VA: International Technology Education Association, 1995.

•Brownstone, Douglass L. *A Field Guide to America's History.* New York: Facts on File, 1984.

•Caney, Steven. *Steven Caney's Invention Book.* New York: Workman Publishing, 1985.

•Copeland, Rolaine, Marcy Abhau, and Greta Greenberger, eds. *Architecture in Education.* Philadelphia, PA: Foundation for Architecture, 1986.

•D'Alelio, Jane. *I Know That Building.* Washington, DC: Preservation Press, 1989.

∞Davis, Meredith, and Robin Moore. *Education Through Design: Middle School Curriculum.* Raleigh, NC: School of Design, North Carolina State University, 1994.

∞Dunn, Susan, and Rob Larson. *Design Technology: Children's Engineering.* Bristol, PA: Taylor & Francis Publishers (The Falmer Press), 1989.

∞Durbin, Gail. *A Teacher's Guide to Using Historic Houses.* London: English Heritage Education Service, 1993.

∞Durbin, Gail, Susan Morris, and Sue Wilkinson. *A Teacher's Guide to Learning From Objects.* London: English Heritage Education Service, 1990.

∞English Heritage. *Resources 1994.* London: English Heritage Education Service, 1994.

∞Eriksen, Aase, and Marjorie Wintermute. *Students, Structures, Spaces: Activities in the Built Environment.* Reading, MA: Addison-Wesley Publishing Co., 1983.

•Glenn, Patricia Brown. *Under Every Roof: A Kid's Style and Field Guide to the Architecture of American Houses.* Washington, DC: Preservation Press, 1993.

∞Graves, Ginny. *Walk Around the Block.* Prairie Village, KS: Center for Understanding the Built Environment, 1992.

∞•Hubel, Vello, and Diedra Lussow. *Focus on Designing.* New York: McGraw-Hill, 1984.

•Isaacson, Philip M. *Round Buildings, Square Buildings & Buildings That Wiggle Like Fish.* New York: Alfred A. Knopf, 1994.

∞•Kimbell, Richard, et al. *Craft, Design, and Technology.* London: Thames/Hutchinson, 1987.

•Lewis, Barbara A. *A Kid's Guide to Social Action.* Minneapolis, MN: Free Spirit Publishing, 1991.

∞McCrory, David, and Karen Todd. *Understanding and Using Technology.* Worcester, MA: Davis Publications, 1985.

∞Nelson, Doreen. *Transformations. Process and Theory: A Curriculum Guide to Creative Development.* Santa Monica, CA: The Center for City Building Education, 1982.

∞Olsen, Gary, and Michelle Olsen. *Archi-Teacher: A Guide to Architecture in the Schools.* Champaign, IL: Educational Concepts Group, 1985.

Pollard, Jeanne. *Building Toothpick Bridges.* Palo Alto, CA: Dale Seymour Publications, 1988.

∞Salvadori, Mario. *Architecture and Engineering: An Illustrated Teacher's Manual on Why Buildings Stand Up.* New York: New York Academy of Sciences, 1993.

•Salvadori, Mario. *The Art of Construction.* Chicago: Chicago Review Press, 1990.

∞Sandler, Alan, ed., *The Sourcebook II: Learning by Design.* Washington, DC: The American Institute of Architects Press, 1988.

∞•Shadrin, Richard. *Design and Drawing: An Applied Approach.* Worcester, MA: Davis Publications, 1995.

∞•Stoops, Jack, and Jerry Samuelson. *Design Dialogue.* Worcester, MA: Davis Publications, 1995.

∞Sutton, Sharon. *The Urban Network Instructional Portfolio: An Urban Design Program for Elementary Schools.* Ann Arbor, MI: University of Michigan.

∞Taylor, Anne. *Architecture and Children: Learning by Design, Teachers Guide and Poster Sets.* Albuquerque, NM: American Institute of Architects, 1991.

∞Tickle, Les. *Craft, Design and Technology in Primary School Classrooms.* Bristol, PA: Taylor & Francis Publishers (Falmer Press), 1990.

∞Urban Land Institute. *Dilemmas of Development* (1990) and *Urban Plan* (1991). Available at the Planners Bookstore, Chicago.

•Weitzman, David. *Windmills, Bridges, and Old Machines: Discovering Our Industrial Past.* New York: Charles Scribner's Sons, 1982.

•Wilson, Forrest. *What It Feels Like to Be a Building.* Washington, DC: Preservation Press, 1988.

∞Winters, Nathan. *Architecture Is Elementary: Visual Thinking Through Architectural Concepts.* Salt Lake City, UT: Gibb Smith Publishers, 1986.

DESIGN/DESIGN HISTORY/ENGINEERING

The American Institute of Architects Committee on the Environment. *The Environmental Resource Guide.* Washington, DC: American Institute of Architects.

The American Institute of Architects Committee on the Environment. *Healthy, Productive Buildings: A Guide to Environmentally Sustainable Architecture.* Washington, DC: American Institute of Architects.

•Bender, Lionel. *Invention.* New York: Alfred A. Knopf, 1991.

Brand, Stewart. *How Buildings Learn: What Happens after They're Built.* New York: Viking Press, 1994.

Burke, James. *Connections.* Boston: Little, Brown and Co., 1980.

Caplan, Ralph. *By Design.* New York: McGraw-Hill, 1982.

Clay, Grady. *Close Up: How To Read the American City.* 2nd ed. Chicago: University of Chicago Press, 1980.

•Hellman, Louis. *Architecture for Beginners.* New York: Writers and Readers Publishing, 1988.

Hollis, Richard. *Graphic Design: A Concise History.* London: Thames and Hudson, 1994.

Levy, Matthys, and Mario Salvadori. *Why Buildings Fall Down.* New York: W. W. Norton, 1992.

•Macaulay, David. *Castle.* Boston: Houghton Mifflin Co., 1977.

•Macaulay, David. *Cathedral.* Boston: Houghton Mifflin Co., 1981.

•Macaulay, David. *Pyramid.* Boston: Houghton Mifflin Co., 1982.

•Macaulay, David. *The Way Things Work.* Boston: Houghton Mifflin Co., 1988.

•Macaulay, David. *Underground.* Boston: Houghton Mifflin Co., 1976.

Meinig, D. W., ed. *The Interpretation of Ordinary Landscapes: Geographical Essays.* New York: Oxford University Press, 1979.

Papanek, Victor. *Design for the Real World: Human Ecology and Social Change.* 2nd ed. New York: Van Nostrand Reinhold, 1985.

Petroski, Henry. *The Pencil: A History of Design and Circumstance.* New York: Alfred A. Knopf, 1992.

Pevsner, Nikolaus. *The Sources of Modern Architecture and Design.* London: Oxford University Press, 1977.

Poppeliers, John. *What Style Is It? A Guide to American Architecture.* Washington, DC: Preservation Press, 1984.

•Purcell, John. *From Hand Ax to Laser.* New York: Vanguard Press, 1982.

Reynolds, Terry, ed. *The Engineer in America: A Historical Anthology from Technology and Culture.* Chicago: University of Chicago Press, 1991.

Schlereth, Thomas J. *Material Culture Studies in America*. Nashville, TN: The American Association for State and Local History, 1982.

Tishler, William, ed. *American Landscape Architecture: Designers and Places*. Washington, DC: Preservation Press, 1989.

Upton, Dell, ed., *America's Architectural Roots: Ethnic Groups That Built America*. Washington, DC: Preservation Press, 1987.

Willis, Delta. *The Sand Dollar and the Slide Rule: Drawing Blueprints from Nature*. Reading, MA: Addison-Wesley Publishing Co., 1995.

Whyte, William. *City: Rediscovering the Center*. New York: Doubleday, 1990.

Wurman, Richard Saul. *Information Anxiety*. New York: Bantam Books, 1990.

DRAWING/TECHNICAL SKILLS

•Hanks, Kurt, and Larry Belliston. *Rapid Viz: A New Method for the Rapid Visualization of Ideas*. Menlo Park, CA: Crisp Publications, 1980.

Kliment, Stephen, ed. *Architectural Sketching and Rendering: Techniques for Designers and Artists*. New York: Watson-Guptill Publications, 1984.

EDUCATION

∞Dunn, Rita, and Kenneth Dunn. *Teaching Students Through Their Individual Learning Styles: A Practical Approach*. Englewood Cliffs, NJ: Prentice Hall, 1978.

Gardner, Howard. *Multiple Intelligences: The Theory in Practice*. New York: Basic Books, 1993.

∞Mayfield, Marlys. *Thinking for Yourself: Developing Critical Thinking Skills Through Reading and Writing*. Belmont, CA: Wadsworth Publishing Co., 1994.

∞McCarthy, Bernice. *The 4Mat System: Teaching to Learning Styles with Right/Left Mode Techniques*. Barrington, IL: Excel, Inc., 1987.

∞Williams, Linda Verlee. *Teaching for the Two-Sided Mind: A Guide to Right Brain–Left Brain Education*. Englewood Cliffs, NJ: Prentice Hall, 1983.

FUND-RAISING

The Foundation Center. *The Foundation Grants Index*. New York: The Foundation Center, 1989.

Million Dollar Directory: America's Leading Public and Private Companies. New York: Dunn and Bradstreet, 1990.

MAPS/AERIAL PHOTOGRAPHY

American Library Association. *Guide to U.S. Map Resources*. 2nd ed. Chicago: ALA, 1990.

∞Boyce, Jesse, et al. *Ground Truth Studies: Teacher Handbook*. Aspen, CO: Aspen Global Exchange Institute, 1992.

Carrington, David, and Richard Stephenson. *Map Collections in the United States and Canada: A Directory*. 4th ed. New York: Geography and Map Division of the Special Library Association, 1985.

Muehrcke, Philip. *Map Use*. Madison, WI: J. P. Publications, 1992.

U.S. Geological Survey, EROS Data Center, P.O. Box 1298, Sioux Falls, SD 57101-9914
800-USA-MAPS [872-6277]
The four main categories of maps are topographic maps (show the shape and elevation of the terrain and name prominent natural and cultural features), photoimage maps, (present multicolored aerial photographic images), geologic maps (show the composition and structure of earth materials and their distribution across and beneath the earth's surface), and national atlas maps (include thematic reference maps and charts). Write to USGS Map Distribution at the address above or call the 800 number to get the appropriate index, price list, and order form for the type of map you want. Availability of new USGS maps is announced in the monthly list "New Publications of the U.S. Geological Survey." A free subscription to this list is available from USGS New Publications, 582 National Center, Reston, VA 22092.

MEDIA COVERAGE

Levey, Jane Freundel. *If You Want Air Time*. Washington, DC: National Association of Broadcasters, 1987.

MULTIMEDIA (FILMS/COMPUTER/CD-ROM)

•Call It Home. *The House That Private Enterprise Built*. New York: The Voyager Company. (Laser disc)

•Children's Television Workshop. *3-2-1 Contact: Architecture*. Lincoln, NE: GPN. Originally produced for broadcast by the Children's Television Workshop. (Video)

•*Connections.* 10-part video series. Alexandria, VA: PBS. (Video)

•*Craft, Design & Technology.* Thames Television Series. San Diego, CA: Creative Learning Systems. (Video)

•*Exploring Ancient Architecture.* Redmond, WA: Medio Multimedia. (CD-ROM)

•Guggenheim Productions. *America by Design.* 5 parts. Alexandria, VA: PBS, 1987. (Video)

•Macaulay, David. *Castle; Cathedral; Pyramid;* and *Roman City.* Alexandria, VA: PBS. (Video)

•National Audubon Society. *Building Green.* New York: National Audubon Society, 1994. (Video)

•*Shaping Our Land.* Available at Landscape Architecture Bookstore, Washington, DC, 1991.

•*Skyscraper.* 5-part video series. Princeton, NJ: Films for the Humanities, 1989. (Video)

•*The Challenge of Change.* Available at the Planners Bookstore, Chicago. 1990. (CD-ROM)

•*The Great Buildings Collection.* New York: Van Nostrand Reinhold, 1994. (CD-ROM).

•White, William. *The Social Life of Small Urban Spaces.* Available from Direct Cinema. (Video)

SCIENCE/ENVIRONMENTAL EDUCATION

•Allison, Linda. *The Reasons for Seasons: The Great Cosmic Megagalactic Trip Without Moving from Your Chair.* Boston: Little, Brown and Company, 1975.

∞American Forest Foundation. *Project Learning Tree.* Washington, DC: American Forest Foundation, 1993. (Must take workshop to receive curriculum materials.)

Brown, Lester R. *State of the World: A Worldwatch Institute Report on Progress Toward a Sustainable Society.* New York: W. W. Norton, 1995.

Canter, Larry. *Environmental Impact Assessment.* 2nd ed. New York: McGraw-Hill, 1995.

∞Collins, Martin. *Urban Ecology: A Teacher's Resource Book.* New York: Cambridge University Press, 1984.

∞Cornell, Joseph. *Sharing Nature with Children.* Nevada City, CA: Dawn Publications, 1979.

Cox, George. *Conservation Ecology: Biosphere and Biosurvival.* Dubuque, IA: Wm. C. Brown Publishers, 1993.

Ehrlich, Paul, Anne Ehrlich, and John Holdren. *Ecoscience: Population, Resources, Environment.* New York: W. H. Freeman and Co., 1977.

•Forsyth, Adrian. *The Architecture of Animals: The Equinox Guide to Wildlife Structures.* Willowdale, Ontario: Firefly Books, Ltd., 1989.

MacEachern, Diane. *Save Our Planet: 750 Everyday Ways You Can Help Clean Up the Earth.* New York: Dell Publishing, 1995.

McPhee, John. *The Control of Nature.* New York: Farrar, Straus and Giroux, 1989.

•Mitchell, John, and the Massachusetts Audubon Society. *The Curious Naturalist.* Englewood Cliffs, NJ: Prentice Hall, 1980.

•Parker, Steve. *The Random House Book of How Nature Works.* New York: Random House, 1993.

Reisner, Marc. *Cadillac Desert: The American West and Its Disappearing Water.* New York: Penguin Books, 1993.

Sagoff, Mark. *The Economy of the Earth: Philosophy, Law and the Environment.* New York: Cambridge University Press, 1988.

Smith, Robert. *Ecology and Field Biology.* 4th ed. New York: HarperCollins Publishers, 1990.

Wallace, Aubrey. *Green Means: Living Gently on the Planet.* San Francisco: KQED Books, 1994.

∞Western Regional Environmental Education Council. *Project Wild.* Western Association of Fish and Wildlife Agencies, 1986. (Must take workshop to receive curriculum materials.)

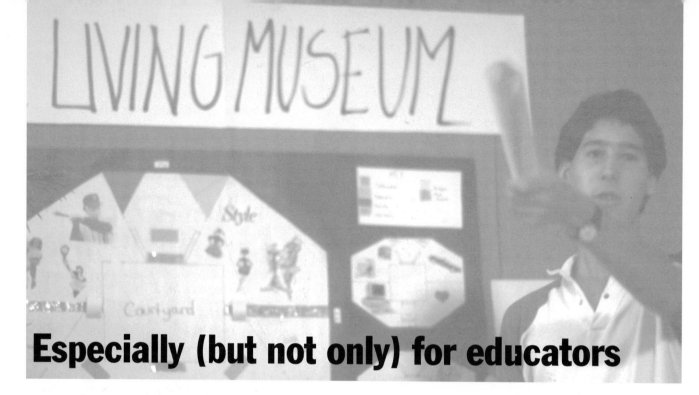

LIVING MUSEUM

Especially (but not only) for educators

HOW TO USE THIS BOOK IN YOUR TEACHING

If you ask your students what they think design is, they'll probably mention something about the look or make of their jeans. But as this book demonstrates, it is much more. It is a tool for examining our culture and our environment. Therefore, it will enable you to teach more effectively what you *already* teach—whether it is traditional classroom curriculum, or the subject matter addressed in museums, camps, and nature and recreation centers.

This section contains ideas and tips for using the two parts of this book, **Design awareness** and **Designing**. These will enable you to

• teach skills, such as critical and creative thinking; problem solving; written, verbal, and graphic communication; negotiation and conflict resolution; leadership; and teamwork;

• provide students with real-world applications for a wide range of skills, facts, and concepts;

• use everyday artifacts as tools for cultural analysis;

• address students' diverse learning styles, abilities, and cultural backgrounds;

• teach thematically and apply an interdisciplinary approach; and

• provide students with the means to understand their environment and equip them with many of the skills needed to change it.

THE CONCEPTUAL FRAMEWORK THAT UNDERLIES THIS BOOK

The four concepts that follow were developed by Ken Baynes, former head of the Design Education Unit at the Royal College of Art in Great Britain. They provide a valuable philosophical and educational rationale for incorporating design study into your work.

1. People consciously change their environments in order to satisfy their physical, emotional, social, and cultural needs and desires.

2. Design is the work of imagining the environments, products, and communications that would meet these needs.

3. Design awareness and design ability are inherent capacities of all human beings and can be developed through education. These capacities are

• the ability to imagine the world being different from the way it is. This relies on the human ability of cognitive modeling (the

Design education is teaching the potential for change—the ability to plan for oneself. Design empowers students.
—*Teacher*

ability to form complex models of reality in our minds). Using these models, people can address the future as well as the past.

• the ability to externalize these imaginings through language and models (drawings, plans, photographs, exhibits, reports, and prototypes), so that they can be shared by others and then made real.

• the ability to use tools and natural resources to make these imaginings physical reality. This requires social action.

• the ability to learn from experience. This ability is based on the use of language and models to record, store, interpret, and communicate lessons learned in one situation for use elsewhere.

4. Design education, therefore, attempts to foster people's ability to imagine, to externalize, to act socially, to construct, and to learn from experience so that they can

• enjoy with understanding and insight the made world of places, products, and images;

• take part in the personal and public design decisions that affect their lives and the life of the community;

• design and criticize design at their own level for their own material and spiritual needs; and

• bring an understanding of design into their work.

WORKING WITH DESIGN PROFESSIONALS
Design professionals are interested in increasing public understanding of design. Therefore, many will eagerly volunteer time to work with you. Pages 168–172 list professional design organizations and how to get in touch with them. Many of these organizations have local chapters, which often have education committees. The American Institute of Architects, for example, has a group of environmental education coordinators for regions of the country. Or you can always look in the yellow pages and call a local designer.

You can work with designers in a variety of ways:

• They can teach (or help you teach) technical skills, such as model making, that you might not feel comfortable teaching.

• They can partner with you in guiding students through the process of identifying and solving design problems in your community.

• They can serve as creative catalysts for you, assisting you in developing methods and techniques for incorporating design activity into what you teach.

182

Design awareness contains activities that enable you to use everyday objects and systems—from houses to waste disposal systems—to teach history, geography, current events, government, science, math, and art. The **Educators' index** on page 194 lists many of the skills, subjects, and topics addressed by the activities.

Any activity can be made simpler or more complex to accommodate your students' age level. And though you may find that an activity is focused toward a different discipline, with a little creative thinking, it can be adapted to meet your needs. Most of the activities require the use of a journal (described on page 5), which can be used as a tool for assessing student work.

The ideas that follow are meant simply as inspiration—to get you thinking creatively about how to incorporate the activities into your teaching.

SOCIAL STUDIES
Cultural diversity
Take a look at the activity, **Routine or special**. It asks students to think about the meaning people bring to designed objects, and has them use design to turn one of their routine activities into a special one. This is a great jumping-off point for studying the daily life of people in different cultures and the many objects cultures create to meet their everyday needs. It can be used to study how cultures use ceremony and how objects are used in the ceremony. It enables students to practice their skills of **observation** and **writing**.

If you are doing a whole unit on cultural diversity, add the activity **I remember it well**. It asks students to think about a place that had a special meaning to them when they were younger, to visually communicate why it has meaning (including all the sounds and smells that come to mind when they think about it), and to share their description with others in the group. If you work with a culturally diverse group, this is a wonderful tool for discovering what people of different backgrounds find important. Not only is this activity a good icebreaker for groups, it also lets students creatively express themselves and what is important to them through **writing** and **drawing**.

You could also add **An apple isn't just an apple**, which examines how culture affects our understanding of symbols, and **They don't build 'em like they used to**, which explores the effect of the environment on American houses.

Geography
The activity **I remember it well** can also be used to compare the vegetation and building types found in the geographic locations the students describe.

Also, try the activity, **Can't beat the system**, which has students **research** the physical, social, and governmental **systems** people develop to deal with natural disasters. Students can investigate the natural systems at work in their hometown and discover the impact those systems have on their lives.

In **What a piece of junk!**, students use a variety of criteria to evaluate a designed object and decide whether or not it is worthwhile. It provides a base from which to talk about **cultural attitudes** towards the use of **resources**, and it enable students to **weigh alternatives** and **make decisions**.

Government
Say you want to examine the role of local, state, and federal government in the life of an individual. Using the activity **Can't beat the system**, students can investigate the systems their community has developed to deal with natural disasters.

Current events

"Paper or plastic?" examines the environmental dilemma generated by the use of paper or plastic bags in the grocery store. It asks students to examine the **pros** and **cons** of each material and create a public awareness campaign based on what they discover. Not only is this activity a good tool for examining an issue that affects them, but it also enables you to address **value-based decision making**—the factors that affect the choices each of us makes—and our culture's attitudes toward the environment. This activity requires that students use their skills of **research, persuasive writing, weighing alternatives**, and **visual communication**.

Economics

"Paper or plastic?" also addresses the idea of "opportunity costs." This activity can begin a discussion about how our economy functions in comparison with other economic systems.

World history

To make history come alive, try **Back to the future . . . again**. It uses designed objects to show how our society changes over time. Students determine the need met by a contemporary object, trace how that need was met at different points, and **speculate** about how it might be met in the future. This **research** activity makes understanding the past relevant to the student's life. It can be a springboard for studying invention and creativity and for discussions about how our society is planning for the future. You can enhance the activity with a field trip to a local museum to see if students can find the "real thing" that they researched.

Lawmaking and public policy

Hey bikers, take a hike! looks at how design can be a focus of community conflict. Not only is this a real-life example of the role special-

interest groups play in affecting public policy, but it also provides students with practice in the skills of **negotiation** and **mediation**. You can use this activity just as it is or adapt it to address an issue that's causing conflict in your own community. Students can then **research** the issue and write arguments for two **different points of view**. You can even take students on a field trip to the local town council meeting or court house to watch democracy in action.

To look at the effect of a new **law** on society, try the activity **Disabled by your environment**. Students spend a day restricting one of their senses or their mobility, and experiencing their daily routine. This provides excellent material for discussing **cultural values** and how our society deals with disabilities. You can expand this by having students **research** the law and find case studies illustrating the effect it has had. This is a good way to reach students who learn best **kinesthetically**.

Community

In the activity **Wish you were here**, students **design** a postcard that illustrates what makes their community special and then **write** a note to someone who has never been to their town. In doing so, students must **observe** and **analyze** their town from a variety of perspectives, identify criteria for making a decision about what they think makes their town unique, and use their skills of visual communication (**drawing, collage**, or **photography**) to create their postcard. **Forms following functions?**, has students look at different building types in their town and determine the factors that affected their design.

Town meeting—Where to put the park has students advocate different locations for a community park and simulates the political process.

SCIENCE

Biodiversity

The activity **Mother Nature knows best** asks students to examine how different plants, animals, and natural systems solve fundamental **biologic** design problems, sketch the examples and how they work, and then apply those ideas to solving human problems. This provides an entry point for the study of **evolution** and **adaptation**.

Mechanics of sensory perception

Sensory treasure map asks students to create a multidimensional, multisensory map to a special place selected by the student. With this activity you can examine the physiology of the senses, while developing students' **creative thinking**, **mapping**, **drawing**, and **kinesthetic skills**.

Environmental issues

With a slight twist, **Getting there from here**, can be used to explore the **environmental impact** of local design choices. Students are asked to examine and rank the transportation choices people in their community are making, **imagine** what the community would look and be like if the choices were reversed, and **sketch** what this might look like. This could easily be expanded by having students study the effect of these choices on **air and noise pollution** and on **energy** consumption. A writing component could be added in which students write a letter to the editor of the local newspaper about their findings.

You could also add **Still can't beat the system**, which uses a newspaper article about the floods of 1993, to look at the impact of natural disasters on the design of communities. With **Hey bikers, take a hike!**, which explores the conflict caused by the mountain bike's use in recreational areas, you could teach mediation and conflict resolution skills.

Chemistry

In the activity **"Paper or plastic?"** you can require that as part of their argument, students explain the **chemical composition** of paper and plastic, and the processes of **decomposition** that each undergoes.

Physics and civil engineering

Lean on me, provides a straightforward way for students to **experiment** with these concepts using paper. You could also turn this into a competition and expand it so that students must use the paper to develop other forms that are strong enough to support a specific weight.

Scrambled or over easy? also addresses these concepts. By creating a container to protect an egg that will be dropped from a great height, students can focus on **gravity**, and on the strength and use of **materials** as well as on the problem-solving process.

Natural systems and earth sciences

Can't beat the system has students examine the physical, social, and governmental systems people develop to deal with natural disasters. Students can **compare** the human-developed systems to the natural systems. Students can also investigate the local **geology**, **climatology**, and **hydrology** of their hometown and the impact of these factors on their lives.

Anatomy and physiology

Learning how you learn, which explores how learning style affects perception, is a good springboard for studying how the brain works. Simultaneously, it enhances student understanding of why people are different and serves as a good icebreaker for new groups.

The activity **Mother Nature knows best** provides an entry point for students to examine and compare the anatomy and physiology of different species.

Designing describes a step-by-step process for solving problems. It can be used to turn topics like the study of water or the railroad into challenging design problems for students to solve. These can be either historical or contemporary; ones that you assign or the students select. Or, you can use the step-by-step process to explore community issues.

The examples below are based on the work of secondary school teachers in Washington, D.C., Virginia, and Maryland, who experimented with incorporating design into the biology, social studies, and art curricula.

Using the design process to explore science

WATER STUDY

In one school, students explored how people use water and how water is important to human life. They brainstormed study sites in the area that had water resources, developed project ideas, and then chose the study groups in which they wished to work. Students followed the steps—from identifying the problem to communicating their proposed solutions. The study groups included: stream study (they examined whether it was viable to alter the flow of a stream to improve an area for recreational purposes), recreation area study (they designed a beach for an area that didn't have one), water tower study (they designed an aesthetically pleasing water tower), and park study (they designed an educational nature center). Each group was responsible for researching its site, submitting progress reports to the teacher, and presenting a final project

> **Quality learning, like design, is messy. It is not packaged or predictable.**
> —*Teacher*

model. In addition, each group had to develop a projected budget for its project and write a persuasive letter applying for funding.

DEVELOP AN IMAGINARY ORGANISM

Individual students designed a new organism and detailed three of its physiologic systems (skeletal system, muscular system, and a system of the student's choice). They then constructed the skeletal system based on criteria set by the teacher. These included: it must be structurally sound, stand on its own, maintain a posture that permitted the use of anatomical terms when describing it (dorsal, posterior), have at least one moveable joint, be transportable, and be prepared with materials from home. They also developed an ideal habitat for the creature, and a two-paragraph abstract to describe the fundamental concepts of the skeletal system and the skeletal design. Each skeletal system was presented to the class, photographed for documentation and displayed. Students then evaluated the learning process of the entire project.

Using the design process to explore social studies

THE HISTORY OF THE RAILROAD

In order to discover how the railroad developed and understand its impact on society, students used the design process outlined to actually design a transportation system for the late 1800s. This required them to investigate the available technology, political systems, and cultural factors of the time period in order to determine alternative designs. They needed to examine social issues, such as who would benefit from their design and how it would affect other people, animals, and the environment. They were required to gather facts, generate ideas, evaluate alternatives, and make judgments. In the end, some decided that the railroad was an appropriate solution, and some came up with an alternative transportation solution.

MEDIEVAL STUDIES

Students at one school planned a medieval town and built models of one site at different points in time using a pop-up book format. The unit culminated with a medieval festival for which students created objects, food, and costumes.

TRANSPORTATION SYSTEMS

One group conducted a study of the Washington, D.C., subway to evaluate its effectiveness as a transportation and communication system. They found that certain neighborhoods were not being served by the subway. To communicate their findings, they designed a model of a new station for an ethnically diverse neighborhood that also served as a cultural celebration of that section of town. Their problem and solution was presented as a skit with the audience playing the role of subway riders.

THE U.S. CONSTITUTION: INTERDISCIPLINARY PROJECT (SOCIAL STUDIES AND VISUAL ARTS)

An art teacher and a social studies teacher team-taught a project in addition to their regular courses. Titled "We, the Designers," this yearlong project received a special grant, secured by the visual art teacher. The project's goal was to use design awareness and design activity to help students learn about the United States Constitution.

The theme of "choices" was selected with the goal of helping students understand the Constitution as a document granting freedom of choice to American citizens. Teachers emphasized that freedom of choice carries with it a responsibility to make informed, responsible decisions. The two classes came together biweekly to hear guest speakers, attend dramatic presentations, and go on field trips in order to build their knowledge base about the Constitution as a document, and about the context in which it was developed. A Constitutional celebration was planned for the end of the school year to demonstrate what they had learned. Students then broke into eight committees:

• event organization (planned overall celebration and coordinated all other committees),

• costume (researched costumes and made appropriate attire, worked on life-size cutout people and dressed them appropriately),

• entertainment (planned music, drama, readings, debate, and/or dance events),

• logo/poster (designed T-shirt logo and "We, the Designers" poster),

• monument (studied monuments and created a model to commemorate the bicentennial of the Constitution),

• communications (informed people about the celebration through the newspaper and wrote invitations, the evening program, and thank-you notes),

• banner (designed and created a "We, the Designers" banner), and

• menu (researched, planned, and arranged traditional food and drink from 1787).

Students, parents, school staff, and community members attended the culminating event. Other resources used for this project included the school librarian, who taught the students calligraphy; the school music teacher, who helped a student write a musical ode to the Constitution; older students, who had participated in the DesignWise Summer Institute at the National Building Museum, served as junior teachers; and parents, who helped raise funds and attended and organized field trips.

Using the design process to explore art

SPATIAL AWARENESS

This project required students to work in small groups to select and study an area of the school. Students evaluated the quality of the area and its surroundings by observing the good, bad, and ugly aspects of this environment. Their observations were guided by a teacher-generated list of objects, elements, and concepts that affect design and space. The teams then presented their proposals for change. The presentations incorporated models, drawings, and lists, and these were mounted in the hallway of the school.

DESIGN REFLECTS CULTURE

Over a three-month period, students independently researched a topic they selected and designed a visual presentation that later became part of a whole-class exhibition. Individual projects included:
• jewelry study (student presented a photo-essay on people wearing jewelry and jewelry displays in store windows, and created a line of paper jewelry),
• graffiti study (student presented a photo-essay about New York City graffiti, a 5 x 4–foot graffiti mural, and a jean jacket designed with graffiti),
• hairstyle study (student focused on hairstyles as expressions of different cultural attitudes and perceptions),
• African heritage study (as reflected in clothing, furniture, and personal objects),
• the sexual revolution and American advertising,
• skateboard design,
• children at play in the 1980s, and
• bridges.

The culminating activity was an exhibition in the school's gallery. Students wrote an introduction to the exhibit that explained the concept of design as a reflection of culture and introduced the individual displays. They used the introduction to create a flyer and an invitation to the exhibition, which they circulated to students, school faculty, and students' families.

You can combine the parts of the book to create in-depth programs that examine a range of topics. Two such program descriptions follow. The first is a four-week, all-day program exploring architecture, graphic design, and product design. The second is a four-week, all-day program in which students identify, and propose design solutions to community-based problems. It is followed by examples of how this program has been adapted for the Central Park Conservancy in New York City, the National Building Museum, and the Chicago Architecture Foundation.

Both of these programs were taught by the institution's education staff and a faculty of design professionals. These programs can be easily adapted to the time and space needs of different institutions.

Exploring architecture, graphic design, and product design (four weeks, all day)

INTRODUCTION—3 DAYS
Introduce design and the design process with a selection of activities from **Design awareness**, such as:
• **I remember it well**
• **Scrambled or over easy?**
• **Design detective**
• **Wanted: The Design Gang**

ARCHITECTURE—1 WEEK
• **On a scale of 1 to 10**
• **Forms following functions?**
• **They don't build 'em like they used to**
• Students can redesign their bedrooms or design and fabricate a portable bedroom, using the steps outlined in chapter four.

PRODUCT DESIGN—1 WEEK
• **Learning how you learn**
• **Lean on me** (expand on this by adding the structural challenge of designing and building a paper beam)
• Students can solve a packaging challenge by designing a "fish taxi" (a container used to move tropical fish), using the steps outlined in chapter four.

• Students can design a product for another audience—either a play vehicle or playground equipment for toddlers—using the steps outlined in chapter four.

GRAPHIC DESIGN—1 WEEK
Student teams can do one large project, competing to research and design a mural that conveys an idea about your institution to the people who live and work in the neighborhood. The faculty or institution staff can serve as client and jury and select one of the designs. If you have the space, the whole group can then collaborate on the creation of a real mural, which can be painted onto large sheets of plywood. To pay for the supplies, you can solicit donations from local merchants or write a grant application to a local foundation. Preparatory activities can include:
• **An apple isn't just an apple**
• Design technical skills such as collage and model making (see chapter five, **Design technical skills**).

WRAP-UP—2 DAYS
Pull together the design concepts students have learned with a selection of activities from **Design awareness**, such as:
• A replay of **Scrambled or over easy?** (redesign and redrop the egg containers for students to see if they can improve on their past designs).
• **Town meeting—Where to put the park**

Identifying and proposing solutions to design problems for sites in the community (four weeks, all day).

This program uses the problem-solving steps and skill-building activities outlined in chapter four of **Designing**, interspersed with activities from **Design awareness**

GETTING ORGANIZED

Select a site—it can be a park or neighborhood—and divide it into sections. The size of the site you choose will depend on the number of participants you have, because they will explore it in teams. For example, one team of four could handle a four-block section.

WEEK 1

Step 1: Identify the need for change: *Does someone have a problem?*
Step 2: Investigate the need: *Are you solving the right problem?*

Have the teams explore their site, identify the existing design problems, and present them to the whole group. To engage and invest students let them select the design problem they wish to solve. This then creates new teams, who will need to identify the additional information they must acquire in order to fully understand the problem. Whenever possible, include opportunities for the teams to make informal presentations. This will help them refine their ideas and give them practice presenting their ideas. Faculty can serve as catalysts and resources for the students.

Intersperse activities from **Design awareness**. These should provide an introduction to and overview of design, and be appropriate to the setting and the problems that might eventually be solved. A combination of these activities could include:
• **Scrambled or over easy?**
• **Design detective**
• **Who says it's ugly?**
• **Satisfied customer**
• **Back to the future . . . again**

WEEK 2

Step 3: Establish the performance criteria: *What defines a successful solution?*
Step 4: Write the design brief: *How can stating the problem make it easier to solve?*
Step 5: Generate ideas: *How can you expand your thinking?*
Step 6: Edit and develop ideas: *Which ideas have the most potential?*

Field trips to offices and work sites of design professionals, other relevant sites, and museums can also be included.

WEEK 3—SKILL ACQUISITION

In many cases, students will need to learn or practice basic technical skills to create their sketches or build the models needed to communicate their ideas. A series of workshops led by the faculty will prepare students to create a design solution. Many of these are described in chapter five, **Design technical skills**. Topics can include:
• Drawing and collage
• Model making
• Materials
• Photography

Workshops should also address interpersonal skills such as group dynamics, conflict resolution, and negotiation.
• **Hey bikers, take a hike!**
• **They're such a pain to work with!**

WEEK 4

Step 7: Test ideas: *How can feedback improve your solution?*
Step 8: Communicate proposed solution(s): *It's show time! How can you "sell" your ideas?*
Step 9: Evaluate your process: *Did you do what you needed to do?*

Toward the end of this week, hold a town meeting simulation in which the design teams present their final design solutions to a "town council." The council can be made up of institution staff and peers. The council can select one solution it thinks should be implemented based on the institution/community's budget, concerns, and need. This serves as practice for a final presentation to local decision makers.

Conclude the program with a presentation and reception at which students present their ideas to their parents and to a panel of people responsible for making decisions in the institution or community. The panel can serve as the "design review committee," asking students questions about their designs and their rationale for the choices they made. This process enables students to experience what is required to implement a design idea in the real world.

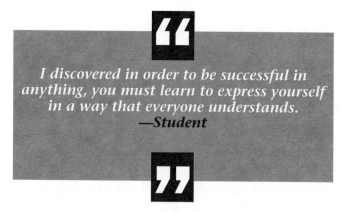

> **I discovered in order to be successful in anything, you must learn to express yourself in a way that everyone understands.**
> **—Student**

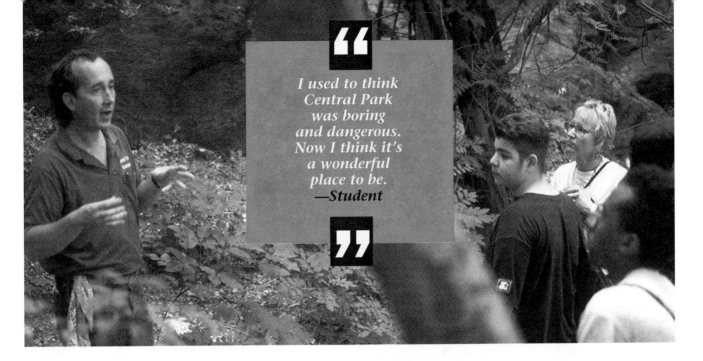

> "I used to think Central Park was boring and dangerous. Now I think it's a wonderful place to be.
> —Student"

*Example: Solving problems in a park
(Central Park, New York City)*

Students participating in this collaboration between the Central Park Conservancy and the National Building Museum, were led by a faculty composed of park staff, an architect, a graphic designer, a visual artist/urban designer, a landscape architect, and a product designer. Students created solutions to three diverse design problems they determined were critical within the park: how to prevent "desire lines" created when pedestrians wear down the grass into new, unpaved paths; how to bring one of the park's historic structures, the Blockhouse (a fort built in 1812), back to life and attract visitors to the much-neglected, ill-used area of the park where it is located; and how to increase use of seriously underused sections of one of the park's largest and oldest playgrounds.

A solution to the "desire lines" problem included a redesign of the Columbus Circle (main) entrance to the park. The research into the Blockhouse dilemma resulted in a "master plan" for the north end of the park, including a series of historic trails linking all the forts, and a series of family-based nature trails. The plan included detailed designs for creating paths, signage, and trash containers. It also included a plan for landscape maintenance and a publicity plan to attract visitors through links to other park programs. The playground solution involved connecting the popular part of the playground to the underused section with new, innovative equipment such as a "spider climb," slides into a "ball pit," and a "gerbil cage." The group also suggested adding traditional equipment that interviews, research, and observation showed attracts children. The park was given a water theme, with fountains containing dolphin sculptures.

Students presented their proposals to a panel of community board members, the executive director of the Art Commission of the City of New York, members of the Parks and Landmarks Committee, and park and recreation planners. A display of the students' work was on view at the Cooper-Hewitt, National Design Museum, for several days. An article in *New York Newsday* successfully captured the spirit of the students throughout the program.

Example: Solving problems in a neighborhood (Washington, D.C.)

On Saturdays for three months, National Building Museum staff, students from Howard University School of Architecture and Planning, and design professionals led middle-school students through the process of examining design problems in their neighborhood—the Shaw community of Washington, D.C. Students thoroughly explored their neighborhood and compared it to another, and interviewed residents, workers, and visitors. They also took field trips to places that make the city work—the water treatment plant, the design center, a local business, and their city council. Students presented the problems they identified and chose three to tackle: (1) too much litter, (2) a vacant parking lot and empty building that attracted vagrants, and (3) graffiti that made the neighborhood look rundown, discouraged people from visiting, and was bad for local business. They broke into problem-solving teams, based on personal interest.

Team one's research into the litter problem determined that trash receptacles at fast-food restaurants were usually near the door—not near where people ate. They also found public receptacles were few in number and not emptied regularly, and private ones were often locked. Solutions included getting the city to empty the receptacles more frequently, raising public awareness by erecting signs in stores, and setting an example for the community by holding cleanup parties. To encourage people to use trash cans, the team developed new, interactive designs. One had a basketball hoop that urges people to score with the slogan "Dunk your junk!" Another came with a hockey stick that said, "Try your luck, use garbage as a puck!" To pay for these, the team suggested yard and bake sales, as well as a raffle or contest with the theme "How many pieces of garbage are in this can?"

Team two decided that the vacant lot and empty building would be better utilized as a park/playground and a boys' and girls' club. Their park plan included a gazebo, basketball courts, playground equipment, and a place to screen movies. The boys' and girls' club contained a gym, dance hall, and cafeteria. They also proposed using the empty building behind the lot as a temporary shelter and drug rehabilitation center for the vagrants.

Team three proposed a mural to cover a large area of graffiti. It would depict many of Shaw's historic buildings, most notably the Lincoln theater and the famous entertainers who performed there. To further discourage this kind of vandalism, the team wrote a song encouraging neighborhood pride, which they planned to sing at local schools.

All three groups presented their findings and solution ideas to their parents, peers, and a panel of local residents, government officials, and professors from area universities. A simple exhibition of their work was mounted and remained on display for several weeks.

Example: Solving problems on downtown streets (Chicago, Illinois)

The Chicago Architecture Foundation (CAF), whose mission is to educate the public and raise awareness of the architectural history and design of Chicago, offered a six-week architecture and urban design course to area high- school students. The program was offered through Gallery 37, an innovative educational program sponsored by Chicago's Department of Cul-

tural Affairs. The program offers both art education and employment for city youth, giving them an opportunity to learn and practice essential work skills. The program took place in temporary studios housed in large, colorful tents occupying one vacant (unbuilt) city block in the heart of Chicago.

CAF faculty asked the students to investigate the real problems facing Chicago's State Street,

a major thoroughfare in the heart of the city's shopping and financial district, and envision their own solutions. The students were divided into teams of four members and given the task of developing a plan of the street; creating a photographic mosaic that identified historic buildings and considered the nature of each block; and constructing a model showing the traffic patterns, street furniture, and landscape architecture that might be considered. Under team names such as Architects with Attitude, Creative Energy, and Constructive Minds, students undertook a lengthy investigative process—including touring State Street, meeting with members of the Department of Planning, visiting architects' offices, touring the Art Institute of Chicago to see examples of architectural models and learn about the architectural history of Chicago, and conducting interviews with pedestrians. Coursework included architectural lettering; architectural photography; how to carve, cut, and assemble simple materials into architectural models; and how to create plot plans.

The students' efforts culminated in a presentation of 14 models, each representing a one-block section of State Street, which included elevation drawings and scale models of building and transportation innovations. The final presentation was attended by city officials including the mayor and several of Chicago's planning commissioners.

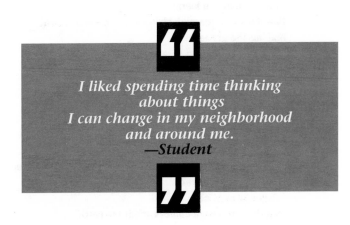

I liked spending time thinking about things I can change in my neighborhood and around me.
—Student

Educators' index

to activities found in part one: **Design awareness**

●● Major focus of activity
○○ Minor focus of activity

PAGE	Activity	Art	Earth science	Economics	Geography	Government	History	Life science	Mathematics	Physical science	Aesthetics	Animals/Plants	Architecture	Civil engineering	Community
73	An apple isn't just an apple: How does culture affect our understanding of symbols?	●					●								
26	Back to the future . . . again: Design is a tangible way to show how our society changes through time.	○			○		●						○		
98	Can't beat the system: How do natural systems affect design decisions?		●	○	●	●	●		○	○			●	●	●
19	"Can't get no satisfaction": Design is frustrating when it doesn't work.	○									●		●		
49	Checking out the neighborhood: How does the design of your neighborhood meet community needs?	●	○	●	●	●	●				●	●	●	○	●
14	Design detective: Design is graphics, places, products, and systems created to satisfy a need.	●		●			○				●		○	○	
65	Disabled by your environment: How does the designed environment work for people with special needs?												●	○	
29	Eye of the beholder: Design is capable of pleasing your senses.	●					●	○			●		○		
63	Feeling spaces: How can listening to inanimate objects tell us something about our needs?										●				
56	Forms following functions?: How can forms suggest a response to different needs?	●		○	●	○					●	●	●	●	●
111	Getting there from here: What influences our transportation choices?	●		●	●	○				●	○		●		●
40	Hey bikers, take a hike!: Design is often a source of conflict.			○	○	○	○	○			○	○			●
89	Hunit city: How can you affect an experience by changing spatial relationships?	●						●					●	○	
104	I remember it well: How do emotion and memory affect your attitude toward design?	●				○	●	●	●		●		●		
96	Lean on me: How do the laws of nature affect design?								●	●			○	●	
71	Learning how you learn: How does your learning style affect your perception?	●							●		○		●		
54	Making the grade: How successfully do components work as a system?	○		○	●	●					○		●		●
24	Mother Nature knows best: Design is natural.	○	●		○			●	○	○	○	●			
31	Need another trash can?: Design is most successful when the problem is fully analyzed.	●		○	○	○			●						●
91	On a scale of 1 to 10 . . .: How do choices of color, scale, and material affect your perception?	●							●		●		●	●	●
48	One-way bridge: How do you decide which designs you need and which you desire?	●									●		○	○	
94	"Paper or plastic?": How do your design choices affect the earth?	○		●		○	○			○	●				●

Legend: ● = filled (black), ◐ = filled (gray), ○ = open

	Consumerism	Cultural perspectives	Environmental issues	Evolution/Adaptation	Graphic design	Interdependence	Landscape architecture	Land use planning	Materials	Natural resources	Product design	Sensory perception	Stereotypes	Symbolism	Systems/Ecosystems	Technology	Transportation	Values/Attitudes	**SKILLS** Conflict resolution	Creative thinking	Critical thinking	Data collection	Debating	Drawing	Interviewing	Mapping	Model making	Observing	Problem solving	Public speaking	Researching	Team building	Writing	**ACTIVITY CONSTRAINTS** Indoor	Outdoor	One session (approx. 50 minutes)	Two or more sessions	Requires more than one person
73		●			◐								◐	●				○		◐	○			◐							○			●		●		
26		●		◐	●	●				○	◐			○	○	●		●		◐	●				○						●			●			◐	
98		●	◐		●				●	◐	●			◐	●						○				○	●		◐						●	○		◐	
19	◐				●					◐	◐					○			●		●								◐	●		●		●		●		
49		●				●	●	◐	○		○				◐	●		●			●	●			●	●		●			○						◐	
14	◐	○	◐	●	●	●	●	●	●	●	◐					○		●			●	●			●	●		●			○				○	●	◐	
65		●		◐		●	●	●	●			●	○			◐		●			○	○							◐				●	●	◐			●
29		●			◐			◐		◐		◐	●	○				●			●								◐		●			●		◐		
63		○				●		◐					○		◐			●	○	◐	●				●				●	◐	●	○	●	●				●
56		●												●		○		●			●	○							◐		●						◐	
111		●	◐		●		●			○				◐	◐			●			●				●									●			◐	
40		●	◐					●		●			◐	●	●			●			●			●					●					●		●		◐
89		●																		◐				○			●	◐						●	○		◐	
104		●			◐				●					●	○			●										◐				○	●	●		●		
96																					○	○					●	◐						●				
71		●											◐					●	○	●	○				●	○		○	●		○	◐		●		●		●
54	○	○	○		◐	●	○	●	◐					◐	●	◐					●			○		◐		◐			●			●	◐		◐	
24		●	○	●	○	●				◐	◐				◐	○		●		●	●	◐		○		○		◐	●		●			●	○		◐	
31	◐	●	◐		●	●				●	●	○			◐			○			●	◐		○				◐			●			◐		◐	◐	
91		○	●		◐	●	◐	◐		◐			○		●			●			○			○										●	○	◐		
48	◐	●				●				○				◐	●	○					○								●					●	●			
94	◐	●		●		●	●	◐	◐				○	●	●	○		●	○		●			○	○	●					●	●					◐	

WHY DESIGN? Activities and Projects from the National Building Museum

#	Activity	Art	Earth science	Economics	Geography	Government	History	Life science	Mathematics	Physical science	Aesthetics	Animals/Plants	Architecture	Civil engineering	Community
75	Rethinking your primary sense: How does our reliance on sight influence the designed environment?	○						●			○	○	●		●
83	Routine or special: How can design influence your quality of life?	●					○				●	○	●		
18	Satisfied customer: Design—when it works—is capable of improving your life.	●		○		○					●		●	○	
38	Scrambled or over easy?: Design is a plan and a process.	●					○	◐	●						
77	Sensory treasure map: How can using all your senses affect the quality of an experience?	●			◐			●			●	◐	●		●
100	Still can't beat the system: How do natural systems affect design decisions?		◐	●	◐	●	●				○		●	●	●
28	Thank you, Mr. Gecko: Design is creative thinking, not necessarily making something new.	○				◐						◐			
8	The designing animal: Design is intrinsically human.	○	○	●	◐	●	●	○			○		◐	●	●
67	The Goldilocks Syndrome: How well do objects fit your needs physically?	○		○					◐					○	
108	They don't build 'em like they used to: How has the environment shaped American houses?		◐	●	●		●				○		●	○	○
79	They're such a pain to work with!: How do diverse personalities affect communication?		○			○			○		●		●		●
20	Town meeting—Where to put the park: Design is a political process.	○		●	◐	●									●
69	Utopia: What would your perfect world be like?	●		○		●	○	○			●		○		
33	Wanted: The Design Gang: Design is affected by the decisions of many people.	●		●		●	◐				●		●	◐	●
36	What a piece of junk!: Design is making responsible choices.			●							○		●		
17	What if?: Design is moving from the existing to the preferred.	●													
105	Who says it's ugly?: What influences your attitudes toward design?	●			○		○	○			●		●	◐	
88	Why are stop signs "read"?: How do colors affect each other?	●						○	◐						
87	Wish you were here: How does design make your hometown special?	●			◐	○					●		●		●
84	You're not my type: How do communication needs affect typeface selection?	●									●				
35	Zeitgeist objects: Design is an expression of cultural values.	●					◐				○			○	●

	Consumerism	Cultural perspectives	Environmental issues	Evolution/Adaptation	Graphic design	Interdependence	Landscape architecture	Land use planning	Materials	Natural resources	Product design	Sensory perception	Stereotypes	Symbolism	Systems/Ecosystems	Technology	Transportation	Values/Attitudes	**SKILLS**	Conflict resolution	Creative thinking	Critical thinking	Data collection	Debating	Drawing	Interviewing	Mapping	Model making	Observing	Problem solving	Public speaking	Researching	Team building	Writing	**ACTIVITY CONSTRAINTS**	Indoor	Outdoor	One session (approx. 50 minutes)	Two or more sessions	Requires more than one person
75	○	●	○		◐	●	◐		◐		●	●	○		◐	●	◐	●		●	●			○									●			●		●		
83	○	○			○	●		◐	●		●			●				●		●	●			○				◐								●	○		◐	
18	◐	●	○		◐					◐				○		○		●		●				○								●				●		●		
38									●					○				●			●			○			●	◐				○	●	●		●	○			●
77		○			◐	●			◐		○	●			◐			●		●	●			○		○	◐	●	●		●	●	●			●	◐			●
100	●	●	●	●		●		●		●				●	◐	●		●	○		●			○							●		●			●				●
28	○	●									◐			○				●		◐	○			○				●	●							●		●		
8		●	●	●	●			●		●				○		◐		●		●							◐				○					●		●		
67		○								◐											○	●									●									
108		●		●				○	◐	●				○	●	●				●			○		○		●		●		●			●	○					
79												●		○		○		●	○		●		●		●	◐	◐	◐			●			●				●		
20		○	○			●	◐	●						○		○		●		●	●			●			●	◐		◐		●			●		◐	●		
69	○	●	○		◐	●		○						○				●		●							●		●				●		●		◐			
33		○			◐	●	◐	◐	●					○		○		●	○		●		◐		○	○	◐		●		●	●	◐	◐		●				
36	●	○	○								◐							●			●			●									●			◐				
17		●			◐				●					◐		○				◐	●					◐	●	●	○				●			●				
105	○	●			◐				◐	◐			◐	●				●			●												●			◐				
88		○				●	◐			○	●			◐						○	◐			◐		●	◐					●			●	◐		●		
87		●			◐	●												●			●			●			◐					●		●		○	●			
84		●			◐								○	○		○		●			●					◐	◐				○		●			◐				
35	○	●			○		○				◐			●		○		●			○			●								●			●		●			

Feedback?

*Give us your opinions of **Why Design?** Tell us what worked for you and what didn't.*
Send your responses to: Why Design? Feedback,
The National Building Museum, 401 F Street, N.W., Washington, DC 20001.
Or you can fax it to 202-272-2564.

TELL US ABOUT . . .

How you found out about <u>Why Design</u>?

Which activities you enjoyed the most and why.

Which activities you enjoyed the least and why.

Which activities you learned the most from and why.

Which activities you learned least from and why.

How you have used the book.

Any variations you have created for the activities.

Any problems you solved in your community.

Whether <u>Why Design?</u> helped you improve your ability to identify and/or solve design problems.

How could <u>Why Design?</u> be changed to work better for you. (Consider the content and layout.)

Anything else you want to tell us?

What is your age?   **Male/Female?**   **Hometown?**

Occupation?

If you'd like more information about the National Building Museum, please provide your name, address, and phone number. We'll put you on our mailing list.